THE KURDS A~~SCENDING~~

THE KURDS ASCENDING

THE EVOLVING SOLUTION TO THE KURDISH PROBLEM IN IRAQ AND TURKEY

SECOND EDITION

MICHAEL M. GUNTER

FOREWORD BY DAVID ROMANO

First published in hardcover in 2008 by
PALGRAVE MACMILLAN®
in the United States—a division of St. Martin's Press LLC,
175 Fifth Avenue, New York, NY 10010.

Where this book is distributed in the UK, Europe and the rest of the world,
this is by Palgrave Macmillan, a division of Macmillan Publishers Limited,
registered in England, company number 785998, of Houndmills,
Basingstoke, Hampshire RG21 6XS.

Palgrave Macmillan is the global academic imprint of the above companies
and has companies and representatives throughout the world.

Palgrave® and Macmillan® are registered trademarks in the United States,
the United Kingdom, Europe and other countries.

ISBN: 978–0–230–11287–2

Library of Congress Cataloging-in-Publication Data is available from the
Library of Congress.

A catalogue record of the book is available from the British Library.

Design by Newgen Imaging Systems (P) Ltd., Chennai, India.

Updated and expanded paperback edition first published by PALGRAVE
MACMILLAN in June 2011

10 9 8 7 6 5 4 3 2 1

Printed in the United States of America.

Transferred to Digital Printing in 2011

*To my many students
at Tennessee Technological University
and elsewhere*

CONTENTS

FOREWORD

Professor Gunter has been following, analyzing, and writing about the Kurdish question for almost thirty years. To my knowledge, he was the very first American scholar to write extensively on these issues in a modern context, and thankfully for us, he still writes on the Kurds today. Gunter's work on Kurdish issue offers the reader a clear, level headed and authoritative account.

The second edition of *Kurds Ascending* draws on more of Professor Gunter's most recent work to provide a very up-to-date, riveting accounting of the monumental changes occurring vis-à-vis the Kurdish issue today. Chapters eight ("The KRG's Delicate Balance") and nine ("Turkey's Kurdish Initiative") offer completely new analyses of the most recent developments in the Iraqi and Turkish Kurdish regions. These chapters form a very welcome addition to the book, given how fast things have been moving in the region.

The Kurds Ascending should prove particularly appealing to readers who want more information, more analysis, and more facts than journalistic treatments of the topic generally provide, but who don't want the overly dense jargon of many academic publications. Written in easily understandable prose, brimming with interesting up-to-date information, Michael Gunter's book should be of great interest to both those previously unfamiliar with the Kurds and specialists in Middle East politics as well. I enjoyed it thoroughly, especially the chapter on the "shadow state" in Turkey—the best I have read on a difficult, murky question. Gunter's new chapter on "Turkey's Kurdish Initiative" may in fact offer readers a roadmap showing how Turkey may eventually put its shadow state to rest.

DAVID ROMANO
Thomas G. Strong Professor of Middle East Politics
Missouri State University

INTRODUCTION

For the first time in their modern history, the Kurds in Iraq and Turkey, at least, are cautiously ascending. This is because of two major reasons. (1) In northern Iraq the two U.S. wars against Saddam Hussein have had the fortuitous side effect of helping to create a Kurdistan Regional Government (KRG). The KRG has become an island of democratic stability, peace, and burgeoning economic progress, as well as an autonomous part of a projected federal, democratic, post–Saddam Hussein Iraq. If such an Iraq proves impossible to construct, as it well may, the KRG is positioned to become independent. Either way, the evolution of a solution to the Kurdish problem in Iraq is clear. (2) Furthermore, Turkey's successful European Union (EU) candidacy would have the additional fortuitous side effect of granting that country's ethnic Kurds their full democratic rights, which have hitherto been denied. Although this evolving solution to the Kurdish problem in Iraq and Turkey remains cautiously fragile and would not apply to the Kurds in Iran and Syria because they have not experienced the recent developments their co-nationals in Iraq and Turkey have, it does represent a strikingly positive future that until recently seemed so bleak.

I first became interested in the Kurdish problem while I was a Senior Fulbright Lecturer in International Relations in Turkey during 1978–79. Over the years I became possibly the only Western scholar to meet and interview arguably the three main Kurdish leaders of the past thirty years: (1) Massoud Barzani, the current president of the KRG as well as president of the Kurdistan Democratic Party (KDP) in Iraq; (2) Jalal Talabani, the current president of Iraq as well as the secretary general of the Patriotic Union of Kurdistan (PUK) in Iraq; and (3) Abdullah Ocalan, the imprisoned president of the Kurdistan Workers Party (PKK) in Turkey. In addition, I count as friends a number of other important Kurdish leaders including: (1) Nechirvan Idris Barzani, the current prime minister of the unified KRG; (2) Barham Salih, the current deputy prime minister of Iraq and former prime minister of the PUK-administered KRG; (3) Noshirwan Mustafa Amin, for many years possibly the number two leader of the PUK; (4) Kosrat Rasul, another long-time leader of the PUK; (5) Hoshyar Zebari, the current foreign minister of Iraq; (6) the late Ibrahim Ahmed, the long-time leader of the KDP Politburo and father-in-law of Jalal Talabani; (7) the late Muhammad "Sami" Abdulrahman, another well-known KRG leader; (8) Mahmud Othman, who is still active as a member of the Iraqi parliament, and (9) Najmaldin O. Karim, probably the most prominent spokesman for the Kurdish cause in the United States, as well as such members of the next generation of KRG leaders as Masrour Barzani and Qubad Talabany, among many others. Furthermore, as the only U.S. member of the Advisory Council of the EU Turkey Civic Commission—an NGO advocating Turkish accession to the EU as a possible solution to the Kurdish problem in Turkey—I have had the opportunity to meet and interact with a number of new Kurdish leaders in Turkey including the dynamic young mayor of Diyarbakir, Osman Baydemir, and the leader of the Democratic Society Party, Ahmet Turk, as well as Kariane Westrheim who chairs the EUTCC.

In addition, I personally know and interact with many of the leading scholars (mostly Western) who have been studying the Kurdish problem over the past thirty years. A partial list includes Mohammed M.A. Ahmed, Henri Barkey, Hamit Bozarslan, Joyce Blau, Nader Entessar, Edmund Ghareeb, Amir Hassanpour, Mehrdad Izady, Farideh Koohi-Kamali, Janet Klein, Philip Kreyenbroek, Sheri Laizer, Charles MacDonald, David McDowall, Lokman Meho, Brendan O'Leary, Denise Natali, Kendal Nezan, Robert Olson, Khaled Salih, the late Maria O'Shea, David Romano, the late Vera Saeedpour, Gareth Stansfield, Nouri Talabany, Abbas Vali, Nicole Watts, Ismet Cheriff Vanly, and Kerim Yildiz, among others I am sure I have inadvertently omitted. Finally, there are many Turkish scholars I know, respect, and have learned much from too including Feroz Ahmad, Tozun Bahcheli, Michael Bishku, Palmira Brummett, the late Kathleen Burrill, George Gruen, George Harris, Metin Heper, Kemal Karpat, Heath Lowry, Paul Magnarella, Michael Rubin, Sabri Sayari, the late Stanford Shaw, and M. Hakan Yavuz, among others. My oldest friend, Joseph Blair, as well as Aram Nigogosian and Charles Bolden, Jr. have given me numerous insights over the years. From all of these Kurdish leaders, Kurdish scholars, and others, I have learned much about the Kurdish problem and what it will take to begin to solve it in a manner fair to all involved including the existing states of Iraq and Turkey.

A number of excellent studies on the Kurds have recently appeared. However, this is the first book that will be primarily directed at analyzing the evolving solution to the Kurdish problem in Iraq and Turkey.

ABBREVIATIONS

AK (AKP)	AK Party (Turkey)
ANAP	Motherland Party (Turkey)
ARGK	Peoples Liberation Army of Kurdistan (PKK)
BDP	Peace and Democracy Party (Turkey)
BEM	Big Emerging Market
CHP (RPP)	Republican Peoples Party (Turkey)
CIA	Central Intelligence Agency (USA)
CSMs	Combined Security Mechanisms
DEHAP	Democratic Peoples Party (Turkey)
DEP	Democracy Party (Turkey)
DSP	Democratic Left Party (Turkey)
DTK	Democratic Society Congress (Turkey)
DTP	Democratic Society Party (Turkey)
DYP	True Path Party (Turkey)
ECHR	European Convention on Human Rights
ECtHR	European Court of Human Rights
EU	European Union
EUTCC	EU Turkey Civic Commission
GAP	Southeast Anatolia Project (Turkey)
HADEP	Peoples Democracy Party (Turkey)
IHD	Human Rights Association (Turkey)
KCK	Kurdistan Communities Union (PKK)

KDC	Kurdistan Development Council (KRG)
KDP	Kurdistan Democratic Party (KRG)
KDPI	Kurdistan Democratic Party of Iran
KHRP	Kurdistan Human Rights Project (Great Britain)
KIU	Kurdistan Islamic Union (KRG)
KNK	Kurdistan National Congress (PKK)
KRG	Kurdistan Regional Government
KSDP	Kurdistan Socialist Democratic Party (KRG)
MGK (NSC)	National Security Council (Turkey)
MGSB	National Security Policy Document (Turkey)
MHP (NAP)	National Action Party (Turkey)
NATO	North Atlantic Treaty Organization
OSCE	Organization for Security and Cooperation in Europe
PJAK	Kurdistan Free Life Party (Iran)
PKK	Kurdistan Workers Party (Turkey)
PUK	Patriotic Union of Kurdistan (KRG)
RAF	Royal Air Force (Great Britain)
TAK	Kurdistan Freedom Hawks/Falcons (PKK?)
TAL	Transitional Administrative Law (IRAQ)
TESEV	Turkish Economic and Social Studies Foundation
TOBB	Turkish Chamber of Commerce and Commodity Exchange
TMY	Anti-Terrorism Law (Turkey)
TSK	Turkish Armed Forces

CHAPTER 1

HISTORICAL OVERVIEW

Introduction

Straddling the borders where Turkey, Iran, Iraq, and Syria converge in the Middle East, the Kurds constitute the largest nation in the world without its own independent state.[1] Long a suppressed minority, the wars against Saddam Hussein in 1991 and 2003 resulted in the creation of a virtually independent KRG in a federal Iraq. This KRG has inspired the Kurds elsewhere to seek cultural, social, and even political autonomy, if not independence. Furthermore, Turkey's application for admission into the EU also has brought the Kurdish issue to the attention of Europe. On the other hand, the states in which the Kurds live greatly fear Kurdish autonomy as a threat to their territorial integrity. The purpose of this initial chapter is to present a brief but necessary historical overview of the Kurdish problem in Iraq and Turkey before proceeding with the analysis of how a solution to the Kurdish problem is presently evolving in those two states.

Population

The Kurds are a largely Sunni Muslim, Indo-European-speaking people. Thus, they are quite distinct ethnically from the Turks and

Arabs, but related to the Iranians with whom they share the *Newroz* (new year) holiday at the beginning of spring. No precise figures for the Kurdish population exist because most Kurds tend to exaggerate their numbers, whereas the states in which they live undercount them for political reasons.[2] In addition, many Kurds have partially or fully assimilated into the larger Arab, Turkish, or Iranian populations surrounding them. Furthermore, debate continues whether such groups as the Lurs, Bakhtiyaris, and others are Kurds or not. Thus, there is not even complete agreement on who is a Kurd.

Nevertheless, a reasonable estimate is that there may be as many as 12 to 15 million Kurds in Turkey (18 to 23 percent of the population), 6.5 million in Iran (11 percent), 4 to 4.5 million in Iraq (17 to 20 percent), and 1,000,000 in Syria (9 percent). At least 200,000 Kurds also live in parts of the former Soviet Union (some claim as many as 1,000,000 largely assimilated Kurds live there) and recently a Kurdish diaspora of more than 1,000,000 has risen in western Europe. More than half of this diaspora is concentrated in Germany. Some 25,000 Kurds live in the United States. (Again, it must be noted, however, that these figures are simply estimates given the lack of accurate demographic statistics.) Finally, it should be noted that numerous minorities also live in Kurdistan. These minorities include Christian groups such as the Assyrians and Armenians, Turkomans and Turks, Arabs, and Iranians, among others.

The Kurds themselves are notoriously divided geographically, politically, linguistically, and tribally. In all of the Kurdish revolts of the twentieth century, for example, significant numbers of Kurds have supported the government because of their tribal antipathies for those rebelling. In Iraq, these pro-government Kurds have been derisively referred to as *josh* (little donkeys); in recent years the Turkish government created a pro-government militia of Kurds called village guards. Thus, their mountains and valleys have divided the Kurds as much as they have ethnically stamped them.

Historical Background

The origin of the Kurds is uncertain, although some scholars believe they are the descendants of various Indo-European tribes, which settled in the area as many as 4,000 years ago. The Kurds themselves claim to be the descendants of the Medes who helped overthrow the Assyrian Empire in 612 BCE, and also recite interesting myths about their origins involving King Solomon, *jinn*, and other magical agents. Many believe that the Kardouchoi, mentioned in his *Anabasis* by Xenophon as having given his 10,000 such a mauling as they retreated from Persia in 401 BCE, were the ancestors of the Kurds. In the seventh century CE, the conquering Arabs applied the name "Kurds" to the mountainous people they Islamicized in the region, and history also records that the famous Saladin (Salah al-Din), who fought so chivalrously and successfully against the Christian Crusaders and Richard the Lionheart, was a Kurd.

Early in the sixteenth century, most of the Kurds loosely fell under Ottoman Turkish rule, and the remainder was placed under the Persians. Badr Khan Beg, the ruler of the last semi-independent Kurdish emirate of Botan, surrendered to the Ottomans in 1847. Some scholars argue that Sheikh Ubeydullah's unsuccessful revolt against the Ottoman Empire in 1880 represented the first indication of modern Kurdish nationalism, whereas others consider it little more than a tribal-religious disturbance.

Turkey

Background

In 1891, Ottoman sultan Abdul Hamid II created the *Hamidiye*, a modern pro-government Kurdish cavalry that proved significant in the emergence of modern Kurdish nationalism. Nevertheless, the Kurds supported the Ottomans in World War I and Mustafa Kemal (Ataturk) during the Turkish War of Independence following that conflict.

During World War I, one of U.S. President Woodrow Wilson's Fourteen Points (Number 12) declared that the non-Turkish minorities of the Ottoman Empire should be granted the right of "autonomous development." The stillborn Treaty of Sevres signed in August 1920 provided for "local autonomy for the predominantly Kurdish area" (Article 62) and in Article 64 even looked forward to the possibility that "the Kurdish peoples" might be granted "independence from Turkey." Turkey's quick revival under Ataturk—ironically enough with considerable Kurdish help as the Turks played well on the theme of Islamic unity—altered the entire situation. The subsequent and definitive Treaty of Lausanne in July 1923 recognized the modern Republic of Turkey without any special provisions for the Turkish Kurds.

Ataturk's creation of a secular and purely Turkish state led to the first of three great Kurdish revolts: the rising in 1925 of Sheikh Said, the hereditary chief of the powerful Naqshbandi sufi Islamic order. Sheikh Said's rebellion was both nationalistic and religious as it also favored the reinstatement of the Caliphate. After some initial successes, Sheikh Said was crushed and hanged.[3] In 1927, *Khoyboun* (Independence), a transnational Kurdish party that had been founded that year in Lebanon, helped to launch another major uprising under General Ihsan Nuri Pasha in the Ararat area; the uprising was completely crushed, this time with Iranian cooperation. Finally, the Dersim (now called Tunceli) rebellion from 1936 to the end of 1938, and led by Sheikh Sayyid Riza until his death in 1937, also ended in a total Kurdish defeat.

Although many Kurdish tribes either supported the Turkish government or were at least neutral in these rebellions, the Turkish authorities decided to eliminate anything that might suggest a separate Kurdish nation. A broad battery of social and constitutional devices was employed to achieve this goal. In some cases what can only be termed pseudo-theoretical justifications were offered to defend what was being done. Thus, the so-called Sun Theory taught that all languages derived from one original primeval Turkic language in central Asia. Isolated in the mountain fastnesses of eastern Anatolia, the Kurds had simply forgotten their mother tongue. The much-abused and criticized appellation "Mountain Turks" when referring to the Turkish Kurds served as a code term for these actions. Everything that recalled a separate Kurdish identity was to be abolished: language, clothing, names, and so on.[4]

The present (1982) constitution contained a number of specific provisions that sought to limit even speaking or writing in Kurdish. Its preamble, for example, declared: "The determination that no protection shall be afforded to thoughts or opinions contrary to Turkish national interests, the principle of the existence of Turkey as an indivisible entity." Two articles banned the spoken and written usage of the Kurdish language without specifically naming it.

Although restrictions on the usage of the Kurdish language were eased following the Gulf War in 1991, Article 8 of the Anti-Terrorism Law, which entered into force in April 1991, made it possible to consider academics, intellectuals, and journalists speaking up peacefully for Kurdish rights to be engaging in terrorist acts. Similarly, under Article 312 of the Turkish Penal Code, mere verbal or written support for Kurdish rights could lead one to be charged with "provoking hatred or animosity between groups of different race, religion, region, or social class." Similar restrictions have continued into the twenty-first century and are analyzed in chapter 5.

PKK

Beginning in the 1970s, an increasingly significant portion of Turkey's population of ethnic Kurds has actively demanded cultural, linguistic, and political rights as Kurds. Until recently, however, the government ruthlessly suppressed these demands for fear they would lead to the breakup of the state itself. This official refusal to brook any moderate Kurdish opposition helped encourage extremism and the creation of the *Partiya Karkaren Kurdistan* (PKK) or Kurdistan Workers Party, headed by Abdullah (Apo) Ocalan on November 27, 1978. In August 1984, the PKK officially launched its insurgency that by the beginning of 2000 had resulted in more than 37,000 deaths, as many as 3,000 villages partially or completely destroyed, and some 3,000,000 people internally displaced.

For a short period in the early 1990s, Ocalan actually seemed close to achieving a certain degree of military success. In the end, however, he overextended himself, and the Turkish military spared no excesses in containing him. Slowly but steadily, the Turks marginalized the PKK's military threat. Ocalan's ill-advised decision in August 1995 to also attack Massoud Barzani's Kurdistan Democratic Party (KDP) in northern Iraq because of its support for Turkey further sapped his strength. The final blow came when Turkey threatened to go to war against Syria in October 1998 unless Damascus expelled Ocalan from his long-time sanctuary in that country.

Ocalan fled to Italy where U.S. pressure on behalf of its NATO (North Atlantic Treaty Organization) ally Turkey pressured Italy and others to reject Ocalan as a terrorist undeserving of political asylum or negotiation. Indeed for years the United States had given Turkey intelligence training and weapons to battle against what it saw as the "bad" Kurds of Turkey, while ironically supporting the "good" Kurds of Iraq against Saddam Hussein. With U.S. and possibly Israeli aid, Ocalan was finally captured in Kenya on February 16, 1999, flown back to Turkey for a sensational trial, and sentenced to death for treason.

Recent Events

Instead of making a hard-line appeal for renewed struggle during his trial, however, Ocalan issued a remarkable statement that called for the implementation of true democracy to solve the Kurdish problem within the existing borders of a unitary Turkey. He also ordered his guerrillas to evacuate Turkey to demonstrate his sincerity. Thus, far from ending Turkey's Kurdish problem, Ocalan's capture began a process of implicit bargaining between the state and many of its citizens of Kurdish ethnic heritage as represented by the PKK and the Peoples Democracy Party (HADEP). HADEP had been founded in 1994 as a legal Kurdish party and had elected numerous mayors in the Kurdish areas during the local elections held shortly after Ocalan's capture.

At this point, Turkey's potential candidacy for membership in the EU entered the picture. If implemented, EU membership would fulfill Ataturk's ultimate hope for a strong, united, and democratic Turkey joined to the West. Until Turkey successfully implemented the so-called Copenhagen Criteria of minority rights for its Kurdish ethnic population and suspended Ocalan's death sentence to conform to EU standards, which banned capital punishment, however, it was clear that Turkey's long-treasured candidacy would be only a pipe dream. As some have noted, Turkey's road to the EU lies through Diyarbakir (the unofficial capital of Turkish Kurdistan).

There are unfortunately still powerful forces in Turkey, which do not want further democratization because they fear it would threaten their privileged positions as well as Turkey's territorial integrity. The military's favored position in Turkey has been a prime example of this continuing situation. Thus, Turkey's passage of reform legislation beginning in August 2002 to harmonize its laws with EU norms and allow significant Kurdish cultural rights in theory as well as the commutation of Ocalan's death sentence to life imprisonment in October 2002, did not solve the continuing Kurdish problem in practice. The tremendous electoral victory of the moderate Islamist AK Party (AKP) on November 3, 2002, however, brought an even stronger Turkish determination to implement the necessary reforms for the EU, resulting in Turkey finally being given October 3, 2005 as a specific date for its candidacy talks with the EU to begin.

Although HADEP was finally closed down in 2003, its place was taken first by the Democratic Peoples Party (DEHAP), and since November 2005 the Democratic Society Party (DTP). Leyla Zana—a Kurdish leader elected to the Turkish parliament in 1991 but imprisoned in 1994 for her nonviolent support of the Kurdish cause—was finally released in 2004 after her case had become a *cause celebre* for Kurdish human rights. In August 2005, Prime

Minster Recep Tayyip Erdogan became the first Turkish leader to admit that Turkey had a "Kurdish problem." In a dramatic speech in Diyarbakir, he added that Turkey had made "grave mistakes" in the past and called for more democracy to solve the problem.[5] Violent riots throughout many parts of Turkey in March 2006, however, have dampened further movement on the Kurdish issue as of this writing in March 2007. Much work still has to be done both on the part of Turkey and the EU if Turkey is ever going to enter the EU and in so doing help solve the Kurdish problem in Turkey.[6]

Arguing that Turkey has not implemented the necessary reforms, for example, the PKK ended its cease fire it implemented after Ocalan's capture and renewed low-level fighting in June 2004. In addition, opposition to Turkish membership in the EU seems to be growing in such EU members as France, Germany, and Austria, among others. New EU members must be approved unanimously, so any one member of the EU could veto Turkey's membership, which many now see as not possible until some time in the distant future. Nevertheless, the promise of eventual EU membership offers a realistic solution to the Kurdish problem in Turkey. The year 2007 proved to be very significant for Turkey as it held extremely important presidential and parliamentary elections. These events are analyzed more thoroughly in chapter 4.

U.S. Alliance

Turkey's opposition to the Kurdish identity and Turkey's strong strategic alliance with the United States since the days of the Truman Doctrine first promulgated in 1947 have arguably been two of the main reasons for the inability of the Kurds to create any type of an independent state in the modern Middle East that began to develop after World War I. Although the United States paid lip service to the idea of Kurdish rights, when the chips were down, again and again the United States backed its strategic NATO ally Turkey when it came to the Kurdish issue.

Only when the United States perceived the Iraqi Kurds to be a useful foil against Saddam Hussein did it begin to take a partially pro-Kurdish position, at least toward the Iraqi Kurds. However, this U.S. support for the Iraqi Kurds did not prohibit Turkey from unilaterally intervening in northern Iraq in pursuit of the PKK during the 1990s. U.S. support for the de facto state of Kurdistan in northern Iraq, disagreements over sanctions against Saddam Hussein's Iraq, and the future of Iraq itself helped begin to fray the long-standing U.S.–Turkish alliance.

The U.S. war to remove Saddam Hussein from power in 2003 furthered this process and even partially reversed alliance partners. For the first time since the creation of Iraq, the Iraqi Kurds now—at least for the present—have a powerful ally in the United States. This ironic situation was brought about by Turkey refusing to allow the United States to use its territory as a base for a northern front to attack Saddam Hussein's Iraq in March 2003. Courtesy of Turkey, the Iraqi Kurds suddenly were thrust into the role of U.S. ally, a novel position they eagerly and successfully assumed. Quickly, the Iraqi Kurds occupied the oil-rich Kirkuk and Mosul areas, which would have been unthinkable encroachments upon Turkish "red lines" had Turkey anchored the northern front. What is more, Turkey had no choice but to acquiesce in the Iraqi Kurdish moves.

The new situation was further illustrated in July 2003 when the United States apprehended eleven Turkish commandos in the Iraqi

Kurdish city of Sulaymaniya who were apparently seeking to carry out acts intended to destabilize the de facto Kurdish government and state in northern Iraq. Previously, as the strategic ally of the United States, Turkey had had *carte blanche* to do practically anything it wanted to in northern Iraq. This is no longer true. The "Sulaymaniya incident" caused what one high-ranking Turkish general call the "worst crisis of confidence"[7] in U.S.–Turkish relations since the creation of the NATO alliance. It also illustrated how the United States was willing to protect the Iraqi Kurds from unwanted Turkish interference. What is more, the United States now began to reject Turkish proposals that either the United States eliminate the PKK guerrillas holed up in northern Iraq or permit the Turkish army to do so. Previously, the Turkish army had entered northern Iraq any time it desired in pursuit of the PKK.

Iraq

Background

The Kurds in Iraq have been in an almost constant state of revolt ever since Great Britain artificially created Iraq—according to the Sykes–Picot Agreement of World War I—out of the former Ottoman *vilayets* (provinces) of Mosul, Baghdad, and Basra. There are three major reasons for this rebellious situation.[8]

First, the Kurds in Iraq long constituted a greater proportion of the population than they did in any other state they inhabited. Consequently, despite their smaller absolute numbers, they represented a larger critical mass in Iraq than elsewhere, a situation that enabled them to play a more important role there than they did in Turkey and Iran. Second, as an artificial, new state, Iraq had less legitimacy as a political entity than Turkey and Iran, two states that had existed in one form or another for many centuries despite their large Kurdish minorities. Thus, discontent and rebellion came easier for the Iraqi Kurds. Third, Iraq was further divided by a Sunni–Shiite Muslim division not present in Turkey or Iran. This predicament further called into question Iraq's future.

For its part, the Iraqi government has always feared the possibility of Kurdish separatism. Kurdish secession would not only deplete the Iraqi population; it would also set a precedent that the Shiites, some 60 percent of the population, might follow and thus threaten the very future of the Iraqi state. In addition, since for many years approximately two-third of the oil production and reserves as well as much of the fertile land were located in the Kurdish area, the government felt that Kurdish secession would strike at the economic heart of the state. Thus were sown the seeds of a seemingly irreconcilable struggle between Iraq and its Kurdish minority.

To further their goals, the British, who held Iraq as a mandate from the League of Nations, invited a local Kurdish leader, Sheikh Mahmud Barzinji of Sulaymaniya, to act as their governor in the Kurdish *vilayet* (province) of Mosul. Despite his inability to overcome the division among the Kurds, Sheikh Mahmud almost immediately proclaimed himself "King of Kurdistan," revolted against British rule, and began secret dealings with the Turks. In a precursor to subsequent defeats at the hands of the Iraqi government in Baghdad, the British Royal Air Force (RAF) successfully bombed the sheikh's forces, putting down several of his uprisings during the 1920s.

Although the Treaty of Sevres (1920) held out the possibility of Kurdish independence, as mentioned above, the definitive Treaty of Lausanne (1923) made no mention of the Kurds. What is more, the British already had decided to attach the largely Kurdish *vilayet* of Mosul to Iraq because of its vast oil resources. The British felt that this was the only way Iraq could be made viable.

With the final defeat of Sheikh Mahmud in 1931, Mulla Mustafa Barzani began to emerge as the leader almost synonymous with the Kurdish movement in Iraq. Although the Barzanis's power was originally founded on their religious authority as Naqshbandi sheikhs, they also became noted for their fighting abilities and still wear a distinctive turban with red stripes. For more than half a century, Barzani fought the Iraqi government in one way or another. Despite his inherent conservatism and tribal mentality, he was the guiding spirit of the Kurdistan Democratic Party (KDP) founded on August 16, 1946; spent a decade in exile in the Soviet Union (1947–58); and at the height of his power in the early 1970s negotiated the March Manifesto of 1970, which theoretically provided for Kurdish autonomy under his rule. Kurdish infighting against such other leaders as Ibrahim Ahmed and his son-in-law Jalal Talabani and continuing government opposition, however, finally helped lead to Barzani's ultimate defeat in 1975. Barzani's defeat also occurred because the United States and Iran withdrew their support in return for Iraqi concessions, an action U.S. National Security Advisor Henry Kissinger cynically explained as necessary covert action not to be confused with missionary work.[9]

Following Barzani's collapse in March 1975, his son Massoud Barzani eventually emerged as the new leader of the KDP, while Talabani established his Patriotic Union of Kurdistan (PUK) on June 1, 1975. Divided by philosophy, geography, dialect, and ambition, Barzani's KDP and Talabani's PUK have alternated between cooperation and bloody conflict ever since. They also have suffered grievously from such horrific repression as Saddam Hussein's genocidal *Anfal* campaigns of 1987–88, and the chemical attack against the city of Halabja on March 16, 1988.

After the 1991 Gulf War and failure of the ensuing Kurdish uprising in March 1991, the mass flight of Kurdish refugees to the mountains reluctantly forced the United States to create a safe haven and no-fly zone in which a de facto Kurdish state began to develop in northern Iraq. In addition, the unprecedented United Nations Security Council Resolution 688 of April 5, 1991, condemned "the repression of the Iraqi civilian population...in Kurdish populated areas" and demanded "that Iraq...immediately end this repression." As symbolic as it may have been, never before had the Kurds received such official international mention and protection.

Despite the de facto Kurdish state that emerged in northern Iraq following Saddam Hussein's defeat in the Gulf War, the KDP and PUK actually fought a civil war against each other from 1994 to 1998. As a result of this internal Kurdish fighting, there were two separate rump governments in Iraqi Kurdistan after 1994: the KDP's in Irbil and the PUK's in Sulaymaniya. Inevitably, the resulting instability and power vacuum drew in neighboring Turkey and Iran, among others such as the United States, Syria, and of course, Iraq, since for reasons of state none of the powers wanted to see a Kurdish state established in northern Iraq.

The United States finally brokered a cease-fire by bringing Barzani and Talabani together in Washington in September 1998. The Kurds also began to receive thirteen percent of the receipts from the oil Iraq was allowed to sell after 1995. Peace, relative prosperity, and democracy began to grow in the de facto state of Kurdistan in northern Iraq. In October 2002, the reunified parliament of the de facto Kurdish state met for the first time since 1994 and declared that Iraqi Kurdistan would be a federal state in a post–Saddam Hussein Iraq.

The 2003 War

On March 19, 2003, the United States finally launched a war against Iraq that quickly overthrew Saddam Hussein's regime. Establishing a stable new Iraqi government has proven much more difficult. As Peter W. Galbraith recently explained: "The fundamental problem of Iraq is an absence of Iraqis."[10] As analyzed in chapters 2 and 3, the Iraqi Kurds were determined to establish at least an autonomous federal state in post–Saddam Hussein Iraq. If this failed, they would then opt for complete independence. The interim constitution—known as the Transitional Administrative Law (TAL)[11]—promulgated on March 8, 2004, for a democratic federal Iraq proved only a temporary compromise given the majority Shiites' insistence on what they saw as their right to unfettered majority rule. Thus, United Nations Security Council Resolution 1546 of June 8, 2004, which authorized Iraq's new interim government, failed even to mention the Transnational Administrative Law (TAL) and federalism as a solution for the Kurdish problem in Iraq. Grand Ayatollah Ali al-Sistani, the de facto Shiite religious leader, in general felt that the TAL should not tie the hands of the interim Iraqi parliament elected on January 30, 2005, and specifically objected to Article 61(c) in the TAL that gave the Kurds an effective veto[12] over the final constitution, which nevertheless provided for meaningful federalism and was adopted on October 15, 2005.

Moreover, Turkey feared the demonstration effect on its own restless Kurds of any Kurdish entity on the Turkish border. Indeed,

General Ilker Basbug, Turkey's deputy chief of staff, declared that "if there is a federal structure in Iraq on an ethnic basis, the future will be very difficult and bloody."[13] Turkish prime minister Recep Tayyip Erdogan accused the Iraqi Kurds of "playing with fire"[14] by trying to annex the oil-rich Kirkuk area to their prospective federal state. Turkish opposition to ethnic or multinational federalism in Iraq reflects its long-standing security fears that any decentralization there—especially in favor of the Kurds—will inevitably encourage the Kurds in Turkey to seek autonomy and eventually separation. Given the adoption of the Iraqi Constitution in October 2005 and its institutionalization of federalism, however, Turkey has begrudgingly come to accept the existence of the KRG.

Elections

A number of other problems faced the prospective Kurdish federal state. Unofficial referenda held in February 2004 and again in January 2005 almost unanimously called for independence despite the opposition of the KDP and PUK leaders who argued that independence would not be practical.[15] In maintaining this position, Massoud Barzani and Jalal Talabani ran the risk of losing control of the Kurdish "street" and thus their long-term grip on power. For the present, however, the two leaders seem secure in their positions.

In the immediate aftermath of the three national elections held in 2005—January 30, 2005, for an interim parliament (that then chose a new interim government and began to write a new permanent constitution for Iraq), the ratification of the permanent constitution on October 15, 2005, and the election of a permanent parliament on December 15, 2005—the Kurds held the balance of power. To form the necessary two-third majority coalition government, the majority Shiite coalition had to accept the Kurdish demands for strong Kurdish rights in a democratic federal Iraq. These demands included one of the two main Kurdish leaders, Jalal Talabani, as the president of Iraq, while the Shiites gained the leading office of prime minister. Other Kurdish demands included the so-called Kurdish veto over approving or amending any future Iraqi constitution, the limited role of Islam, the rights of women, no Arab troops in Kurdistan, and Kirkuk, among others. The Kurds also decided that the other Kurdish leader, Massoud Barzani, would become president of the unified KRG. If these demands would not be met, the Kurds could simply wait until they were, while maintaining their de facto independence. On paper, it seemed a win/win situation.

After a great deal of debate and against strong Sunni Arab opposition, the permanent constitution finally was concluded at the end of August 2005 and then approved by nearly seventy-nine percent of those who voted in a referendum held on October 15, 2005. Sunni Arab opposition almost derailed the document, however, as the Sunnis achieved a two-third negative note against the constitution in two governorates and fell just short of doing so in a third.[16] As noted above, a two-third negative vote in any three governorates would have scuttled the constitution.

On December 15, 2005, elections were held to choose the first permanent post–Saddam Hussein parliament and government. After a great deal of haggling, a Shiite Arab, Nouri al-Maliki, finally emerged as the new prime minister in May 2006, and Jalal Talabani was chosen as the largely ceremonial permanent president. Several other prominent Kurds also joined the new Iraqi government. Among others, Barham Salih was tabbed as one of the two deputy prime ministers and Hoshyar Zebari remained the foreign minister. The Kurdish role in Baghdad was a hedge against renewed Arab chauvinism.

On May 7, 2006, a supposedly unified KRG was chosen headed by Nechirvan Idris Barzani, the nephew of Massoud Barzani. It consisted of thirteen ministries headed by the KDP and fourteen by the PUK. Islamists held three ministries, and Turkmans and Assyrians were granted one each. The main problem with the new unified KRG was that four of its major ministries remained divided between the PUK and the KDP: Interior, Finance, Justice, and Peshmerga (Defense). Each portfolio had two ministers, one from the PUK and the other from the KDP. It remained to be seen how successful this mechanism would prove. Even more problematic would be the interrelationship between the KRG and the national government in Baghdad. These issues are analyzed more thoroughly in chapters 2 and 3.

CHAPTER 2

THE IRAQI KURDS'
FEDERALISM IMPERATIVE

The Iraqi Constitution—adopted by a referendum held on October 15, 2005, over bitter Sunni Arab opposition and the resulting elections held on December 15, 2005—might ultimately prove stillborn. Until recently at least the numerically majority Shiite Arabs sought simple majoritarian rule and at heart still do. This is a formula totally unacceptable to the numerically minority Kurds who—after enjoying more than a decade of de facto independence—do not welcome reincorporation into a centralized unitary state that had carried out genocide, ethnic expelling, and forced assimilation at their expense. For their part, the Sunni Arabs continue to seek to preserve as much of their former prerogatives as possible, while particularly fearing their economic marginalization. Moreover, Sunni Arab Iraq has also become a deadly wartorn region involving U.S. and Iraqi government (actually Shiite Arab and Kurdish) troops against Sunni Arab Iraqi and foreign jihadist insurgents. The Sunni Arab region is also suffused with an unemployed, dispossessed population that resents foreign occupation and looks upon the Kurds as U.S. collaborators or worse. All these problems are magnified by Iraq's lack of any meaningful democratic experience. Indeed, one wit has summed up the problem of negotiating an acceptable permanent government as "Iraq lacking any Iraqis." Under such circumstances, analyzing Iraq's attempt at constitutional development may be an exercise in futility. The TAL—Iraq's interim constitution that set up the rules for adopting the permanent constitution and government—may be "the first, very best, and very likely the last constitution Iraq will ever have."[1] Unless the United States suddenly abandons its role in Iraq and the insurgents manage to come to power, however, the current exercise in constitutional struggle will continue.

As part of the rush to finish the draft constitution by August 15, 2005 (a date eventually extended until the end of August), some of the basic constitutional issues were fudged or simply ignored. Thus, the constitutional struggle will now simply move to the permanent National Assembly that was elected on December 15, 2005. Here the Kurds will hopefully prove strong enough to preserve their many hard-won, theoretical rights in the constitution that was adopted over bitter Sunni Arab opposition on October 15, 2005.

The type of federalism the new Iraq will finally adopt constitutes the paramount constitutional debate for the Kurds because it largely will determine the disposition of the other main constitutional issues involving the role of Islam and women; Kirkuk; the peshmerga; the sharing of oil, water, and other natural resources; the official languages; and the name of the country, among others. Therefore, the debate over what type of federalism is to be adopted permanently will be imperative for the Iraqi Kurds.

Federalism

Federalism is a form of government in which power is divided and shared between the central (national or federal) government and the constituent (state or regional) governments. Individuals are citizens of both the central and constituent governments, and they elect at least some parts of both governments. A federal form of government is convenantal. This simply means that the authority of each level of government—central and constituent—derives from the constitution, not from the other level of government. Thus, neither level of government can take away the powers of the other.[2]

Broadly speaking, there are two types of federalism being broached for Iraq: (1) majoritarian (also known as mono-national, nonethnic, territorial, or administrative), and (2) ethnic (also known as multinational or pluralist). The United States is an example of the first type, and Switzerland and Canada are examples of the second type. Different variations of each model, of course, exist. In general, however, the first model tends toward greater centralization than the second. As is explained below, the Shiite Arabs would tend to favor the first type of federalism because this would allow them to exercise the maximum amount of power inherent in their majority status. The Kurds, however, would prefer the second type of federalism because this would best enable them to preserve their ethnic unity and protect their political, cultural, and social existence. It also would grant them the closest thing to the independence they almost all desire but cannot now achieve given geostrategic realities. For their part, the Sunni Arabs tend to mistrust federalism as dividing Iraq and initiating the slippery road to secession. They also fear that federalism might leave them without any of Iraq's oil.

Nonethnic Federalism

Both the United States and the Shiite Arabs favor the first type of majoritarian or nonethnic federalism. Under this model, internal regional boundaries are purposely drawn to deny self-government to national or ethnic minorities. Thus, the Kurds—as well as the Shiites and Sunnis—would be divided into a number of different administrative units making it less likely that any one of them might secede or, in the case of the Kurds, act as a magnet for their ethnic kin across international borders. Kanan Makiya as well as Adeed Dawisha and Karen Dawisha have argued that such a system would create crosscutting allegiances among different ethnic groups and thus prevent secession.[3] Donald L. Horowitz has maintained that in general such an arrangement would tend to dilute the strength of any one ethnic group by creating constituent governments that would encourage interethnic cooperation.[4] Elaborating, Horowitz more recently argued that splitting ethnic groups into different regions "heightens intraethnic divisions, for fractions of groups may have greater incentives to cooperate across group lines than do entirely cohesive groups."[5] Thus, nonethnic federalism would supposedly result in the advantages James Madison articulated in *Federalist #10* of facilitating the construction of crosscutting interethnic alliances, increasing the chances for shifting coalitions, and thus strengthening Iraqi nation-building at the expense of Kurdish nation-building. These advantages of nonethnic federalism also have recently been recommended by Dawn Brancati,[6] Andreas Wimmer,[7] and M. Hakan Yavuz.[8] Finally, the success of nonethnic U.S. federalism matched against the recent failures of such ethnic federations as the Soviet Union, Yugoslavia, and Czechoslovakia constitutes yet another reason to favor nonethnic federalism.

One of the main criticisms of nonethnic, territorial federalism in Iraq is that it simply would not be able to prevent ethnic or sectarian majorities from dominating regional units unless absurdly crescent-shaped units running from north to south were artificially created. Furthermore, although Adeed Dawisha and Karen Dawisha would base their administrative federalism on Iraq's preexisting eighteen governorates, most of these units clearly are dominated by one ethnic or sectarian group. The Kurds, for example, are an overwhelming majority in at least three of the governorates (Irbil, Sulaymaniya, and Dohuk) and probably are a slight, but overall majority in a fourth, Kirkuk. Partitioning the Kurdistan region in the name of nonethnic federalism would be a sure recipe for renewed conflict. The Shiites are a majority in at least nine of the other governorates, and the Sunnis dominate in at least four. Only Baghdad at present comes close to having no clear majority, although the Shiites probably have a slight edge. The virulent violence in Iraq, however, has resulted in a de facto partition even of Baghdad. Thus, in practice, it would be virtually impossible to create federal units in Iraq that were not dominated by one ethnic or sectarian group or another.

The TAL tried to compromise on this issue of what type of federalism by declaring in Article 4 that "the federal system shall be based upon geographic and historic realities and the separation of powers, and not upon origin, race, ethnicity, nationality, or confession." Seldom has one sentence so blatantly contradicted itself in the name of compromise! The Kurdish opponents of nonethnic federalism probably held the initial advantage, however, because chapter eight of the TAL was entitled "Regions, Governorates, and Municipalities" and specifically mentions the "Kurdistan Regional Government" and its considerable powers in "the design of the federal system in Iraq." In addition, the Shiite majority has now expressed an interest in creating its own federal state, which would constitute, in effect, the disavowal of nonethnic federalism.[9] The permanent constitution adopted on October 15, 2005, simply postponed the final decision on the federalism imperative for the new permanent government that emerged from the December 15, 2005, elections. Gripped in a struggle to maintain its very existence, however, the Nouri al-Maliki government is in no position to settle the federalism question.

Ethnic Federalism

The Kurds have favored a version of the second type of federalism, namely ethnic federalism or a loose binational federation consisting of one Kurdish unit and one Arab unit with a weak central government in which the Kurds would also participate.[10] Although appealing for the Kurds at first glance, such a scheme would present few opportunities for shifting alliances among different ethnic and sectarian groups as issues would more likely be viewed as zero-sum in nature. Binational federations such as Pakistan and Czechoslovakia have broken up, while Serbia and Montenegro also recently split apart. Even Canada has often witnessed franco-phone Quebec pitted against the anglophone remainder of the country.

Just because a Kurdistan in federal Iraq would work best does not mean that the Arabs would be best off or even desire their own single unit. In the first place, the Arab region is famously divided between the Shiites and Sunnis. Second, there are probably still Arab nationalists who identify with all of Iraq and not just with the Arab portion of it. Such Arab nationalists would probably be satisfied by Iraq's central government and not desire a separate Arab government for just part of the country. The English in the United Kingdom present an analogous situation, especially in light of the recent quasi-federalism implied by the creation of regional parliaments for Scotland, Wales, and once again Northern Ireland, but not for just England. Third, the much larger Arab population would probably resent the concept of national parity with the much smaller Kurdish population implied by a binational federation. These arguments would suggest the division of Arab Iraq into several provinces or what will be explained below as a type of de facto federacy. Indeed, Iraq would probably be more likely to find stability by having a number of separate Arab units, which could offer the chance for crosscutting alliances between Kurds and parts of the Arab population; this would not be as likely if the Arabs were united in just one unit.

Quebec

Quebec's position in the Canadian federal system may present a more acceptable model for the Kurds in the new Iraq.[11] Although Canada at first glance is a type of majoritarian administrative federalism, in practice Quebec has achieved a special role that enjoys the advantages of ethnic federalism.[12] Certainly, no one in Canada would argue that the country's stability would be enhanced by partitioning Quebec as the mono-national federalists would do to Kurdistan in Iraq. As a result, ethnonational federalism for Quebec successfully combines with territorial federalism for anglophone Canada's nine provinces. Indeed, sometimes a combination of anglophone Ontario (Canada's largest province) and Quebec opposes the provinces of western Canada, while the four maritime provinces on the Atlantic coast also can play a role in alliance forming. As most anglophone Canadians view the national government in Ottawa as their government, they—like the English in the United Kingdom—have no need for their own separate anglophone government to complement francophone Quebec.

Consociation

Despite its formal model of a Westminster plurality-election government imposing its rule upon the state, informal consociational politics that result in power-sharing among the leaders of different ethnic groups has been key to the working of the Canadian federal system.[13] Consociational politics in Canada date back to the union of Upper and Lower Canada (Ontario and Quebec) between 1841 and 1867.[14] Power-sharing involved dual premiers with executives requiring the support of both language communities through concurrent majorities. When the formal system was dissolved in 1867, the new Canadian federal government (now joined by the maritime provinces of Nova Scotia and New Brunswick) continued consociational practices informally. By the end of the nineteenth century it had become the custom for the federal prime minister to be bilingual. In recent years, the prime minister has frequently come from Quebec, a situation that has probably contributed strongly to keeping Quebec within Canada. The customary power-sharing in the executive is also reflected in the bureaucracy, and the Supreme Court Act of 1949 mandates that three of the court's nine judges have to come from Quebec. Further, there are formal rules that require that the federal legislature, courts, and bureaucracy operate both in English and French. The

Charter of Rights and Freedoms entitles all Canadian citizens where their numbers warrant it to receive federal government services in either language no matter where they live. Bilingualism also covers public education and broadcasting, as well as the labels for all goods sold in Canada.

Canada's consociational politics offer an obvious model for the Kurds in Iraq. Given Iraq's lack of a culture of trust and cooperation, however, it would be necessary to mandate constitutionally those aspects of it that depend on mere custom in Canada. Indeed, such constitutional provisions already exist in Belgium where the federal cabinet must be composed of an equal number of French and Flemish speakers. Switzerland combines a formal Federal Council of seven persons with informal consociational politics. The Good Friday Agreement in Northern Ireland provides that the First and Deputy First Minister be elected as a team by a concurrent majority of unionist and nationalist Assembly members as well as that the cabinet of ten members be in proportion to their share of seats in the Assembly. In the Middle East, the Taif Accords in 1989 for war-torn Lebanon transferred more executive authority to the Muslims while establishing parity between them and the Christians in the legislature. All these constitutional powers for minorities in the national government, however, simply guarantee a blocking role on that level of government. Important minorities such as the Kurds in Iraq will demand significant powers in their own federal unit as Quebec enjoys and ethnic federalism can bestow.

Natural Resources

The Canadian federal system also offers a model for distributing Iraq's natural resources such as oil in a fair and acceptable manner.

Indeed this issue concerning oil is also an important component of the dispute over multiethnic Kirkuk and the Kurdish determination to reverse previous Arabization policies there and then add it to their region. One reason the Sunni Arabs have opposed federalism for the Kurds and now the Shiite Arabs is that federal arrangements for these two groups who have such rich oil reserves in their regions might leave the formerly ruling Sunnis with only the sands of Anbar, which lack oil.[15]

Although the provinces own the natural resources in Canada, the federal constitution establishes an equalization program that shares the wealth with the other provinces. A constitutional provision could provide a similar situation for Kirkuk and the even richer Rumailah oil fields in the Shiite south. In Canada, for example, though the province of Alberta owns its oil deposits, it also constitutionally shares them with the other provinces. Indeed, Article 25 (E) of the TAL spoke about "the natural resources of Iraq, which belongs to all the people of all the regions and governorates of Iraq." Similarly, Article 111 of the permanent Iraqi Constitution directs that oil and gas extracted from "current fields" be distributed "in a fair manner in proportion to the population distribution in all parts of the country." Early in 2007, after months of hard bargaining, all parties including the KRG agreed to implement this constitutional principle. Thus, Kirkuk eventually could become part of the KRG, but its oil resources would be shared with the Sunnis and Shiites to the south. Such an outcome should make the Kurds' federalism imperative more palatable for the Sunni Arabs. This sharing principle also would enable the Kurds to receive a fair portion of the Rumailah deposits in the south.

Federacy

Although the Kurds seek to enter a multinational or ethnic federal system in Iraq, they should not try to impose such a system upon unwilling partners. A federacy might be an imaginative solution to this problem. Under such a system, the Kurdistan region in Iraq could enter a federal arrangement with the central Iraqi government, while the rest of the country would not be federally organized. Federacy might satisfy the Kurds' federalism imperative, while accommodating the Arabs' wish to maintain the essence of a unitary state if that is what they want. Indeed, a type of informal federacy or asymmetrical federalism in effect already exists for the Kurds in Iraq and Quebec in Canada.

Federalism or Independence?

Given the extraordinary divisions in Iraqi society, the haste with which the permanent constitution was drafted and then approved in an attempt to meet specific datelines, the perception that the document was being overly influenced by the United States, and the need for the permanent government that emerged from the December 15, 2005, elections to renegotiate important elements of the constitution, it will be difficult, but not impossible, for a permanent Iraqi government to be successfully implemented. These limited chances for success will be reduced to a cipher if the constitution does not meet the Kurdish federalism imperative as analyzed in this chapter. Given the genocidal history and earlier repression of the previous Iraqi regime and de facto Kurdish independence since 1991, no surer recipe for failure and subsequent civil war exists than to force the Kurds to accept anything less than meaningful ethnic federalism. The Kurds would either have vetoed anything less in the ratification process or would walk away from Iraq if this issue were to be revisited for the mere majority to decide unfavorably upon in the future permanent government. Unfortunately for the future of Iraq, the Kurdish gain seems to be the Sunnis Arabs' loss. The constitution the Kurds have demanded as their price to remain in Iraq is the very constitution the Sunni Arabs will probably not accept.

Many Arabs consider the Iraqi Kurds traitors for having supported the United States in the 2003 War. On the other hand, many Kurds see the Arabs as chauvinistic nationalists who oppose Kurdish rights because they would end up detaching territory from the Arab world. The future of Iraq, of course, has become even more uncertain given the virulent insurgency against the current Iraqi government and its U.S. ally. Those who criticized the so-called Kurdish veto power in the recent referendum to ratify the constitution should remember that Article VII of the U.S. Constitution provided that it would not be ratified until at least nine of the thirteen states ratified it and then only for those who had voted affirmatively. If such an extraordinary majority were called for given the relatively miniscule divisions then present in the United States, surely a similar right exists for the Kurds today.

What is more, Iraq lacks a democratic tradition. For one to develop requires the existence of an implicit consensus on the legitimacy of the underlying order and trust on the part of the minority that the majority will not abuse its power. These, however, are the very ingredients that have been in pitifully short supply in modern Iraq. Moreover, federalism is a sophisticated division and sharing of powers between a central government and its constituent parts; it would probably demand, as a prerequisite for its successful implementation, a democratic ethos. Trying to establish federalism in Iraq before that state is able to imbue a democratic tradition may be placing the cart before the horse.

Therefore, if a federal Iraq proves impossible to construct, why not an independent Iraqi Kurdish state? What would be so sacred about the territorial integrity of a failed state like Iraq that was becoming increasingly unstable?[16] Indeed, within the past fifteen years, both the Soviet Union and Yugoslavia broke up into numerous new states. Earlier, Singapore split off from Malaysia, Bangladesh from Pakistan, and more recently, Eritrea broke away from Ethiopia and East Timor from Indonesia. The United Nations also has in the past officially approved self-determination for the Palestinians[17] and black South African majority.[18]

Why do the Arabs so rightfully demand a state for the Palestinians, but so hypocritically deny one for the Iraqi Kurds? Why do the Turks demand self-determination for the Turkish Cypriots, but deny the same for the Iraqi Kurds? For the Kurds and their supporters, the current situation is neither fair nor logical. Indeed, a strong case can be made that the injustice done to the Kurds contributes to the instability in the Middle East.

The Iraqi Kurds, however, would be well advised to proceed with the consent of the United States, Turkey, and the other involved regional neighbors because without their consent an independent Iraqi Kurdistan would prove impossible to sustain for obvious geopolitical reasons. The first step to achieve this seemingly impossible task is for the Iraqi Kurds to be seen giving their all in trying to make a democratic federal Iraq work. If such an Iraq proves impossible to achieve, the Iraqi Kurds then would be seen as having the right, in the name of stability that also would benefit the United States, Turkey, and other neighboring states, to move toward independence.

At that point, the Iraqi Kurds must convince these states that in return for their support for Iraqi Kurdish independence, an independent Iraqi Kurdistan would not foment rebellion among the Kurds in neighboring states either directly or indirectly. These states' guarantee of an independent Iraqi Kurdish state would be a powerful incentive for the Iraqi Kurds to satisfy them on this point. Furthermore, the Iraqi Kurds must proceed in a manner that their neighbors including the Iraqi Arabs would perceive to be fair to them. This will probably mean compromise on the Kurdish demands for complete control of oil-rich Kirkuk.

In addition, the Iraqi Kurds should encourage Turkey's begrudging democratic reforms that will help lead to eventual Turkish membership in the EU and thus help solve the Kurdish problem in Turkey without secession, as discussed above. If Turkey joins the EU, its fears about an independent Iraqi Kurdish state would most likely abate gradually since EU membership would guarantee Turkish territorial integrity. Furthermore, once Turkey joins the EU, the influence of the Turkish military on political decisions regarding such issues as the Iraqi Kurds would diminish, a work already in progress as Turkey's candidacy proceeds. A more civilian-directed Turkish government within the EU would be less likely to fear an independent Iraqi Kurdish state. The late Turkish president Turgut Ozal's imaginative initiatives toward the Kurds during the early 1990s illustrate that these arguments concerning Turkish–Kurdish cooperation are not divorced from reality.[19] On the other hand, if Turkey were kept out of the EU, it would be more likely to continue to view the Kurdish issue through traditional national security issues hostile to an independent Iraqi Kurdish state. Cast adrift from both the EU and the United States, Turkey would be more likely to seek succor from Syria and Iran, both of which remain very hostile to any concept of an independent Iraqi Kurdish state.

In addition, the Kurds must avoid having their continuing divisions exploited. Repeatedly in the past, when presented with a strong Kurdistan in Iraq, the governments in Baghdad and the surrounding states of Turkey, Iran, and Syria have used Kurdish divisions to divide and rule them. In September 1996, for example, Massoud Barzani's KDP invited Saddam Hussein's army into Kurdistan to help temporarily defeat Jalal Talabani's PUK. After this unfortunate event, the Kurds gradually accepted their division as a way to avoid further suicidal conflict. Indeed, they stumbled upon "a consociational model of multi-party elite [and] political accommodation within a divided administrative and territorial system."[20]

So far, the Kurds have proven adept at maintaining their unique unity in the January and December 2005 elections as well as in the processes of negotiating an interim government, permanent constitution, and now permanent government. On the other hand, despite lengthy efforts, the Kurds have not yet been able to create a completely united administration. Ironically, however, they may have found a way to avoid further intra-Kurdish strife by the paradoxical method of partially maintaining their division under the umbrella of the loose formal unity finally achieved when Massoud Barzani became president of the KRG in June 2005, and his long-time rival Jalal Talabani became interim president of Iraq.

CHAPTER 3

THE CHANGING DYNAMICS IN THE KURDISTAN REGIONAL GOVERNMENT OF IRAQ

Who Are the Emerging Leaders?

Identifying emerging leaders can quickly become an exercise either in the obvious or obscure. For years, any such list would simply catalog the Barzanis, Talabanis, and their closest allies. Since the creation of the KRG of Iraq[1] in 1992, however, an emerging civil society has considerably broadened this exercise. Nevertheless, nepotism continues. Thus, any list of the emerging leaders must still start here, while also recognizing that one needs financial resources to become a leader.

Massoud Barzani—the president of the KRG since June 2005 and the sole leader of the KDP since his elder half-brother Idris Barzani suddenly died in 1987—turned sixty on August 16, 2006. For some time his heir apparent has been his nephew and current prime minister of the supposedly unified KRG, Nechirvan Idris Barzani, born in 1966. Nechirvan Idris Barzani represents an interesting merging of the progressive and conservative factions of the KDP in that his ideas seem modern whereas his late father Idris

Barzani was notably traditional. Much less known is Massoud Barzani's eldest son Masrour Barzani. Masrour Barzani speaks excellent English, was educated at the American University in Washington, DC, and has already been a member of the KDP Politburo for several years as well as the leader of the KDP's intelligence branch. In addition, there is an entirely new generation of Idrises, Mustafas, and so on, in the Barzani family.

Jalal Talabani—the long-time leader of the PUK and presently the president of Iraq—was born in 1933 and thus is approaching his mid-seventies.[2] Recently, his second son Qubad Jalal Talabany (born in 1977) has emerged as a promising future leader. Qubad was educated in Britain, speaks excellent English, has an American wife, and is presently the most prominent Iraqi Kurdish representative in Washington, DC.

Norshirwan Mustafa Amin, often mentioned as a possible number two leader of the PUK, is now in his sixties, speaks English well, but is a heavy smoker. The other frequently mentioned number two member of the PUK is Kosrat Rasul, somewhat younger than Norshirwan Mustafa Amin but now partially crippled. Rasul's successor as the PUK regional prime minister and currently the deputy prime minister of Iraq is the much younger Barham Salih (born 1960). Barham Salih earned a Ph.D. in statistics and computer modeling from the University of Liverpool in Britain and speaks flawless English, but lacks the deep party roots possessed by Norshirwan Mustafa Amin and Kosrat Rasul.

The list of the 111 members of the new Kurdistan Regional Parliament elected on December 15, 2005, and roll of the 32 members of the supposedly unified KRG cabinet announced on May 7, 2006, contain the names of some obvious other current leaders as well as candidates for future leaders. These names, of course, are easily available and thus not necessary to mention specifically.[3] Despite exhortations to enlist women, only two were originally appointed to the new KRG cabinet, Ms. Chinar Saad Abdullah as the minister for Martyrs and Victims of the Anfal, and Ms. Nazanin Mohammad Waso as minister for Municipalities. Subsequently, another token woman also has been appointed as Minister of Tourism.

Mahmoud Ali Othman (Osman), a medical doctor by profession and once a top lieutenant of the legendary Mulla Mustafa Barzani (1903–79), is now almost seventy and has become one of the grand old men of Kurdish politics. He has played a prominent role in the various Iraqi governments since 2003 and continues to offer his services. For the future, however, his two sons Hiwa and Botan, both of whom speak excellent English and have worked as journalists in Britain, bear scrutiny. Hiwa is currently the Media Advisor in the Office of the Iraqi president, Jalal Talabani, and Botan is the director general of Information Technology for the KRG Council of Ministers.

Bayan Sami Abdulrahman—the daughter of the long-time prominent KDP leader Sami Abdul Rahman assassinated in February 2004—is the KRG representative to Britain, speaks excellent English, and is also a former journalist. Given her pedigree and the perceived need for female leaders, she also bears watching.

Mohammed Ihsan—the former KRG minister for Human Rights and presently the KRG minister for Regions outside the KRG in Iraq—won Massoud Barzani's gratitude for discovering the bodies of Barzani family members murdered and buried by the Baathist regime in southern Iraq. Ihsan has a doctorate in law from the University of London, speaks excellent English, and just recently turned forty. Fuad Hussein is Massoud Barzani's chief of staff and has a Ph.D. from the University of Amsterdam. Latif Rashid is the competent Minister of Water Resources in the Iraqi government of Nouri al-Maliki and a son-in-law of Jalal Talabani. He has a Ph.D. in engineering from Manchester University in Britain and is now over sixty years old. Khaled Salih, a former academic, has become the advisor to KRG prime minister Nechirvan Idris Barzani and is the KRG's first official government spokesman. He has a Ph.D. in politics, speaks excellent English, was a consultant for the Iraqi Reconstruction and Development Council, and served in Kurdistan as a constitutional advisor to the KRG.

Kamran Karadaghi, another former journalist with a wealth of experience and able to speak good English as well as Russian, is presently serving as a close advisor to Iraqi president Jalal Talabani. Dr. Mohammed Khosnaw Sadik, is the president of Salahaddin University in the KRG capital of Irbil and thus represents an entirely new potential list of possible leaders from the universities. His tribal connections suggest yet another area from which potential leaders might emerge. Dr. Abbas Vali, a prominent Kurdish scholar who formerly taught at the University of Wales in Swansea, is the president of the University of Kurdistan (Hewler [Irbil]), a new private university financially backed by the KRG and scheduled to open in October 2006. Dr. Rebwar Fatah, who writes the much-read website <KurdishMedia.com> currently lives in Britain and epitomizes possible leaders from the Kurdish diaspora. Dr. Najmaldin O. Karim, the president of the Washington Kurdish Institute in the United States where he is also a prominent neurosurgeon is particularly well connected to most of the current Kurdish leaders and also has good relations with numerous prominent U.S. politicians and officials. Indeed, several of the current Kurdish leaders lived in the Kurdish

diaspora for a long time before recently returning to Iraqi
Kurdistan. Barham Salih is a good example. This, of course, is
only a very partial listing. Many future leaders are probably
almost completely unknown at this time. Finally, the United
Nations, United States, and EU discreetly should play a role in
developing future leaders.

The Dynamics between the KRG
and the Iraqi Government

At the present time, the Iraqi Kurds not only possess their most
powerful regional government since the creation of Iraq following
World War I, but also play a very prominent role in the Iraqi gov-
ernment in Baghdad including the posts of president (Jalal Talabani),
deputy prime minister (Barham Salih), foreign minister (Hoshyar
Zebari), and six other cabinet positions (Fawzi Hariri—Industry;
Latif Rashid—Water Resources; Bayan Dazee—Housing and
Construction; Narmin Othman—Environment; Assad Kamal
Mohammed—Culture; and Ali Mohammed Ahmed—Minister of
State). This dual governmental role stands in mark contrast to the
situation that existed before the events of 1991 and 2003, when the
Kurds were treated as second-class citizens and worse. The ultimate question, of course, is for how long this unique Kurdish
position of strength will last. Many Arabs still resent the Kurdish
claims to autonomy as a challenge to the Arab patrimony and a
federal state for the Iraqi Kurds within Iraq as simply a prelude to
secession. Indeed, most Kurds would quickly opt for independence
when they perceive the time as ripe. When will the Iraqi Arabs get
their act together and start trying to reduce the Kurds again? For
the Kurds, on the other hand, their current role in Baghdad is a

hedge against renewed Arab chauvinism. The current interplay between these two governmental roles for the Kurds is very interesting and instructive. A brief analysis follows.

The long struggle for ultimate power in Iraqi Kurdistan between Massoud Barzani and Jalal Talabani—a contest that led to a bloody civil war between the two as recently as the mid-1990s and even saw Barzani call upon Saddam Hussein for help in 1996—for now has been put on hold by ceding Barzani the presidency of the KRG and Talabani has assumed the largely ceremonial presidency of Iraq. Thus, the Barzani–Talabani rivalry potentially has been grafted partially onto the dynamics for power between the KRG and the Iraqi government.

The Iraqi Constitution approved by a hotly contested referendum on October 15, 2005, establishes a federal structure for Iraq that grants significant powers to the regions.[4] Indeed, for the first time ever most Kurds now think of their government in Irbil, not the one in Baghdad, when the concept of government is broached. The actual division of power between the Iraqi government and the KRG, however, remains in potential dispute. These contested powers include the ownership of natural resources and the control of the revenues flowing from them, the role of the KRG army or peshmerga (militia), and the final status of Kirkuk (see below) as well as several other disputed territories such as Sinjar and Makhmur, among others. Mosul, Iraq's third largest city, has a big Kurdish population in its eastern part and is also likely to be contested.

Dr. Ashti A. Hawrami, the KRG minister for Natural Resources and a well-known former international oil executive, addressed the issue of natural resource ownership in a wide-ranging interview in the KRG capital of Irbil on June 14, 2006.[5] He argued strongly that Article 115 of the new Iraqi Constitution "states the supremacy of regional laws over federal laws, and can be invoked if no agreement is reached on the management of oil and gas resources and the distribution of proceeds." He also argued that Article 112 of the constitution only permits the Iraqi government "an administrative role confined to the handling, i.e. exporting and marketing, of the extracted oil and gas from existing producing fields.... The elected authorities of the regions and producing governorates are now entitled to administer and supervise the extraction process; in other words local oilfield managers are answerable to the local authorities." Hawrami went on to maintain that since the new constitution was silent on undeveloped fields or any new fields, "the regions and governorates will have all the controls." Although he stated that the KRG and the government in Baghdad would be able to cooperate, the possibility for conflict over the issue of natural resources is obvious and is already occurring.

After months of heated bargaining a compromise solution seemed to be emerging early in 2007 that would allow the KRG to initiate the process of tendering contracts before sending them to a new Federal Council on Oil and Gas for review, which includes a Kurdish official and follows exacting criteria. Disputes might also be taken to a new group of independent advisors who might include foreign experts.[6] All revenues would flow into a new federal oil fund and then be distributed among all regions and governorates in proportion to their populations. What remained unclear, however, was whether the federal government merely would sign off on contracts reached by the KRG or would actually have the power to approve or disapprove them.

Given the security problem to the south, many foreign investors have been attracted to the Kurdistan region. Chief among them have been Turkish firms, which have been heavily involved in such projects as building international airports in Irbil and Sulaymaniya (each of which was handling more than seventy flights per week as of March 2007) as well as cement plants, among other projects. Ilnur Cevik has been one of the most important of these Turkish entrepreneurs. In 2004, Cevik resigned as the editor of the English-language *Turkish Daily News* to pursue his family's construction business in Iraqi Kurdistan. As the chief columnist of the *New Anatolian*, Cevik increasingly became an advocate of Turkish–KRG economic relations for at least two additional reasons. (1) Such economic relations would help alleviate the economically depressed situation in southeastern Turkey and lessen Turkish Kurds' support for radical Kurdish groups such as the PKK. (2) Turkish–KRG economic relations also would help bind the two, with Turkey, of course, as the senior partner. By the end of 2005, Turkish–Iraqi trade (much of it involving the KRG) had reached $2.6 billion.[7] In January 2006, Vakifbank and Akbank (two of Turkey's largest banks) announced that they would open branches in Irbil, Sulaymaniya, and Dohuk, as well as Kirkuk. Turkish trade and economic relations with the KRG were expected to reach $3 billion in 2006.[8]

From the Turkish point of view, these economic relations with the KRG would diminish Kurdish nationalism by encompassing it within Turkey's overall Middle Eastern economic initiatives, which also included the Arab states and Israel. On the other hand, Turkey still feared that a Kurdish federal state in Iraq would incite rebellion among the Kurds living across the border in southeastern Turkey. Thus ironically, while Turkey has presented major political problems to the legitimacy and thus future of the KRG, Turkish businesses have brought much-needed investments and thus implicit legitimacy to the region. Chinese, Russian, and English investments, among others, also have bolstered the economy of the KRG.

On July 7, 2006, the KRG parliament unanimously approved a new foreign-friendly investment law in the hope of attracting more foreign capital to the region.[9] Before, two different investment laws had been in force allowing foreign companies in the region to hold only minority stakes, a provision that deterred many foreign investors. Under the new legislation, foreign firms will be permitted to hold up to 100 percent of a company. In addition, foreigners will also be allowed to own land, while also enjoying a five-year tax holiday exempting them from import duties, income taxes, and taxes on repatriated profits. Dier Haqi Shaways, the head of the KRG parliament's economic and financial committee, argued that "this [new] law will offer investors guarantees and facilities with regard to taxation and custom tariffs." Douglas Layton, the director of the Kurdistan Development Corporation (KDC)—a joint public–private company that seeks to promote economic investment in the region—agreed.[10] Layton warned, however, that the bureaucracy remained cumbersome, the infrastructure dilapidated, and education unable to prepare graduates to enter the business world. Nevertheless, he argued that all of these problems presented opportunities for foreign investment, rather than deterrents. Hersh al-Tayyar, the chairman of the Iraqi Businessmen's Union based in Irbil, too has promoted the Kurdistan region as a gateway to the remainder of Iraq. The process, however, may also lead in the opposite direction toward even greater KRG independence.

On June 7, 2006, KRG president Massoud Barzani declared that the Kurds had not sought to use their successful experience in promoting security in their region by trying to nominate a Kurd for the post of interior minister in the new Iraqi government of Nouri al-Maliki: "A Kurdish interior minister...will still be accused of being biased to a certain side or of committing crimes against this sect or that party." Barzani cited how Kurdish soldiers were accused of killing Arabs in Fallujah and concluded that "the past circumstances were not encouraging."[11] On June 17, 2006, KRG prime minister Nechirvan Barzani pointed to still other problems between his government and Baghdad involving training courses or scholarships abroad offered to Iraq as well as the receipt of medicines. Barzani concluded that "this is occurring because federalism is very new to Iraq, and we need time to develop necessary mechanisms and to learn how to work within a federal system."[12]

As sectarian violence increased in Baghdad in July 2006, Iraqi prime minister Nouri al-Maliki journeyed to Irbil to plead for several thousand Kurdish peshmergas as a possible way to help the situation. The new Iraqi prime minister was accompanied by one of his two deputy prime ministers, the prominent Kurdish official Barham Salih, and his minister of oil, Hussain al-Shahristani. Al-Maliki's appeal was particularly ironic given his recent promises to curb the militias and the disdain with which the Arabs held the Kurds in the past. In addition, of course, what had happened to the much-proclaimed new Iraqi forces trained by the United States? For their part, however, the Kurds appeared to be in no hurry to respond to al-Maliki's appeal. After all why should they become involved in the Arab Shiite–Sunni conflict when they were relatively secure within their own region and even the potential benefactors if Iraq completely collapsed?

KRG prime minister Nechirvan Barzani explained that the Kurds did not consider their peshmerga forces to be militia that must be integrated into the Iraqi national army. He also found constitutional sanction in the new Iraqi Constitution for his view, declaring that "due to past injustices, our people have the right to possess a regular army trained up to the latest military standards."[13] In February 2007, however, as part of the U.S. surge to stem the raging civil war, some 1,800 Kurdish troops were added to a brigade already there for a few weeks as backup in a Shiite area of Baghdad and as guards for a nearby airport. Such action was very unpopular among the KRG population and obviously had the possibility of involving the Kurds in the deadly violence to their south.

Barzani did welcome al-Maliki to the Kurdish region and promised that mechanisms would be put in place to strengthen regional–federal relations. He added that a KRG delegation would soon visit Baghdad and a KRG representation office would be established to address budget and other issues.[14] Already Dr. Dindar Zebari holds the position of Kurdistan Regional Coordinator to the United Nations and has called upon the United Nations to appoint a political advisor to the KRG.

As for the future status of Kirkuk, al-Maliki promised that Baghdad would accept the outcome of the referendum to be held before the end of December 2007 under the provisions of Article 140 of the new Iraqi Constitution.[15] Many Kurds remain skeptical of Baghdad's ultimate intentions because the new Iraqi Constitution does not specifically acknowledge the previous Arabization that had occurred there as a crime. In addition, the Kurds do not like how al-Maliki appointed a member of the Iraqi Turkmen Front as the head of the committee of normalization for Kirkuk. Early in 2007, al-Maliki also declared that all newcomers to Kirkuk since 1968 including Kurds should not be allowed to vote in the upcoming referendum.

Kirkuk

Kirkuk is on the cusp where most of Iraq's Arab, Kurdish, and Turkmans ethnic factions and Sunni, Shiite, and Christian sectarian divisions meet. It also possesses incredibly large oil reserves.

Thus, the Iraqi government and the Kurds have never been able to agree on whether Kirkuk should be included in a Kurdish autonomous region. The uncompromising position Barzani and Talabani seem to be taking on Kirkuk being part of Kurdistan is probably at least in part a result of their fear of losing control of the Kurdish "street," which considers Kirkuk to be the Kurdish "Jerusalem."

Kirkuk voted against Faisal becoming king of Iraq during the referendum of 1921. Turkey also claimed it until the League of Nations finally handed it over to Iraq as part of the former Ottoman *vilayet* of Mosul in 1926. Indeed, the 1957 census indicated that Kirkuk city (as distinguished from Kirkuk province or governorate) had a slightly larger Turkmans (39.8 percent) than Kurdish (35.1 percent) population. The Arabs (23.8 percent) constituted only the third largest group. The 1957 census, however, also showed that Kirkuk province had a Kurdish majority of 55 percent, whereas the Arabs numbered only 30.8 percent and the Turkmans 14.2 percent.[16]

During the 1960s and 1970s, Kirkuk was perhaps the most important point of disagreement between Mulla Mustafa Barzani (Massoud Barzani's legendary father who died in 1979) and the Iraqi government. Illustrating how strongly he felt about the issue, the elder Barzani reputedly declared that even if a census showed that the Kurds were only a minority in Kirkuk, he would still claim it. Showing his ultimately poor judgment on the matter, Barzani also stated that he would allow the United States to exploit its rich oil fields if the United States would support him.[17] Thus, the Iraqi government had reason to believe that—given the Kurdish links to the United States, Israel, and then pro-Western Iran—handing Kirkuk to the Kurds, in effect, would be giving it and its rich oil reserves back to the West.

Given its oil and geostrategic location, Kirkuk's Kurdish majority was diluted over the decades by Saddam Hussein's Arabization policies so that when Saddam Hussein fell from power in 2003, the city had roughly equal populations of Kurds, Arabs, and Turkmans, as well as a considerable number of Christians. Indeed, the census that had been taken in 1977 even showed that Kirkuk province had an Arab plurality of 44.41 percent, whereas the Kurds numbered 37.53 percent and the Turkmans 16.31 percent.[18] Saddam Hussein accomplished this demographic legerdemain by expelling and killing many Kurds, replacing them with Arab settlers, and gerrymandering the province's boundaries. The Iraqi government even officially renamed Kirkuk as Tamim (Nationalization), supposedly in honor of the nationalization of the oil fields in 1972.

In a theoretical victory for the Kurdish position, Article 58 of the TAL declared that "the Iraqi Transitional Government...shall act expeditiously to take measures to remedy the injustice caused by the previous regime's practices in altering the demographic character of certain regions, including Kirkuk, by deporting and expelling individuals from their places of residence, forcing migration in and out of the region, settling individuals alien to the region, depriving the inhabitants of work, and correcting nationality." Although tens of thousands of Kurds have returned to Kirkuk and filed claims for homes and property lost when they were expelled, as of January 2007, few claims have been settled. Indeed, as early as 2005, Jalal Talabani, then the interim president of Iraq, complained formally to Ibrahim Al-Jafari, the (Shiite) interim prime minister of Iraq, about the situation.[19] As for taking a census, the Kurds, of course, argued that one should only be taken after all the expelled Kurds have been allowed to return to Kirkuk and the Arab newcomers returned to their original homes. To summarily oust the new Arab population after it has lived in Kirkuk for some thirty years, however, would simply create new injustice. In addition, what would it say about the future of Iraqi unity if most Iraqi Arabs were not allowed even to live in Kirkuk? Furthermore, the Turkish military has suggested that it would take it only eighteen hours to reach Kirkuk if the Kurds insisted on tampering with the city's population to their own benefit and to the detriment of the Turkmans.[20]

In a partial victory for the Kurds, the Independent Electoral Commission of Iraq authorized some 100,000 Kurds to return to Kirkuk and vote in the elections held on January 30, 2005. The result was a resounding Kurdish electoral victory in the Kirkuk municipal elections. Article 140 of the permanent constitution adopted on October 15, 2005, provided that a referendum to determine the final status of Kirkuk would be held by the end of 2007. The U.S. Iraqi Study Group report issued in December 2006, however, recommended that the referendum be postponed in order to prevent further conflict.[21] The Kurds bitterly denounced the proposal, particularly with regard to Kirkuk.[22] Clearly, Kirkuk constitutes one of the main stumbling blocks in the effort to create a successful post–Saddam Hussein Iraq, especially given the lack of any group manifesting willingness to compromise on their maximal demands. Indeed, if the Kurds did annex Kirkuk they might be disastrously annexing the Iraqi violence to the south into their largely peaceful KRG. The tentative agreement reached early in 2007 to share Iraq's oil resources proportionally to its entire population did offer a reasonable compromise that might allow the KRG to include Kirkuk while sharing its oil resources with the Sunnis and Shiites to the south. As this book went to press in July 2007, however, it seemed likely that the referendum on Kirkuk would be postponed given the continuing problems in Iraq.

Troubles in Kurdistan

Despite many rosy depictions and prognostications, all is not well in Iraqi Kurdistan. The riot in Halabja on March 17, 2006, aptly demonstrated this situation.[23] Hundreds of stone-throwing protesters—most of them students from universities in the Kurdistan region home for vacation—beat back government guards, stormed, and then destroyed a museum dedicated to the memory of the chemical attack on Halabja on March 16, 1988. "We've had enough of these liars and we don't want to see them in our town," cried one protestor. The demonstrators also marched through Halabja chanting "we don't want any government officials here" and waved banners declaring "you have done nothing for the city" and "all government officials are corrupt."[24] It was arguably the most serious popular challenge to the KDP-PUK-run KRG in its fifteen-year history.

Amazingly, the prominent PUK leader Kosrat Rasul suggested that all of the party's highest-ranking officials, including him, should resign except Talabani. This would pave the way for new, younger party staff.[25] In December 2006, Norshirwan Mustafa Amin, often mentioned as the number two leader of the PUK, actually did resign from his post as the deputy secretary general of the party. However, it was not the first time he had taken such a "sabbatical," so it remained unclear what the long-term implications of his resignation might mean. If the PUK did manage to reform itself by initiating an elected succession as well as achieving greater transparency, the process and result could enable it to give more Kurds a sense of being true stakeholders in the party and help it surpass the more hidebound KDP. For his part, Massoud Barzani recently suggested that both the KDP and PUK "should turn into two civil parties and melt within one government."[26]

On August 13, 2006, hundreds of disgruntled young people from across the KRG demonstrated in Sulaymaniya, the second-largest city in the KRG. They demanded an end to corruption and added that the majority of the people were suffering from the shortage of fuel and electricity. "Why do political party and most government officials enjoy a luxurious life and are able to afford everything, while we are deprived of the basic and essential necessities?" queried one demonstrator who declined to give his name. Over 2,000 also demonstrated for basic services such as fuel and electricity in Chamchamal just southwest of Sulaymaniya. The security forces arrested at least forty-five people in this second demonstration.[27]

Earlier, human rights advocates expressed concern about flagrant abuses involving two critics of the KRG. Kamal Said Qadir, an Austrian national of Kurdish origin, was imprisoned in October 2005 for allegedly defaming KDP political leaders such as Massoud Barzani. Qadir claimed that he was only released following interventions by the United States and various human rights organizations. High school teacher Hawez Hawezi is also facing prosecution on similar charges for defaming PUK leaders. Amnesty International called upon the KRG to free the two and amend existing legislation that permitted such abuses.[28] Commenting on the overall situation, *Time* magazine went so far as to characterize the Kurdistan region as "a veritable police state, where the Asyeesh—the military security—has a house in each neighborhood of the major cities, and where the Parastin secret police monitors phone conversations and keeps tabs on who attends Friday prayers."[29]

KRG officials have responded that such security measures are necessary to keep the Kurdistan region free from jihadi and resistance cells plaguing the south from infiltrating the north. Opponents counter that these measures are often used by the ruling parties as a mere excuse to maintain their position in power. KRG president Massoud Barzani recently declared that "civilians have the right to criticize the establishments and institutions of the Kurdistan Regional Government for the current shortcomings but they should also remember that these establishments are there to serve them and it takes time to completely overcome existing problems."[30] Frequent roadblocks serve effectively as security checkpoints throughout the KRG.

Huge discrepancies in wealth have developed and a lot of new millionaires are living in Sulaymaniya and Irbil. As already mentioned, this economic situation has led to inevitable problems. Some blame the shortage of oil on the two ruling parties "using this crisis to their advantage by trading the oil."[31] Others argue that "Kurdistan's economic capacity has neared a point almost incapable of providing more job opportunities, and it is unable to expand further."[32] Denise Natali maintains that the KRG economy remains a highly dependent one due to NGO and United Nations handouts plus a budget that comes from Baghdad. Indeed, she claims that approximately ninety-five percent of the KRG revenues flow from the central government and points out that still there is neither meaningful foreign direct investment nor international banking. Nevertheless, even Natali admits that construction continues and can be expected to accelerate in the coming years.[33]

Considerable popular dissatisfaction also exists over the KRG's perceived compromises with the Baghdad government. Ultimate among these grievances is the deeply felt desire for Kurdish independence. Unofficial referendums in February 2004 and again in January 2005 almost unanimously called for Kurdish independence. The KRG, of course, has opposed independence as premature and therefore dangerous given the virtually universal opposition of the Iraqi Arabs, Turkey, Iran, and the United States. A related problematic element is the question of a pan-Kurdish state that would include portions of Turkey, Iran, and Syria. The lack of such a state, of course, is a historical injustice, but to even hint at such an entity guarantees the strongest reaction from the KRG's regional neighbors. Responsible KRG leaders, therefore, would refuse to support any such notion. Nevertheless, the very existence of the KRG inspires dreams of a pan-Kurdish state among many Kurds.

In an effort to maintain their control over events, the KDP and PUK joined most other smaller Kurdish parties to form a single electoral list of candidates for the seats to be chosen both in the Iraqi national and Kurdish regional elections held on January 30, 2005, and December 15, 2005. The two main Kurdish parties argued that such a single list would avoid splintering the potential Kurdish strength when no Arab electoral group offered to support Kurdish demands. What was not as readily admitted, however, was that such a single list would be most likely to guarantee the continuing dominance of the KDP and PUK because those chosen for the two parliaments would be the KDP and PUK candidates placed highest on the single all-Kurdish list.

Although one observer has argued that compared to a nonbeliever a Kurd is a good Muslim, recent signs indicate a growing popularity for Islamic parties such as the Kurdistan Islamic Union (KIU), which doubled its vote in the Iraqi national elections held on December 15, 2005.[34] Instead of advocating loyalty to Islam over nationalism, Kurdish Islamist parties are attempting to seize the moral high ground by accusing the KDP and PUK of corruption and economic mismanagement. Mohammed Ahmed, a KIU member of the KRG parliament, declared that the "people know that our followers and members are not corrupt." The KIU is also building a large, hi-tech TV studio to run a twenty-four-hour satellite station that should be operational by the end of 2006. If successful, this Islamist TV station will attempt to compete with stations currently run by the KDP and the PUK.

Other minor secular Kurdish parties also exist such as the Kurdistan Toilers Party now led by Qadir Aziz, the so-called Kurdistan Socialist Democratic Party (KSDP) led by former but now disenchanted KDP warlord Muhammad Haji Mahmud, and the Kurdistan Communist Party led by Kamal Shakir, among others. The communists won ten percent of the vote in Irbil municipal elections in 2002; Muhammad Haji Mahmud's KSDP continues to maintain an armed militia just west of Sulaymaniya as does the Kurdistan Democratic Party of Iran (KDPI) led by Mustafa Hejri. The PKK from Turkey also maintains a troublesome military force within the KRG region near the Iranian border in the Kandil Mountains. Finally, a militant PKK offshoot in Iran called the Free Life Party of Kurdistan (PJAK) exists on the KRG–Iran border.

In the spring of 2006 and again in July 2006, Iranian forces bombarded areas of the KRG in an apparent attempt to retaliate against both the KDPI and the PJAK. The PKK's presence in the Kandil mountains of Iraqi Kurdistan and the reputed welfare of the region's Turkmen minority also give neighboring Turkey a potential excuse to intervene in the region. The Iraqi Turkmen Front established in April 1995 and currently led by Faruq Abdullah consists of some twenty-six groups, and the Assyrian Democratic Movement is the main Assyrian party. Although the KRG has some token Turkmen and Assyrian representation, potential problems remain over land claims, voting, and parliamentary representation, among others. The so-called Conservative Party of Kurdistan established in 1991 seeks to represent the still potentially influential tribes. In 1996, the KDP killed an influential Surchi tribal chief in a dispute that led to a bitter split between the KDP and the Conservative Party, which since has operated from the PUK region.

In July 2006, Turkey again threatened to send its army into northern Iraq to root out the PKK. Turkey justified such possible action on the grounds of self-defense while also drawing parallels to the then-concurrent Israeli intervention against Hizbollah in Lebanon, which the United States implicitly supported. The United States and the KRG strongly opposed such Turkish measures, however, on the grounds that they could potentially ignite dangerous fighting between all the parties concerned.[35] The Iraqi Kurds specifically feared that any real offensive against the PKK would create a wave of violence in their own peaceful KRG by turning Kurds against Kurds.[36] In an attempt to assuage Turkey, the KRG prime minister Nechirvan Idris Barzani declared—with reference to PKK attacks upon Turkey from bases in the KRG—that the KRG and Baghdad government "will not permit our country to become a base for attacking neighbouring states."[37]

On August 28, 2006, the United States appointed to Turkey retired air force general Joseph Ralston as its "Special Envoy for Countering the Kurdistan Worker's Party (PKK)." A potential conflict of interest soon emerged, however, when it was revealed that Ralston was a member of the board of directors of Lockheed Martin, which was currently doing billions of dollars worth of business with Turkey. Ralston was also a vice chairman of The Cohen Group, a private lobby with close ties to The American-Turkish

Council, for which he also was a current member of the board of directors. Moreover, during the 1990s, Lockheed's planes had been used freely in the war against the PKK. As a result of these revelations, numerous Kurdish groups called for Ralston's dismissal.[38]

Turkey would be likely to accomplish little by intervening in northern Iraq (the KRG) for several reasons. (1) Previous interventions in the 1990s accomplished little. (2) Turkey would be more likely to get bogged down like the United States has in Iraq. (3) Intervention would largely reverse Turkey's historic and domestically very popular decision of March 2003 not to intervene in northern Iraq in support of the United States. (4) PKK raids in Turkey are partially or even mostly from bases already in Turkey such as Tunceli (Dersim). (5) Intervention might lead to an unwanted clash with the United States. (6) Furthermore, given Turkey's strong criticism of Israel for intervening in Lebanon in August 2006, Turkish intervention into northern Iraq would look hypocritical. In addition, Hizbollah's explicitly announced goal is the destruction of Israel, whereas the PKK has never claimed that it wished to destroy Turkey. Indeed, in recent years, the PKK's stated goal has been to win true democracy for the ethnic Kurds within Turkey's existing territorial integrity. (7) Finally, Turkey's intervention would probably hurt its EU membership chances very badly.

The Unified KRG

It remains to be seen if the new unified KRG established on May 7, 2006, will prove to be a positive step forward for the Iraqi Kurds or more of the same troubling division between the KDP and the PUK. Previous attempts at achieving a unified government for the KRG have always foundered, even leading to a civil war in the mid-1990s. Indeed, some observers such as Gareth R.V. Stansfield have gone so far as to argue that, given the divisions between the KDP and PUK, the quasi-federal arrangements institutionalized by having two separate regional governments based in Irbil and Sulaymaniya served the Kurds better than a forced unified government.[39]

The new unified KRG contains a KDP prime minister and PUK deputy prime minister, thirteen ministries headed by the KDP and fourteen by the PUK. Islamists hold three ministries, and Turkmen and Assyrians hold one each.[40] The main problem with the new unified KRG is that it is not completely united: four major ministries remain divided between the PUK and the KDP: Interior, Finance, Justice, and Peshmerga (Defense) Affairs. Each portfolio has two ministers. A truly unified or single KRG, of course, would have only one minister for each position.[41] The remains of the two former regional governments in Irbil and Sulaymaniya include a grossly overstaffed civil service and ghost employees all collecting salaries, conflicting legislation in personal status laws and foreign investment (the latter seemingly dealt with by the new investment law passed on July 7, 2006), and different cultural practices between civil servants from the two former KRGs.[42]

In addition, the new cabinet has only three female members, lacks new blood, and contains some ministers accused of corruption. The Kurdish people remain frustrated at the lack of services, transparency, women's and youth's rights, institutionalization, and, of course, the continuing corruption. Several ministries should make changes to improve their efficiency. All the security, intelligence, and armed forces should be united under the two ministries of the Interior and Peshmerga Affairs. Furthermore, steps remain to be taken for fashioning these ministries into truly representing

Kurdish interests instead of mere KDP and PUK interests. Party members and functions should not be paid for by public funds. What is more, various bodies that still have any judicial function should be placed under one Justice ministry. A single ministry should be designated as the lead one responsible for the coordination between the Kurdistan Parliament and the Kurdistan bloc within the Iraqi Parliament. The present penal code of Saddam Hussein needs to be revised, and of course, Kurdistan needs a formal constitution.

Despite these continuing problems, the dynamics of change in the KRG are encouraging, especially when compared to the rest of Iraq[43] or for that matter much of the Middle East. The KRG has taken enormously positive steps toward Kurdish unity, democratization, and modernization. Only time will tell, however, whether the achievements of the KRG are permanent or merely a false dawn.

CHAPTER 4

AFTER OCALAN'S CAPTURE

Turkey's dramatic capture in February 1999 of Abdullah (Apo) Ocalan—the long-time leader of the PKK—ironically opened new possibilities for solving its continuing Kurdish problem. The purpose of this chapter is to analyze this evolving situation.[1]

Despite his earlier reputation as a Stalin-like, murderous terrorist, Ocalan, in retrospect, had done more to reestablish a sense of Kurdish self-esteem and nationalism in Turkey (and possibly elsewhere) than any other Kurdish leader in recent years. This was aptly illustrated by the dismay most Kurds and their supporters throughout the world showed upon hearing that he had been apprehended by the Turkish authorities. In the process Ocalan once again illustrated the old adage that one person's freedom fighter is another's terrorist because to most Turks Ocalan seemed bent on destroying Turkey's territorial integrity through terrorist methods.

The final blow came when Turkey threatened to go to war against Syria in October 1998 unless Damascus expelled Ocalan from his long-time sanctuary in that country. After a short, surreptitious stay in Russia, Ocalan landed in Italy on November 12, 1998, where for a brief period it looked like he might be able to turn his military defeat into a political victory by having the EU try him and thus also try Turkey. But in the end U.S. pressure on behalf of its NATO ally Turkey pressured Italy and others to reject Ocalan as a terrorist undeserving of political asylum or negotiation. Indeed for years the United States had given Turkey intelligence training and weapons to battle against what it saw as the "bad" Kurds of Turkey, while ironically supporting the "good" Kurds of Iraq against Saddam Hussein.

Forced out of Italy on January 16, 1999, Ocalan became not only a man without a country, but one lacking even a place to land. During his final hours of freedom, Russia, the Netherlands, and Switzerland all rejected him. Rather pathetically, Ocalan had become like the "Flying Dutchman" of legend whose ship was condemned to sail the seas until Judgment Day. Desperate, Ocalan finally allowed the Greeks to take him to their embassy in Nairobi, Kenya, inundated by U.S. intelligence agents following the U.S. Embassy bombing there the previous summer. The United States then provided Turkey with the technical intelligence to pinpoint his whereabouts and capture him.[2]

During these final hours, the United States ironically stood by Turkey in part because it needed Turkey as a runway for U.S. planes to bomb Iraq in support of the Iraqi Kurds. The United States had to give its Turkish ally something tangible like Ocalan because at that very moment Iraq's deputy prime minister Tariq Aziz was in Turkey in a futile attempt to end Turkey's support for the United States. Given Ocalan's fate, the Iraqi Kurds must have wondered how much longer the United States would continue to support them once Saddam Hussein was eliminated. Ocalan's final hours of freedom illustrate again the old Kurdish maxim: "The Kurds have no friends."

Initial Violence

Against a backdrop of Turkish national pride, Ocalan's capture initially led to a wide spasm of Kurdish violence in Turkey and Europe. Osman Ocalan, Ocalan's younger brother and a senior PKK commander in his own right, called upon Kurds throughout the world to "extract a heavy price from [the] Turkish state for the conspiracy it has engaged in against our leadership. Let no representative of [the] Turkish state have peace at home."[3] The PKK's sixth congress authorized its military arm the Peoples Liberation Army of Kurdistan (ARGK) "to wage a fight against this plot in the true spirit of an Apo fedayee...by attacking all kinds of enemy elements,...to wage a war that will make the enemy tremble,...[and] to proceed incessantly with the *serhildan* [Kurdish intifadah]...by merging it with the guerrillas."[4]

In Berlin, Germany, Israeli guards killed three Kurds and wounded another sixteen when they tried to storm the Israeli consulate. A group calling itself the "Revenge Hawks of Apo" killed thirteen people when it set fire to a crowded department store in Istanbul, Turkey. Further protests occurred in London, Paris, Marseilles, Brussels, Copenhagen, The Hague, Strasbourg, Stockholm, Cologne, Bonn, Hamburg, Frankfurt, Stuttgart, Hanover, Dusseldorf, Bern, Geneva, Milan, Vienna, Leipzig, Moscow, and Yerevan, among other locations.

Despite various reports of a power struggle between "the PKK's mountain [Middle East] cadres and its European wing,"[5] or a "leadership struggle...being waged among [long-time number two] Cemil Bayik, Osman Ocalan, and Mustafa Karasu,"[6] the PKK quickly reconfirmed Abdullah Ocalan as its president or general secretary and named a temporary ten-member presidential council

to act for him: Cemil Bayik, Osman Ocalan, Halil Atac, Mustafa
Karasu, Riza Altun, Duran Kalkan, Nizamettin Tas, Ali Haydar
Kaytan, Murat Karayilan, and Nizamettin Ucan.[7] Although all ten
appeared to be militants based in the Middle East, how long such a
relatively large group could hold together remained unclear. Also
uncertain was the allegiance of PKK members in Europe to a leadership group based solely in the Middle East. Indeed, further initial
reports suggested (erroneously it turned out) that such high-ranking
European leaders as Kani Yilmaz might even have been executed
by the organization for having failed to have found a sanctuary for
Abdullah Ocalan while he was in Europe.[8] These problems and
Abdullah Ocalan's subsequent calls to abandon the armed struggle
and seek a democratic republic notwithstanding, the PKK initially
continued to maintain its unity.

Turkish National Elections

Apparently benefiting from the nationalist pride Ocalan's capture
had elicited among many Turks, ultra-nationalist parties made a
strong showing in Turkey's national parliamentary elections held
on April 18, 1999. Bulent Ecevit's nationalist but leftist Democratic
Left Party (DSP) ran first with some 22.6 percent of the vote, but
the real surprise was the showing made by the Devlet Bahceli's
extreme right National Action Party (MHP), which garnered 18.6
percent and came in second. In the previous elections, the MHP
had not even won enough votes to enter parliament. Now—in a
coalition with Ecevit's party—the MHP formed the core of the
new government. On the other hand, the Islamist Virtue Party and
the two more moderate parties of the right—Mesut Yilmaz's
Motherland Party (ANAP) and Tansu Ciller's True Path Party

(DYP)—all saw significant declines in their vote totals from before. The result was an ultra-nationalist government with a seeming mandate to try Ocalan quickly, execute him, and thus successfully end the PKK's struggle. Instead, a completely different scenario was already in progress.

Initial Violence Ends

When he was first captured, Ocalan, amazingly and not without some consternation to his own followers, declared: "I really love Turkey and the Turkish people. My mother was Turkish. Sincerely, I will do all I can to be of service."[9] As he awaited trial in his prison cell on the island of Imrali near Istanbul, Ocalan next averred: "A solution based on the unity and independence of Turkey, which would guarantee peace and real democracy... is also our innermost wish."[10] He also called upon his followers to refrain from violence in the run up to the Turkish parliamentary elections that were held on April 18, 1999. Despite the attitude of many including some Kurds that Ocalan was merely trying to save his own neck and had shown himself a coward, the initial violence that had broken out upon his capture stopped almost overnight.

Interestingly, while the imprisoned Ocalan had begun calling for a democratic solution to the Kurdish problem, Ahmet Necdet Sezer, the chief justice of the Turkish Constitutional Court, openly criticized the Turkish Constitution for the restrictions it placed on basic freedoms. Sezer specifically mentioned the necessity to defend freedom of speech and eliminate what some have called "thought crimes" to imprison as terrorists those who called for Kurdish cultural rights. He also lashed out at the restrictions still existing against the use of the Kurdish language, insisted on the need to conform to the universal standards of human rights, and asked for the appropriate revision of the Turkish Constitution, among other points.[11] One year later—and largely on the basis of these comments—Sezer was elected the new president of Turkey.

In September 1999, Sami Selcuk, the chief justice of the Turkish Supreme Court of Appeals, made similar pleas to democratize the Turkish Constitution. Indeed, Selcuk went so far as to assert that the present (1982) Turkish Constitution was illegitimate because it was dictated by the military, and no serious debate against it had been allowed. Specifically, he argued that the Constitution limits personal freedom, rather than limiting the power of the state and thus makes Turkey a state with a constitution but not a constitutional state.[12] The similarities between Ocalan's recommendations for democracy to solve the Kurdish problem and the proposals of these two eminent Turkish jurists were striking. Indeed, the PKK responded that "we, as a party and a people, are ready to live with pride in a Turkey, on the essential lines drawn by the chief of the appeals court."[13]

Ocalan's Evolution

When interviewed in March 1998, Ocalan admitted he had used some terrorist methods, but argued that if you looked at the historical record honestly you would see that Turkey was the real terrorist.[14] Indeed, since its creation in the 1920s, Turkey had tried to obliterate the very existence of the Kurds by assimilating them, claiming they were just "Mountain Turks," and legally banning their language, culture, and geographical place names, among numerous other tactics. During the 1960s, Turkish president Cemal Gursel praised a book that claimed that the Kurds were Turkish in origin, and helped to popularize the phrase "spit in the face of him who calls you a Kurd" as a way to make the very word "Kurd" an insult.[15] Peaceful democratic attempts to protest against such policies landed one in prison or worse. By pursuing such actions, Turkey itself radicalized its ethnic Kurdish population and sowed Ocalan's movement.

Although Ocalan had begun his struggle as a violent Marxist committed to establishing an independent pan-Kurdish state for the approximately 20–25 million Kurds in the Middle East (half of whom lived in Turkey), over the years his ideas evolved, so that by the early 1990s, he was asking for only Kurdish political and cultural rights within the preexisting Turkish borders. In part he had mellowed in the face of the hard realities imposed by the Turkish military and the outside world hostile to any independent Kurdish state that might destabilize the volatile but geostrategically important Middle East. The Turkish state, however, saw Ocalan as insincere and felt that if it relented even slightly in its anti-Kurdish stance, the situation would escalate into the eventual breakup of Turkey itself as happened to its predecessor the Ottoman Empire.[16]

Many who really know him understand how Ocalan has come to believe that both the Turks and the Kurds would be better off living together in a Turkey that has become fully democratic. When he declared a unilateral cease-fire in March 1993, for example, Ocalan stated, "Turkish-Kurd brotherhood is about 1,000 years old, and we do not accept separation from Turkey."[17] Rather, the Kurds in Turkey "want peace, dialogue, and free political action within the framework of a democratic Turkish state." Complete democracy would not only solve the Kurdish problem within Turkey, but also fulfill the ultimate goal of Ataturk—the founder of the Turkish Republic—for a modern democratic Turkey that would be accepted as a member of the West.

The key to Turkey's future is to resolve the Kurdish problem democratically. From a zero-sum game that pitted Turks against Kurds, Ocalan's struggle had developed into a win/win proposition for both. Given Turkey's paucity of able political leaders, Ocalan—who after all was born in Turkey and spoke Turkish better than Kurdish—ironically might be seen as a better Turk than the Turkish leaders themselves.

During his recent trial, Ocalan repeated his position. He offered "to serve the Turkish state" by ending the Kurdish insurgency in return for real and complete democracy, which if Turkey spared his life he argued he could then accomplish. Here was a clear strategy to achieve a just democratic peace for everyone within the existing Turkish borders. After all the Kurds are not the only ones suffering from the lack of Turkish democracy and justice.

The Susurluk scandal in 1996, for example, demonstrated how Turkish authorities hired right-wing criminals on the lam to murder hundreds of perceived civilian enemies of the state in return for turning a blind eye to their drug trafficking.[18] In 1999, Oral Calislar, a leading Turkish journalist, was sentenced to prison as a terrorist because of a critical interview with Ocalan he had published more than five years ago. Akin Birdal, the president of the Human Rights Association in Turkey who was shot more than ten times and nearly killed by ultra-Turkish nationalists in 1998, was sentenced in 1999 to prison for calling for a peaceful solution to the Kurdish problem. The state claimed Birdal was guilty of "inciting people to hatred on the basis of class, race, or regional differences." Merve Kavakci, a female member of the Islamist Virtue Party, was expelled from her newly won seat in the Turkish parliament in 1999 for wearing a headscarf into that body. Supposedly, her actions demonstrated a desire to overthrow the secular Turkish Republic and establish a religious dictatorship. She also was stripped of her Turkish citizenship on the grounds that she had illegally obtained U.S. citizenship.

Ocalan's Call for Democracy

Instead of issuing a hard-line appeal for renewed struggle during his trial for treason that ended on June 29, 1999, with a sentence of death, Ocalan issued a remarkable statement that calls for the implementation of true democracy to solve the Kurdish problem within the existing borders of a unitary Turkey and thus fulfills Ataturk's ultimate hopes for a strong, united, and democratic Turkey that can join what is now the EU. As the centerpiece of his new attempt to reach a peaceful settlement of Turkey's Kurdish problem, it would be useful to analyze Ocalan's statement at some length: "The historical conclusion I have arrived at is that the solution for this [Kurdish] problem which has grown so big, is democratic union with the democratic, secular Republic."[19] "The democratic option...is the only alternative in solving the Kurdish question. Separation is neither possible nor necessary" (p. 18).

Throughout what was actually his defense against charges of treason and separatism, Ocalan appealed to a higher, more equitable natural law over what he saw as the narrow positive or man-made law of the Turkish state. "I am not concerned with a legalistic defense for myself" (p. 10) because "the laws [of the Turkish state]...have become an obstacle before society" (p. 46). "Needless to say...legally speaking, [my] punishment is called for" (p. 123). However, "the real dishonesty and the real treason here is not to see what is right and not to undertake any effort towards such ends" (p. 136). "The narrow articles of criminal law...expose...the need for a democratic constitutional law" (p. 144). "Therefore we can talk about its [the PKK's] moral and political legitimacy even if it was illegal" (p. 145). "It should not be seen as a flaw or a dilemma that I have tried to arrive at moral and political values and see them as a solution rather than delivering a defence in the legal sense of the word" (p. 153). "In spite of my conviction...I have no doubt that I will be acquitted morally and politically by history" (p. 155).

Early in his exposition, Ocalan declared that "Leslie Lipson's *The Democratic Civilisation* [New York: Oxford University Press, 1964]...contributed to my understanding" (p. 11). Lipson analyzes how such multiethnic states that are truly democratic such as Switzerland can successfully transcend narrow ethnonationalism and achieve peace, justice, and prosperity for all their citizens. Ocalan cited long passages from Lipson to illustrate why he now believed that "the right of nations for self-determination,...which in practical terms meant establishing a separate state, was, in fact, a blind alley...in the case of Kurdistan" (p. 11). Independence, federalism, and autonomy are "backward and sometimes even obstructive...in comparison to the rich mode of solutions democracy offered" (ibid.). "The idea of setting up a nation state... employed...mainly armed struggle and national wars of liberation....The struggle that is currently going on in the Balkans clearly shows what a diseased approach this is" (p. 55).

In adopting this position, Ocalan freely admitted that he had been mightily impressed with the Cold War victory of the United States and the West over communism. "Victory belongs to democracy....This is clear when one looks at the way the US and Great Britain lead and shape the world" (p. 56). "Democracy...led to the supremacy of the West. Western civilisation can, in this sense, be termed democratic civilisation" (p. 59). "It seems that the democratic system has insured its victory into the 2000s and cannot be stopped spreading in depth to all societies" (p. 17).

Ocalan also readily admitted to having made costly errors: "Many mistakes have been made by us, by myself. They have caused great pain" (p. 114). "I find that my principle [sic] shortcoming was during the ceasefire episode [presumably March–May 1993], in not seeing and evaluating the preparations the state was making and therefore missing an historic opportunity" (p. 104). "In its programme and its practice as well [the PKK] bears the marks of the dogmatic and ideological approach of the radical youth movement of those [Cold War] years" (p. 127). "Especially in 1997, under the name of an offensive against village guards, there were attacks on civilians, among them women and children, that should never have been the target of military attacks" (p. 130).

Ocalan even praised Ataturk, the founder of modern Turkey and the Turkish leader most often identified with the policy of trying to obliterate the Kurds. "Some primitive Kurdish intellectuals...could not share their programme with Mustafa Kemal [Ataturk] and became narrow-minded separatists.... They ended up participating in the [Sheikh Said] uprising of 1925...a weak affair, without a programme, disorganised and leaderless" (p. 24). Ocalan argued that "it is well known that the latter [Kurdish feudal lords] were not really acting out of nationalist fervor but were interested in achieving local dominance for their tribe" (p. 54). "One cannot ascribe to Ataturk either a particular opposition to democracy or to Kurds" (p. 25). "The acceptance of Turkish as the official language and its development were only natural" (p. 73). However, "imposing a ban on the Kurdish language until 1992...is not consistent with Ataturkism.... If Ataturk were alive today, he would take the most appropriate stand, the one that supports a democratic union with the Republic" (p. 82).

Finally, the PKK leader also found praise for the Turkish army. "The army is more sensitive than the most seemingly democratic parties.... The army has taken upon itself to be the protector of democratic norms.... Today the army is not a threat to democracy, but on the contrary a force that guarantees that democracy will move on to the next stage in a healthy manner" (p. 68).

Originally a child of socialism and Marxism, Ocalan further spent considerable time musing philosophically over their practical failures. "Socialists were prey to vapid generalisations and were slipshod in practice" (p. 38). "Coupled with a dogmatic outlook, Marxism lessened the chance of a creative approach to the challenges which faced us" (p. 106). He still felt, however, that "this of course does not mean that socialism left no positive legacy" (p. 36), since "the socialist experiment...left a great experience behind it...and will form a synthesis between its achievements and what it has to achieve" (p. 37). Indeed, Marxist thought patterns clearly remained, as Ocalan explained how "a new synthesis will be born out of the thesis and antithesis. The State-PKK opposition will lead to the synthesis of a Democratic Republic" (p. 46).

Ocalan still maintained, however, that "the PKK's rebellion using its own methods, and leading the movement as a military force was legitimate" (p. 134). "Nowadays everybody talks about the radicalism of the methods of the PKK without actually seeing how the rulers behaved historically and politically" (p. 134). "The legitimacy of uprising against any system of repression as extensive as the 'language ban' of the 1982 Constitution should be kept in mind when discussing this illegal movement" (p. 123). "There was a struggle to legitimately live like human beings and...many sacrifices were made for a more democratic society and republic" (pp. 132–33). "History will demonstrate that this movement [the PKK] did not target the founder of the republic but was a movement aiming at curing a decaying, sick entity.... We oppose[d] ... the oligarchic, undemocratic, feudal values and structures in Turkish society" (p. 114). "The existing legal system and Constitution are an impediment to democratic rights" (p. 121). As for blame, "everybody from the highest organs of the state to the most backward, stupid, cruel persons, are all of us responsible" (p. 133).

How then did Ocalan now see the Kurdish problem and what did he seek? "If the obstacles to the use of the Kurdish language and culture [are removed],... integration of the Kurdish people with the state will occur. Negative perceptions and distrust of the state will change to positive perceptions and trust. The basis for rebellion and confrontation will be finished" (p. 97). Such a "solution will bring wealth, unity and peace" (p. 95). "To win the Kurds as a people is to win the Middle East" (p. 148) and "a Turkey that has solved its internal problems in this manner will be [a] Turkey that has won the capacity to emerge as an internationally powerful force" (p. 151).

Ocalan himself readily admitted that his analysis was "repetitious at times" (p. 11). This is especially true of his concept of a democratic solution to the Kurdish problem. Although he complained that in writing his declaration, "I have not had much opportunity [to have access to research materials]" (ibid.), others might remark on the liberality of the Turkish state in allowing him to write anything, let alone publish it. Indeed, some have argued that since Ocalan had been incarcerated by the Turkish authorities, anything he now said was suspect. To alleviate this problem, these critics suggested that the PKK should have declared, the moment

Ocalan was captured, that he no longer was in a position to speak for the organization.

Replying to skeptics, Ocalan maintained that his declaration "is neither a tactical attempt to save the day or an unprincipled turn-around" (p. 129). "My effort to end the armed conflict is not an attempt to save my skin" (p. 145). Indeed, his arguments were not wholly new. As mentioned above, he discussed most of them in a more embryonic form with the present author when he interviewed Ocalan in March 1998, eleven months before the Turkish authorities captured him. As early as 1991, Ocalan was arguing that independence was an inappropriate solution to the Kurdish problem in Turkey. Ocalan hoped that his declaration "will leave for future [generations] a very precious legacy of solving the problem" (p. 10), and averred that "if I am given the opportunity, I will direct all my efforts towards attaining, and representing the democratic union of free citizens and peoples with the republic, in peace and fraternity" (p. 110).

Implicit Bargaining

Ocalan's death sentence began a process of implicit bargaining between the state and the PKK that in truth had already begun shortly after his capture. It will be recalled that Ocalan told his captors on the flight back to Turkey that he wanted to be of service to the state. A few days later, Prime Minister Ecevit declared that the state would consider changing its policies toward the Kurds if the PKK would lay down its arms: "If and when conditions become more conducive to solving certain problems, then new approaches may prevail. A substantial decrease in terrorism would be conducive to improvements and reforms in the social, economic and political life of the country."[20]

This process of implicit bargaining continued once Ocalan's trial actually began and the PKK leader set forward his vision of a "democratic republic." The PKK presidential council declared that Ocalan "has made all-embracing statements concerning... the solution of the Kurdish Question in a spirit of peace.... His approach is mature, respectful and responsible. Great warriors also know how to be great peacemakers and now to take realistic initiatives."[21] The council also claimed that Ocalan "behaves respectfully towards the Turkish people," but pointedly added that "we have suffered the greater devastation."

Ocalan's death sentence on June 29, 1999, probably met with a restrained reaction from most Kurds—in contrast to the fury his initial capture in February had elicited—because they realized that the court's action was just an initial step in what was going to be a continuing process of implicit bargaining. The PKK presidential council noted, however, that "this decision will never be acceptable to our people and our party," warned "that this dangerous verdict has potential consequences that could ignite an area far wider than that of Turkey and Kurdistan," but for the time being at least called for only "restrained protests."[22] A week later another statement from the PKK council declared that "the death sentence... is a... continuation of the conflict between the Turks and Kurds into the dawn of the 21st Century," claimed that it "will not serve the Turkish nation but will only benefit forces who trade in war," and maintained that "Ocalan, despite all the difficulties, is trying to open doors to the resolution of the Kurdish Question."[23] In a wide-ranging interview, Duran Kalkan, a member of the PKK's presidential council, concluded that "each positive step [from the Turkish side] will be answered with a positive step from our side."[24]

Surveying the situation, the prominent Turkish journalist Mehmet Ali Birand wrote that "Turkish public opinion is changing dramatically in the wake of the Abdullah Ocalan trial."[25] Birand argued that "the most important sign of this change was evidenced when Ertugrul Ozkok, the editor in chief of *Hurriyet*, Turkey's highest-circulation daily and a champion of progovernment opinions, urged that the death sentence be met with circumspection." Birand added that "another sign of change is that some prominent people known to be close to the state are loudly declaring that the Kurdish identity must be recognized."

Shortly after his conviction, in a statement announced by his lawyers, Ocalan ordered his guerrillas to evacuate Turkey by the end of the year and declared that this indicated his sincerity regarding ending the conflict: "I call upon the PKK to end the armed struggle and withdraw their forces outside the borders of Turkey, for the sake of peace, from September 1, 1999."[26] Although responding that "the Turkish side will never negotiate with anyone or any organization [on the Kurdish problem]," Turkish prime minister Bulent Ecevit implicitly did so anyway when he added: "To end separatist terrorism everyone who cares for Turkey must contribute. We do not know how much will be achieved. Time will tell."[27] Analyzing the developing process, *Briefing*, which describes itself as a Turkish "weekly inside perspective on Turkish political, economic and business affairs," concluded that "whether the state likes it, admits it, or even realizes it, it is now, in an indirect fashion, sitting down to the negotiating table with Abdullah Ocalan."[28]

At almost the exact same time, the U.S. assistant secretary of state for democracy, human rights, and labor, Harold Hongju Koh, visited Turkey and met with a wide variety of people. Although recognizing Turkey's right to defend itself against the

PKK, he upset many Turkish officials with his strong and eloquent recommendations concerning some of the very themes Ocalan was now broaching.[29] Koh argued, for example, that "one can oppose terrorism and still support human rights." He added that "most Kurds in Turkey...want to remain Turkish citizens, while enjoying the basic human rights guaranteed to all people under international law, including freedom to express one's language and culture, and freedom to organize political parties that represent their interests." He maintained that "far from hurting Turkey's territorial integrity, an inclusive policy that acknowledged these rights would strengthen the Turkish state by giving the Kurdish community a genuine stake in their country's future." In other words, Koh seemed to be saying that now that Ocalan had been captured and had offered to withdraw his fighters from Turkey, Turkey had no further excuses not to move forward on human rights and democratization. It was time for Turkey to reconcile with its citizens of Kurdish ethnic heritage by recognizing their linguistic, cultural, and political identity.

Surveying the scene, one could not help but notice that where once any quotation printed from Ocalan or another PKK fighter might have left a journalist open to prosecution on the grounds that he was aiding an illegal organization, now none of the media seemed to fear quoting Ocalan at length. This even included his denials that recent violence in Turkey's southeast was the PKK's work. Rather, Ocalan explained it as the work of "provocateurs" and declared through his attorneys that this was one reason he had called on his fighters to withdraw from Turkey. Once this was accomplished, it would become clear who the true provocateurs were, and they would no longer be able to play the state off against the PKK.[30]

In August 1999 yet another event signaled a potentially more conciliatory attitude on the state's part when President Suleyman Demirel received seven HADEP mayors in the presidential palace in Ankara and engaged them in broad discussions. HADEP had been founded in 1994 as a legal Kurdish party after its predecessor DEP (the Democracy Party) had been closed and several of its MPs including Leyla Zana imprisoned for supposedly supporting the PKK. Although it had not received enough votes in the April 1999 national elections to enter the Turkish parliament, it had elected numerous mayors in the local elections that had been held at the same time. By receiving some of these mayors in Ankara, Demirel was sending a clear signal that the state was now willing to recognize openly the legitimacy of certain forms of Kurdish political activity.[31]

Ironically creating an even greater impression, especially on the Turkish public that had always held the state and its institutions in reverent respect, was the devastating earthquake that struck the western part of the country on August 17, 1999. As many as 20,000 or more persons perished, mostly due to substandard buildings corrupt officials had allowed to be constructed and that collapsed like sand castles killing their inhabitants beneath their rubble. The universal outrage and indescribable grief was then compounded when the state seemed virtually paralyzed in its lack of response, while often reviled foreigners such as the Greeks quickly responded with aid that saved thousands. For the first time ever, the average Turk seemed to question the sanctity of the so-called *Devlet Baba* or Daddy State. One unspoken lesson here was that maybe the Kurds had legitimate grievances against the state if average Turks themselves were now questioning it. From his prison cell on Imrali, Ocalan announced that to show its sympathy for the victims of the earthquake, the PKK would begin its withdrawal from Turkey immediately.

Kivrikoglu Statement

At the beginning of September 1999, General Huseyin Kivrikoglu, the chief of the Turkish general staff, seemingly furthered the process of implicit bargaining with his comments on the PKK's partial withdrawal from Turkey during an interview with a select group of journalists: "The leader of the terrorists [Ocalan] admitted, the terrorists have realized they will get nowhere with the use of arms. Now they are contemplating a solution through political means."[32] The general continued, "they [the PKK] do not want federation, either. What they want are cultural rights," and added, "some of these rights have already been given to them. Kurdish newspapers and cassettes are free. Despite the fact that it is banned, radio and TV stations are operating in Kurdish in eastern and southeastern Turkey." Kivrikoglu also noted that "HADEP controls the municipalities in 37 cities and major townships.... No one challenged their election. As long as they do a decent job and serve the people, no one will raise any objections. Turkey has already given them [the Kurds] many rights." Kivrikoglu also refrained from calling for Ocalan's execution: "The army should remain silent. We are a party to the conflict. And when our opinion is sought, we might respond emotionally."

Ocalan welcomed Kivrikoglu's statement as a "positive step in developing cultural freedom and democratization,"[33] and Cemil Bayik, long seen as the PKK's number two man, declared that "in recognition of our positive steps, the Turkish General Staff has now made a gesture in this direction too."[34] Bayik added that the general's word "are in a sense an answer to our party's declaration. We see them as such and follow them very attentively."

Given the resulting speculation that it was implicitly bargaining with Ocalan and the PKK, however, the general staff quickly backed off: "It is out of the question that the general staff accept the PKK terror organization as an interlocutor, discuss its suggestions, or make any concessions."[35] The military declared that "what they [the PKK] really must do is surrender their weapons...and turn themselves in." Shortly afterward, the army further dismissed the PKK's peace offers as "propaganda spread by the terrorist organization in order to maneuver itself out of the dead end it has reached," and declared that "for this reason the Turkish armed forces are determined to continue the battle until the last terrorist has been neutralized."[36]

In reply, the PKK presidential council stated: "While we are making great sacrifices for peace and democracy we reject capitulation," and declared: "We expect positive contributions to peace and democracy from the civil institutions of the state and especially from the Turkish Armed Forces."[37] For his part Ecevit peevishly declared: "Scarcely we have a day without a statement from Abdullah Ocalan. He has almost become one of our mainstream politicians. This is a little bit too much."[38]

Token Surrenders

To restart the process of implicit bargaining, Ocalan next called on a small group of his militants to surrender to the Turkish authorities. The move coincided with Ecevit's visit to Washington, DC, to meet with U.S. president Bill Clinton at the end of September 1999, and was intended to win the PKK publicity as the bearer of peace, democracy, and human rights before a full complement of the local and foreign press. The Turkish authorities refused to play the game, however. Only a reduced group of eight militants led by Ali Sapan, the former PKK spokesman in Europe who had since been demoted, ended up obscurely turning themselves in on October 1, after crossing the border into southeastern Turkey from northern Iraq. On October 29, 1999, a second eight-member group flew in from Vienna, Austria, and surrendered in Istanbul.

Although Ecevit was quoted as saying: "If the armed militants in the mountains deliver themselves to justice, we would regard that as a positive development,"[39] the state largely chose to ignore the token surrenders. Silence after all can be an effective tactic. What is more the state apparently saw itself in a win/win situation. It could simply ignore Ocalan's moves toward dismantling his military struggle, while sitting back and watching the PKK itself possibly fall into internal fighting over the tactics of its imprisoned leader.

The so-called Peace and Democratic Solution Group that turned itself in to the Turkish authorities on October 1, 1999, carried letters addressed to Demirel, Ecevit, Kivrikoglu, and Yildirim Akbulut, the speaker of parliament. Given the bitterness of its long struggle against the state, the content of these letters demonstrated how far the PKK now claimed its position had changed.[40] The PKK declared that it wished to contribute to "the one hundred and fifty years of democratic people's struggle by the people of Turkey," and owned that "whatever its rights and wrongs, the PKK serves the same purpose as part of the Turkish people's struggle to achieve a contemporary society." Continuing, the PKK argued that "our party realised that it could not isolate itself from these developments. Therefore, it decided to change its cold-war inspired political strategy."

After promising that "this change of strategy will be officially approved at its extraordinary [seventh] congress which will be held in the near future," the PKK declared that "our President [Ocalan] has been aware since 1993 that continuing the armed struggle is meaningless and expressed the view of uniting with Turkey within the framework of democracy." Attempting to put the best possible face on its diminished position, the PKK wrote "this could not be achieved until our President was brought back to Turkey. We believe that now that our President is closer to the Turkish state and its people something good will come from it. As the Turkish saying goes 'There is something good in every incident.' "

After praising Demirel for having met with the HADEP mayors the past August and recognizing the "Kurdish reality" in 1992, the PKK suggested that "a general amnesty as part of the democratisation of Turkey will help remove the protracted tension. Also it is obvious that any legal changes conceding cultural and language freedom will assist." Returning to its process of implicit bargaining, the PKK asserted that "we are aware that the armed struggle and sufferings have created a problem of confidence," but claimed that "our current approach and steps have brought a positive development to this issue. There are many examples where, after long wars and conflicts, people have managed to live together in peace after the conflict ended." In closing, the PKK letter averred that "the Kurdish and Turkish people are like flesh and blood and are inseparable," wished Demirel well, and was signed "with respect and sincere feelings."

Europe

Ever since Ataturk himself proclaimed modern Turkey's goal to be the achievement of the level of contemporary civilization, Turkey has sought to join the West. In recent decades this has ultimately meant membership in what has now become the EU. For many years this seemed to be the impossible dream. Ocalan's capture and subsequent proposals for a democratic republic in which the Kurdish problem would be solved, however, suddenly made this vision a possibility.

On November 18–19, 1999, Istanbul hosted the final major conference of the twentieth century when the representatives of more than fifty states gathered there for a summit meeting of the Organization for Security and Cooperation in Europe (OSCE). Although the Kurdish problem was not officially broached, it was certainly on the minds of many. After all eleven of the fifteen members of the EU were currently being ruled by leftist governments that regarded the Kurdish question as a moral cause akin to that of Kosovo for which NATO had just waged war. Until Turkey successfully implemented the OSCE's Copenhagen Criteria of minority rights for its Kurdish population and broad human rights reforms as demanded by the EU, Turkey could not hope to break through the membership logjam set by the EU. In short, Turkish EU membership depended on solving its Kurdish problem to the satisfaction of the EU. And if the truth be told, this was largely another way of declaring that Turkey's EU future depended to an ironic degree on Ocalan.

Ocalan and his associates were certainly aware of this situation. Thus, the PKK presidential council sent a long letter to the OSCE leaders gathering in Istanbul.[41] "It is no more than an illusion to expect the democratisation of Turkey without a resolution of the Kurdish problem.... Countries which have not resolved the Kurdish problem have inevitably had to shape their laws and institutions in an anti-democratic manner in order to keep the Kurds under control. This has meant that these countries, and primarily Turkey, have remained authoritarian and oppressive regimes." If Turkey could solve its Kurdish problem, however, "there will no longer be a need for such anti-democratic laws and institutions." From his prison cell, Ocalan concurred: "Again, I wish to reiterate my conviction that solving the Kurdish question and creating the grounds for democracy in Turkey will be a guarantee for peace in the Middle East and far beyond."[42]

On November 25, 1999, however, the Turkish court of appeals rejected Ocalan's appeal of his death sentence. The European Court of Human Rights (ECtHR)—to which Turkey belonged—quickly issued interim measures asking Turkey to suspend the execution until it could rule on his appeal, a process that was still continuing as of this writing early in 2007. At this point, Turkish candidacy for EU membership entered the picture as the organization gathered in Helsinki, Finland, to considered new members. On December 11, 1999, Turkey was finally accepted as a candidate member, although no date was set for candidacy talks to commence. It was clear, moreover, that Turkey's candidacy hinged on the satisfactory solution of its Kurdish problem and specifically its suspension of Ocalan's death sentence. As the German ambassador to Turkey Hans Joachim Vergau had declared bluntly, "if you execute Ocalan, you can forget Helsinki."[43]

The PKK presidential council was quick to claim some of the credit.[44] "The acceptance of Turkey's candidacy is the result of a process initiated by our President, Abdullah Ocalan...[and] was implemented with the intense efforts of our party." The PKK argued that "our push for a democratic solution of Turkey's problems played a key role in creating a climate that was conducive for the recent EU decision.... Kurdish diplomacy was mobilised to make Turkey's candidacy to EU membership a reality and EU countries overcame their doubts concerning Turkey largely as a result of such Kurdish efforts."

Mesut Yilmaz, a former prime minister and in 1999 the head of one of the three parties forming the Ecevit coalition government, seemed to agree with this assessment of the importance of the Kurds for Turkey's EU future when he declared that "the road to the EU passes through Diyarbakir."[45] Sounding much like Ocalan himself, Yilmaz asserted, "first of all we have to strengthen democracy, not only in its form but in its substance as well," and stressed that "his party does not see the broadening of rights and freedoms as a danger that threatens the state...that this would, on the contrary, strengthen the state apparatus."

Although Ecevit himself was more cautious, his foreign minister Ismail Cem seemingly seconded Ocalan by declaring that Kurdish broadcasting should be allowed: "Everyone should have the right to speak on television in their native language, just as I am sitting here today speaking in my own native tongue."[46] When a private citizen petitioned an Ankara state security court to try Cem for breaching article eight of the antiterror law prohibiting separatist propaganda, the complaint was dismissed on the grounds that in a democracy such topics were open to discussion. At the same time President Demirel continued the confidence-building process by now inviting a group of prominent human rights activists from the southeast to the presidential palace. There some of them made speeches that would have landed them in jail had they been uttered a few years earlier.

On the other hand, someone ordered the police to raid the offices of HADEP in Diyarbakir and four other smaller cities. Police arrested eleven party leaders and seized documents and cassettes. Laws that limited free debate of the Kurdish problem remained in effect. *Ozgur Bakis*, the largest pro-Kurdish daily in Turkey, was still banned in the five provinces under emergency rule, and the distribution of two Kurdish magazines was also halted. Kanal 21, a television station in Diyarbakir, remained shut down for broadcasting music deemed to incite Kurdish separatism.

Nevertheless, the process of implicit bargaining now continued with a new sense of importance. Murat Karayilan, a member of the PKK presidential council, declared that "this is a big chance for Turkey," but warned Ocalan's "execution means the execution of the Kurdish people...a revival of the armed conflict...and it would mean to prevent Turkey from entering the European Union."[47] He further argued "it would be a fatal error to think that the PKK has been defeated.... We also have the power to escalate the war." Ertugrul Ozkok, a leading Turkish journalist with a pulse on official thinking, also spoke out against executing Ocalan: "The three hanging incidents in our history have brought no happiness to our country.... Would it be too much if we just once tried to attain this [happiness and tranquility] by not hanging?"[48] General Kivrikoglu owned that fighting in the Kurdish region had declined "by 90%"[49] since Ocalan had ordered his guerrillas to begin withdrawing the previous summer.

Ismet Berkan, an important leftist journalist, elaborated on the subject of domestic peace when he asserted that "this problem has nothing to do with Europe. It is mostly to do with internal politics."[50] He claimed that "the agencies providing reports to the government on this issue do not quote European reaction at the top of their concerns." Instead, "it is felt strongly that Ocalan's execution would undermine the domestic peace...[and] rekindle terrorism." President Demirel also urged postponement of the execution in deference to "Turkey's higher interests."[51]

Others argued that executing Ocalan would hurt the Turkish economy by refueling galloping inflation and calling into question the government's very stability seen as necessary to maintain the economy's fragile recovery. The allusion to the government's stability referred to the open disagreement between Ecevit who was against execution and his deputy prime minister Devlet Bahceli, the leader of the ultra-nationalist MHP, who favored it. Finally, in a seven-hour coalition summit meeting of the two on January 12, 2000, the government agreed to comply with the request of the ECtHR for a stay of execution until it had ruled on the case. Ecevit warned, however, that "we have agreed that if the terrorist organization and its supporters attempt to use this decision against the high interests of Turkey, the suspension will end and the execution process will immediately begin."[52] Although this warning partially appeased Bahceli, he had clearly compromised a great deal, given his original hard-line position that had initially carried him to such political prominence during the April 1999 national elections. The process of implicit bargaining had reached a new degree.

Ocalan described the conditional stay of his execution as "important" and "historic."[53] Boldly, he asserted that "if they execute me, the EU candidacy, the economy and peace will all go down.... These all depend on my staying alive. I am a synthesis of values, not just a person. I represent democracy." Then, however, he adopted a more modest position. "Let us be humble. Let us display a change of heart and mentality," and promised that "if the government and state officials adopt a correct attitude, we shall not take any wrong steps." He declared: "Now that this summit is over, the most important task awaiting Turkey and needed is carrying out the reforms that will also fulfill the requirements of EU membership." He explained that "there is a need for general amnesty" and "because everyone has suffered,...the healing must be done all together."

The PKK central committee termed the government's action a "decision of the century" that "comforted and created more hope for peace among the two peoples of Turkey."[54] Responding to the government's warning that it would restart the execution process if the PKK would "use the decision against the highest interests of Turkey," the central committee affirmed: "Turkish leaders with common sense, democratic forces and nationalists can be sure that our party will not tolerate any force to weaken Turkey...or harm its interests." The central committee also moved quickly to further the implicit bargaining process toward Ocalan's eventual release, however, by declaring that "free and healthy environments need to be created for Ocalan so he can work for a Democratic Turkey and solving the Kurdish issue in a peaceful way."

Obviously irritated and not yet willing to grant Ocalan any legitimacy, Ecevit responded: "Ocalan and his supporters are trying to dictate to the Turkish government, and they are making statements with this aim. This is unacceptable. It would be to his advantage to keep quiet.... We cannot allow Ocalan to use Imrali as a political pulpit"[55] Nevertheless, this is, of course, exactly what Ocalan was doing, while Ecevit's warnings were largely his responses in the evolving process of implicit bargaining. Although the ultra-nationalists and Islamists still called for Ocalan's execution, most observers such as Sedat Ergin, a prominent journalist writing in *Hurriyet,* concluded that "thus Ocalan has been turned into a strategic card with which...to discourage the PKK from action."[56]

Obviously, Ocalan's sudden and dramatic capture by Turkish commandos in February 1999 had led to a process of continuing implicit bargaining between the Turkish government and the PKK that held out the hope of a win/win result for all the parties involved. If handled skillfully and sincerely, it could not only result in an end to the long and bloody PKK insurgency, but also lead to a more healthy economy and much needed democratization of Turkish politics that would satisfy the requirements for admission into the EU. Once this was effected, Turkey's Kurdish problem would also become the EU's problem and responsibility. In addition, EU admission would help guarantee Turkey's territorial integrity, the very point that has always prevented the government from initiating the steps that would solve its Kurdish problem.

Much, of course, remained to be accomplished, and it was uncertain what paths the continuing process of implicit bargaining would take. Ahmet Turan Demir, the general chairman of HADEP, suggested that "first of all, general amnesty should be declared."[57] Then, "a new constitution with a consensus in accordance with today's universal standards [and] the democratization of all laws, primarily criminal law, will be the issues that we will pursue." Specifics "include the recognition of the Kurdish identity, practicing cultural rights, and the right to have education in Kurdish." Other goals involved the right of Kurds to return to their villages, the lifting of Emergency Rule (OHAL) and the village guard system, and changes in the electoral system that will permit every political party to be represented in the parliament according to the vote it has received. This latter provision meant rescinding the ten-percent rule that eliminated parties such as HADEP from receiving any representation at all. At its extraordinary seventh party congress held January 2–23, 2000, the PKK adopted a "Peace Project" that incorporated several of these points.[58] Other main points announced by the PKK included securing the life and freedom of

Ocalan, increased investment in the southeast, and preservation of historic and environmental treasures threatened by the Ilisu Dam in the southeast.

The Turkish government, of course, continued to pursue its own agenda. Unfortunately, there were still powerful forces in Turkey that did not seek further democratization, or even an end to what for them continued to be a profitable war. On February 19, 2000, for example, three main HADEP majors were suddenly arrested and accused of supporting the PKK: Feridun Celik of Diyarbakir, Selim Ozalp of Siirt, and Bingol mayor Feyzullah Karaslan. Although they were quickly released and allowed to return to their jobs, their trial began two months later. Daniel Cohn-Bendit, the co-chairman of the Turkey–EU Parliamentary Commission, was initially denied permission to visit the imprisoned Leyla Zana, a decision then reversed. The CNN TV affiliate in Turkey was ordered off the air for twenty-four hours because it asked whether history might one day regard Ocalan as a Turkish version of Nelson Mandela. Ocalan himself was no longer permitted to make statements to the press, and access to his lawyers was reduced. Ecevit continued to argue that Kurdish was not a language, only a dialect, and that there was no Kurdish ethnic problem in Turkey, only a question of economic development in the southeast. Despite the PKK's abandonment of the guerrilla struggle, emergency rule in several southeastern provinces continued until the end of 2002, and the village guards have not been disbanded. In addition, it appeared that there would be no peace dividend, as the Turkish military planned to increase spending on modernization and the purchase of tanks and helicopters.

Furthermore, the March 2000 celebration of the Kurdish holiday *Newroz* in Istanbul was banned by Governor Erol Cakir because the application for permission used the non-Turkish letter "w" in the word "*Newroz,*" instead of the preferred Turkish spelling "*Nevroz.*" Ludicrously, of course, the letter "w" appeared on the door of virtually every public toilet in Turkey. Crude threats led to prominent Turkish sociologist Serif Mardin deciding not to participate in an international conference on the Kurds sponsored by American University in Washington, DC, on April 17, 2000. And in May 2000, state minister Mehmet Ali Irtemcelik, who had been instrumental in obtaining Turkey's EU candidacy the previous December, resigned citing deep differences in the understanding of democracy between himself and Ecevit.

On the other hand, the unexpected decision by the Turkish parliament in April 2000 not to extend President Demirel's term for another five years, despite the Turkish military's clear preference for him, was seen as implementing one of the most critical of the Copenhagen Criteria required for EU membership—civilian control of the military. It also demonstrated a willingness to move on from Demirel's tired old platitudes in search of new bolder approaches. That this indeed was the case became clear when the Turkish parliament elected Ahmet Necdet Sezer, the chief justice of the Turkish Constitutional Court, the new president of Turkey in May 2000. As detailed above, Sezer had only come to the attention of the Turkish public a year earlier by criticizing the Turkish Constitution for the restrictions it placed on basic freedoms, including usage of the Kurdish language, and advocating greater constitutionally protected freedom of thought and expression.

Recent Events

As part of its drive to win a date for EU accession talks to begin, Turkey rescinded Ocalan's death sentence and commuted it to life imprisonment in 2002. A series of harmonization laws began to be passed in an attempt to meet the EU *acquis communauataire* or body of economic, social, administrative, and environmental legislation that all EU member states were required to implement. Turkey's sudden economic collapse in February 2001 and the resulting unpopularity of the Ecevit coalition government eventually led to the overwhelming victory of Recep Tayyip Erdogan's moderate Islamic AK Party in November 2002 as Turkey's first majority government since the victory of Turgut Ozal's ANAP Party in 1987. Early in March 2003, by the smallest of margins, the new majority AK-controlled parliament declined to support the U.S. invasion of northern Iraq. This resulted in dramatically important developments for the evolution of the Kurdish issue in Iraq as detailed in chapters 2 and 3.

In a confused attempt to reflect supposed moves toward peaceful politics (and possibly earn itself omission from various lists of terrorist organizations), the PKK changed its name first to KADEK (Kurdistan Freedom and Democracy Congress), then to Kongra Gel (People's Congress), and finally back to the PKK.[59] Although he continued to be recognized as the leader of the PKK, Ocalan's statements from prison often seemed perplexing. One such declaration called for the Kurds to live under a system of "democratic confederalism" where the Kurds somehow would rule themselves within a Turkish state with their rights protected by EU-style laws.[60] Although more than three million Turkish Kurds signed a petition in 2006 calling for Ocalan's release, the PKK clearly was dividing.

In 2005, Ocalan's younger brother Osman Ocalan and several hundred followers established another group called the Patriotic Democratic Front, which was headquartered near Mosul in northern Iraq. Under the leadership of Murat Karayilan, some 5,000

PKK guerrillas remained entrenched in the Kandil Mountains straddling the border between northern Iraq and Iran. A militant new PKK Iranian offshoot called PJAK joined it there. Frustrated by the lack of progress, the PKK began low-level military operations again in June 2004, only to announce another cease-fire in October 2006, which quickly broke down. During 2006, the TAK (Kurdistan Freedom Hawks or Falcons) began to set off bombs in several Turkish cities. It remained unclear whether the TAK was connected to the PKK or a rival breakaway organization. In Europe, the Kongra Gel under the leadership of Zubeyir Aydar acted as a peaceful political wing of the PKK.

In Turkey, HADEP was followed in 2003 by DEHAP and then in 2005 by DTP. Osman Baydemir (born 1971) was elected mayor of Diyarbakir in 2004 and quickly emerged as one of the most successful young ethnic Kurdish politicians in Turkey. Baydemir also carried his message of achieving Kurdish rights peacefully in his travels to Europe and the United States, but was constantly in danger of being arrested for his activities. The off-again, on-again Ilisu Dam project on the Tigris River was touted by the government as a way to help modernize the southeast's agriculture; however, opponents denounced the project as a way literally to drown the Kurdish historical presence in the area. In August 2005, the Turkish prime minister Recep Tayyip Erdogan declared that Turkey had a "Kurdish problem," had made "grave mistakes" in the past, and now needed "more democracy to solve the problem."[61] ROJ TV, a Kurdish television station in Denmark connected to the PKK, stoked Kurdish self-awareness throughout Turkey, the Middle East, and Europe. In March 2007, former president Kenan Evren amazingly proposed federalism as a solution to Turkey's Kurdish problem and general difficulties in implementing democracy.[62] Turkey's secretive Deep State, however, continued to oppose Turkey's democratization and Kurdish rights. In April 2007, Turkey was thrown into a crisis over the election of a new president and its overall future direction. Ironically, the moderate Islamist AK Party favored continued reform and Turkey's EU candidacy, whereas the secularists and military took a more skeptical attitude, fearing that these policies challenged their long-held privileged positions.

On July 22, 2007, Erdogan's AK Party won another tremendous electoral victory, which a month later enabled it to elect in the new parliament its candidate Abdullah Gul as Turkey's new president. Erdogan assured everyone that he would continue to defend secularism and press ahead with EU-mandated reforms. Although he also promised to continue the fight against the PKK, it now even seemed possible to pursue a renewed political solution to the Kurdish problem as the AK Party had further suprised analysts by winning some 52 percent of the vote in Turkey's ethnic Kurdish areas of the southeast. This electoral support was apparently due to the AK Party's economic policies and its conservative religious appeal to many traditional minded Kurds. In yet another important development, for the first time since the early 1990s, avowed Kurdish deputies also entered the Turkish parliament when more than twenty DTP candidates were elected as independents.

CHAPTER 5

TURKEY'S EU PROMISE

On October 3, 2005, Turkey's[1] long-standing Kurdish problem[2] potentially entered a new phase when the EU formally initiated accession negotiations with Turkey.[3] Although this process promises to be long and arduous, it also represents a watershed opportunity for the solution of Turkey's Kurdish problem. The Copenhagen Criteria required for EU membership mandate the stability of institutions guaranteeing democracy, the rule of law, human rights, and protection of minority rights. There is no bargaining on these criteria. Turkey is required to accept them for entry into the EU. For all Turkish citizens (ethnic Turks and ethnic Kurds alike) who want to fulfill Mustafa Kemal Ataturk's ultimate goal of achieving contemporary civilization,[4] EU membership for Turkey would be a win/win situation because it would guarantee truly democratic Kurdish rights within the confines of Turkey's territorial integrity.

Turkey's EU candidacy would also help put the lie to the clash-of-civilizations thesis[5] of inevitable war and even Armageddon between the Christian West and Islamic East. As a member of the EU, Turkey would offer the Muslim world an attractive moderate model of cooperation and prosperity with the West that would benefit all. In addition, young, hardworking Turkish workers would help solve Europe's problem of zero population growth not being able to support the EU's welfare state. Furthermore, Turkey's geostrategic access to the gas and oil supplies of the Middle East and Central Asia would make Turkey invaluable for the EU's future energy needs as well as providing alternative energy routes to Europe.

However, the Turkish EU candidacy should not be supported naively. Kerim Yildiz is the executive director of the Kurdish Human Rights Project in London and a member of the Board of Directors of the EU Turkey Civic Commission (EUTCC), an NGO that is promoting Turkey's EU candidacy as a way to solve the Kurdish problem. Yildiz has aptly demonstrated the many pitfalls that Turkey, the Kurds, and the EU must face along the way.[6] On the one hand, Yildiz optimistically declares that "for the Kurds, the stipulations in the field of minority and human rights attendant to the accession process offer unparalleled scope to achieve long-term justice and security. Already, the prospect of accession has triggered rapid and extensive legislative reforms since 2002."[7] On the other hand, Yildiz warns, "questions must be asked as to whether Turkey has truly changed her colours, and whether the EU's decision to open accession talks was based on a genuinely objective appraisal of Turkish progress on democratization and human rights."[8]

Recent Turkish reforms to meet EU-mandated criteria sometimes appear to be merely paper concessions, tokens, illusory, or simply sham measures. Similarly, in December 1991, Prime Minister Suleyman Demirel declared that "Turkey has recognized the Kurdish reality."[9] Two years later, the new prime minister Tansu Ciller broached the "Basque model" as a potential formula for solving Turkey's Kurdish problem after a meeting with the Spanish prime minister.[10] Then in December 1999, the former prime minister Mesut Yilmaz declared that "the road to the EU passes through Diyarbakir,"[11] the largest city in Turkey's southeast and long considered the unofficial capital of the historic Kurdish provinces in Turkey. Finally, in August 2005, the current prime minister Recep Tayyip Erdogan declared that Turkey had a "Kurdish problem," had made "grave mistakes" in the past, and now needed "more democracy to solve the problem."[12] Unfortunately, none of these official governmental declarations led to any concrete results.

Similarly, a century ago the English diplomat Sir Charles Eliot contrasted the theoretical and real world of Turkish laws: "If one takes as a basis the laws, statistics and budgets as printed it is easy to prove that the Ottoman empire is in a state of unexampled prosperity. Life and property are secure; perfect liberty and toleration are enjoyed by all; taxation is light, balances large, trade flourishing. Those who have not an extensive personal acquaintance with Turkey may regard such accounts with suspicion and think them coloured, but they find it difficult to realize that all this official literature is absolute fiction, and for practical purposes unworthy of a moment's attention."[13] What is new today?

In September 2006, Camiel Eurlings, a Dutch parliamentarian and the Turkey rapporteur of the EU Parliament, submitted a new draft report approved by the Parliament's Foreign Relations Committee.[14] The Eurlings Report harshly criticized Turkey and concluded that it was not ready for EU membership. Specifically, the Report complained that the pace of Turkish reforms had slowed down since 2005. Significant further efforts were required with regard to fundamental freedoms and human rights, in particular with regard to freedom of expression, women's rights, religious freedoms, trade union rights and cultural rights, as well as further measures against torture. In addition, a dispute over the rights of the new EU member (Greek or Southern) Cyprus to use Turkish sea and airports threatened to result in what Olli Rehn, the EU Enlargement Commissioner, termed a "train crash" in Turkey's EU candidacy talks. Turkey, however, refused to accede to the EU demands on Cyprus as long as the EU failed to honor its own pledge to reduce the isolation of the Turkish community in (Turkish or Northern) Cyprus.[15] In November 2006, the EU Commission released its new Progress Report on Turkey that would guide its policies toward it in the following year. This new Report basically reiterated the oft-repeated criticisms—already broached by the earlier Eurlings Report cited above—that Turkey was dragging its heels in implementing required political reforms and demanded significant improvements in 2007 if Turkey were to remain on track to join the EU.[16] In December 2006, the EU appeared close to suspending accession negotiations in several sections because of the Cyprus imbroglio. Nevertheless, candidacy talks would proceed in the other sections and Turkey's EU promise would continue.

Regressive Reforms

A year after EU accession talks began in 2005, only one-third of Turkey's population still believed their state should join the EU, a total dramatically down from merely a year earlier.[17] This negativity was mirrored in the EU itself where a survey in June 2006 showed that 55 percent of the population opposed Turkish membership. In Austria—where memories of the Turkish siege of Vienna in 1683 still linger—81 percent opposed Turkish membership. Turkey's nationalist-statist domestic elite has joined its nationalist-xenophobic counterparts in the EU to oppose Turkey's EU candidacy. In Turkey this has led to disillusionment, slow down, and even regression in the EU-required reform and harmonization process. Demonstrating the volatility of Turkish public opinion, however, a new poll at the end of 2006 measured a rebound in support for the EU as some 55 percent of the population gave an affirmative reply when asked whether the EU has a positive image.[18]

Article 301

During the 1990s, Article 312 of the Turkish Penal Code notoriously could make mere verbal or written support for Kurdish rights cause one to be charged with "provoking hatred or animosity between groups of different race, religion, region or social class." Yasar Kemal, one of Turkey's most famous novelists, and Aliza Marcus, a Reuters correspondent and U.S. citizen, were indicted in 1995 for violating these provisions, a dilemma that came to be known as "thought crime."

The EU harmonization process led to a new Penal Code entering into force in June 2005. Despite some improvements regarding women's rights and the theoretical curtailment of torture, the fundamental problem of putting state security before the rule of law and individual rights remained. This problem has been egregiously illustrated by Article 301, under whose terms even the recent Nobel Prize–winning author Orhan Pamuk was prosecuted for denigrating "Turkishness." Since it has gone into effect, the vagueness of Article 301 has been used by extreme nationalists and statists to accuse writers, scholars, and intellectuals of treason and subversion. Indeed, in the case of Elif Shafak's *The Bastard of Istanbul*, Article 301 has even been used to prosecute the author for remarks made about the Armenian massacres by a fictional character. Much more seriously, Hrant Dink, the recently assassinated Turkish-Armenian writer and editor, was given a suspended prison sentence for violating Article 301 in a piece he wrote about the Armenian issue. Dink was assassinated on January 19, 2007, apparently by an extreme Turkish nationalist, in part, because of the passions aroused by Dink's conviction for violating Article 301. Although nobody has yet actually been imprisoned for violating Article 301, its mere presence and the suits that have occurred have had a chilling effect on freedom of speech and press in Turkey. Indeed, it is difficult to see how Article 301 represents any improvement over its predecessor in the Turkish Penal Code, Article 312.

New Anti-Terrorism Law

During the 1990s, Article 8 of the Anti-Terrorism Law also notoriously made it possible to consider academics, intellectuals, and journalists speaking up for Kurdish rights to be engaging in terrorist acts: "Written and oral propaganda and assemblies, meetings and demonstrations aimed at damaging the indivisible unity of the Turkish Republic, with its territory and nation are prohibited, regardless of the methods, intentions and ideas behind such activities." Under these provisions, practically anybody could be imprisoned for advocating a political solution to the Kurdish problem and hundreds were.

The new Anti-Terrorism Law (TMY) that entered into force in 2006, represents a regressive step backward and constitutes an affront to the rule of law. Its definition of terrorism is too vague, overly broad, and lacks clarity concerning the nature of the crime. Article 6 of the new Law has the potential to make anybody who expresses an idea contrary to the official state ideology guilty of being a "terrorist," even when the accused may be completely opposed to the use of violence. Under Article 6, "terrorists' offences" are broadened to include the carrying of an emblem, signs, or placards of a terrorist organization and attempting to conceal your own identity during a demonstration. Indeed, mere criticism of the Law can result in an accusation of "terrorism." *Info Turk* declared that even the "Turkish media criticized the government's proposal...saying the draft [of the TMY] defined too many actions as terror and could easily be misused."[19] The *Cumhuriyet* newspaper devoted its front page to criticizing the proposed law: "The reforms passed in the European Union process will be erased by a definition of terror that encompasses all crimes.... There is nothing left out in the definition."[20] Furthermore, Article 7 of the TMY defines the offense of "financing terror" too broadly to include providing funds "directly or indirectly" knowing they would "entirely or partially" be used to commit terror crimes. Under such definitions, it will be difficult for the ordinary, law-abiding Turkish citizen to regulate his/her behavior so as to avoid criminal liability. Finally, according to Nalan Erkem, a lawyer for the Izmir Bar Association Prevention of Torture Group (IOG): "The arrangements the draft (TMY) makes with regard to access to an attorney takes away all of the rights of the defendant.... While it opens the way for torture and mistreatment, the draft also aims to prevent lawyers from proving their existence."[21]

Minority Rights

The fundamental legal problem regarding the definition and protection of minorities in Turkey stems from the definition of the term "minority" in the Treaty of Lausanne (1923), under which the West first recognized the new Republic of Turkey. According to this Treaty, only non-Muslims such as Greeks, Armenians, and Jews were granted minority status in Turkey. The seemingly obstinate refusal in the modern Republic of Turkey to admit that its citizens of Kurdish ethnic heritage constitute a minority can be understood in light of the old Ottoman principle that Islam took precedence over nationality among Muslims and that only non-Muslims could hold some type of officially recognized minority status.

This interpretation can be furthered understood against the background of the gradual disintegration of the Ottoman Empire before the onslaughts of various nationalisms during the nineteenth and early twentieth centuries. Indeed, the modern Republic of Turkey itself was established only after a long and terrible struggle against the invading Greeks, who were pursuing their *Megali* Idea of a greater Greece after World War I with British encouragement, and a lesser but still serious war against the Armenians, pursuing their goal of a greater Armenia also with tacit allied backing. Finally, the Kurds themselves, during the Sheikh Said rebellion of 1925, were seen as trying to destroy the new secular Republic by reinstating the Caliph and creating a Kurdish state in the southeast of Turkey.[22]

Even today this concept of minority prevails within Turkey. For example, Necmettin Erbakan—who became modern Turkey's first Islamist prime minister in July 1996—declared: "We have bonds of brotherhood. There is nothing more absurd than ethnic differentiation among Muslim brothers."[23] Articles 14, 26, 27, and 28 of the current (1982) Turkish Constitution allow Turkish authorities to incriminate nonviolent expressions of ethnic identity simply on the basis that they are contrary to the constitutional definition of "Turkish" and a danger to the integrity of the state. In 2005, for example, Professors Baskin Oran and Ibrahim Ozden Keboglu were prosecuted for simply arguing in a report regarding EU harmonization laws and commissioned by the prime minister's own office, that "Turk" is an identity of only one ethnic group and that Turkey also includes other ethnic groups such as "Kurds."

Given the present Turkish position, even Kurdish names containing the common Kurdish letters "w," "x," and "q" cannot be officially recognized and used because children can only be given names that use the Turkish language's alphabet and these three letters do not appear in the Turkish alphabet. In addition, therefore, as noted in chapter 4, the Kurdish New Year's holiday *"Newroz"* is referred to by the government as *"Nevroz"*; while ironically, of course, the letter "W" appears on the door of virtually every public toilet in Turkey. Finally, Article 49(9) of the constitution still mandates that no language other than Turkish can be taught as a mother tongue to Turkish citizens at institutions of training or education. The recent theoretical legalization of Kurdish language classes was in practice prevented by overly onerous technical requirements.

In November 2006, Hans Jorg Kretscher, the outgoing head of the EU Commission in Ankara, called on Turkey to recognize the identity of the Kurds and supported the notion of *Turkiyeli* [of Turkey] as a replacement for the term "Turk."[24] He also declared: "It is necessary to recognize the identity of the Kurds, to recognize that Kurds are Kurds and Kurds are not Turks. They are Turkish citizens and they want to be Turkish citizens, but they are Kurds. You cannot deny that." General Yasar Buyukanit, the new chief of the General Staff, however, refused to countenance the concept of the Kurds as a legally protected minority by replying: "Approaches based on race are a shame in this century. Such approaches are an insult to the Turkey of Kemal Ataturk.... Ataturk would have been deeply saddened if he had lived through these days."

Nobody can say for sure what Ataturk's position would be; it is not necessarily given that he would support the extreme Turkish nationalist position today on the Kurdish issue. Given his documented determination to see Turkey become a modern country and part of the West, it is entirely possible that in today's world a leader of Ataturk's mettle would recognize the tremendous progress Turkey has made since his times to the extent that loyal particularisms were no longer inconsistent with Turkish territorial integrity and thus support Kurdish demands for their rights within Turkey as being in contemporary Turkish self interest. In other words, the Kurds should not so easily dismiss the founder of modern Turkey as their inveterate enemy and even consider adopting him on occasion as one of their rallying points. Indeed, to do so might emphasize Kurdish loyalty to Turkey and begin to attract more support from ethnic Turks. Abdullah (Apo) Ocalan himself, the imprisoned leader of the PKK, agreed with this idea when I interviewed him in March 1998: "I agree that if Ataturk were alive today, he would change Turkey's policy." [25]

Compounding the problem of Turkey's definition of a minority, even the Kurds decline to pursue official minority status within Turkey. Rather, they seek to be a recognized as a "constituent people" of that state. This presumably would imply that, along with the ethnic Turks, the Kurds are equal stakeholders in the Republic of Turkey. Minority status, although guaranteeing full democratic rights, would imply less than full equality as co-founders and co-owners of the Republic of Turkey.

U.S. Perspectives

Despite Turkey's inability to institute adequate reforms for its Kurdish population, U.S.–Turkish friendship persists. Indeed, as noted in chapter 1, it dates back to the late 1940s, when the Truman Doctrine and the Marshall Plan brought U.S. military and economic aid to Turkey to help it withstand Soviet encroachments. For its part, Turkey proved to be a particularly brave and valuable ally of the United States during the Korean War (1950–53). Thus, their shared geopolitical interests paved the way for a mutually valuable strategic alliance that was formalized when Turkey joined NATO in 1952 and began to anchor the alliance's southeastern flank containing Soviet expansion. The United States also began to hold Turkey in high esteem as a secular democratic Muslim state offering an important model for other states in geostrategical terms. Even with the end of the Cold War, the United States has continued to tout Turkey's significance as a strategic ally helping to bring stability to the former Yugoslavia and Somalia, while combating terrorism and political threats from such reputed rogue states as Iraq, Iran, Afghanistan, and Syria. As part of the cooperative effort to further Turkish economic and military self-reliance, for example, the United States has loaned and granted Turkey more than $12.5 billion in economic aid and more than $14 billion in military assistance. U.S.–Turkish relations continue to focus on areas such as strategic energy cooperation, trade and investment, security ties, regional stability, and human rights progress. The United States and Turkey also have had a Joint Economic Commission and a Trade and Investment Framework Agreement for several years. The U.S.–Turkish trade balance is almost even with each state exporting approximately $3 billion to the other. The United States is Turkey's third-largest export market. In 2002, the two states indicated their joint intent to upgrade bilateral economic relations by launching an Economic Partnership Commission. Turkey has been designated a Big Emerging Market (BEM) for U.S. exports and investment by the U.S. Department of Commerce. When the Turkish economy suddenly collapsed in 2001, the United States continued to provide political and economic support, particularly with the International Monetary Fund. This aid proved invaluable for getting Turkey back on its economic feet.

The Kurdish problem in Turkey, of course, occasionally presents difficulties. Every year, for example, the U.S. State Department releases its annual human rights report for every state in the world. Turkey is always near the top of the list. From time to time, the United States also makes further specific references to the Kurdish situation in Turkey. As noted above, in August 1999, U.S. assistant secretary of state for democracy, human rights, and labor Harold Hongju Koh visited Turkey and met with a wide variety of people. Although recognizing Turkey's right to defend itself against the PKK, he upset many Turkish officials with his seemingly strong recommendations concerning the Kurdish problem.[26] Koh argued, for example, that "one can oppose terrorism and still support human rights." He added that "most Kurds in Turkey...want to remain Turkish citizens, while enjoying the basic human rights guaranteed to all people under international law, including freedom to express one's language and culture, and freedom to organize political parties that represent their interests." He maintained that "far from hurting Turkey's territorial integrity, an inclusive policy that acknowledged these rights would strengthen the Turkish state by giving the Kurdish community a genuine stake in their country's future." Given the strong geostrategic U.S.–Turkish alliance, however, one suspects that the two simply agree to disagree on the Kurdish issue without letting it interfere in their overall relationship.

Although Turkey's failure to support the U.S. northern front in the war to overthrow Saddam Hussein in 2003 created difficulties in their alliance, the United States has continued to look upon Turkey favorably and support its EU candidacy. Despite Turkey's continuing human rights problems, for example, Washington still showcases Turkey as an example of a Muslim state that is not only pro-Western, but also secular and democratic.[27] In June 2006, The Council on Foreign Relations, an influential U.S. think tank, issued a report that declared: "A goal of U.S diplomacy with its principal European partners should be to develop a plan for anchoring Turkey in the

West through the EU."[28] Speaking at a meeting of the Izmir Chamber
of Trade, U.S. ambassador to Turkey Eric Edelman also declared that
Turkey joining the EU would create new opportunities for both
European and U.S. companies.[29] At the end of the EU–U.S. summit
of June 26, 2004, in Shannon, Ireland, U.S. president George W.
Bush himself stated: "As Turkey meets the EU standards for membership, the European Union should begin talks that will lead to full
membership for the Republic of Turkey."[30] Turkish foreign ministry
spokesman Namik Tan thanked the United States for this support by
asserting: "The support of the U.S. to Turkey during the...negotia-
tion period with the EU is clear, natural and right. We are pleased
about it."[31] Another senior Turkish official added that the United
States had helped Turkey's cause by emphasizing Turkey's strategic
importance, the benefits of having an overwhelmingly Muslim state
firmly anchored to the West, and thus putting the lie to the inevita-
bility of the clash of civilizations thesis.

U.S. support for Turkey, however, might have aroused EU resent-
ment as unwarranted interference in its affairs. French president Jacques
Chirac, for example, remarked frostily that he would not presume to
advise the United States on its links with Mexico. EU president Bertie
Ahern and EU Commission president Romano Prodi also expressed
their displeasure with Bush's comments.[32] Earlier, Gunter Verheugen,
the EU Enlargement Commissioner, termed U.S. pressure "counterproductive" and added that it would be better for the EU to conduct
its negotiations with Turkey in a more low-key atmosphere.[33] Ironically,
Turkey might have promoted its EU candidacy better by refusing to
join the U.S. attack against Iraq in March 2003 and thus appearing to
line up with its prospective EU counterparts on this defining issue
against the United States. Other reasons, of course, also help explain
why Turkey chose not to support its traditional U.S. ally. Further irony
resulted from Turkey's decision when it enabled the Iraqi Kurds to step

into the role of U.S. ally and reap the corresponding benefits. Further analysis of this situation is presented in chapter 1.[34]

Conclusion

Turkey's long-standing mindset against the Kurdish identity will not end by mere verbal declaration. Frankly, this Turkish prejudice against the legitimacy of the Kurdish identity reminds one in some respects of the former prejudice against African Americans in the United States.[35] Although the United States still has progress to make on this issue, the genuine reforms it has instituted during the past half-century and the resulting stronger state of the nation might serve as a useful model for Turkey.

The EU Commission's unwillingness to address the Kurdish problem as a cohesive issue also is troubling. Instead, the EU implicitly seems simply to agree with Turkey that the Kurdish problem is just a terrorism issue or at most a limited human rights problem. If the EU prematurely accepts Turkey as a member, it will damage its own human rights commitments and jeopardize its long-term credibility. Despite all these serious problems, Turkey's elusive pursuit of EU membership (and its promise of a solution to its Kurdish problem within the confines of Turkey's territorial integrity as well as creating a healthy democratic Turkey that will benefit all of its citizens and the EU too) will continue. After all, in the past we were told that France was too unstable to make democracy work,[36] and Germany was too authoritarian.[37] Today, however, we can see how these characterizations eventually proved untrue. The same can be said for such other states as Spain, Italy, and Japan. A similar evolution is possible for Turkey. This great state can make democracy work for all its citizens, and the entire world will be better for it.

CHAPTER 6

TAMING TURKEY'S
DEEP STATE

The Kemalist Republic of Turkey was founded on the concept of exclusive Turkish national identity that, among other factors, proved hostile to any expression of Kurdish identity.[1] Since it would be a contradiction in terms to maintain such a situation in a true republic, an arcane or Deep State (*Derin Devlet*) developed alongside or parallel to the official State to enforce the ultimate principles of the Kemalist Republic. This Deep State became "an omnipotent force with tentacle-like hands reaching everywhere . . . a state within the legitimate state."[2] The colorful but enigmatic phrase Deep State referred to how this secret "other" state had penetrated deeply into the political, security, and economic structures of the official State.

Today, however, Turkey is seeking to join the EU, a candidacy supported by a large majority of its population and an initiative that promises to help solve Turkey's long-standing Kurdish problem.[3] Clearly, a Republic of Turkey that is truly a pluralistic democracy cannot be constituted along the lines of the Copenhagen Criteria[4] necessary for Turkey to join the EU until the Deep State is dismantled. The first problem in doing so would be to come to grips with what constitutes the Deep State.

What Is the Deep State?

Many observers dismiss the idea of the Deep State as simply a conspiracy theory.[5] Indeed, Turkish citizens (both ethnic Turks and Kurds alike) seem particularly susceptible to such theories. For them, nothing is as it seems. Always there is some deeper, usually more cynical explanation for what is occurring. Only the naïve fail to understand this.

On the other hand, who can doubt that there is more to be known about the motives that drove Mehmet Ali Agca, supposedly a right-wing Turkish nationalist possibly working for the Soviet Union, to attempt to assassinate Pope John Paul II on May 13, 1981, or to murder Abdi Ipekci, the chief editor of the liberal daily *Milliyet*, in 1979 and then escape from prison and make the attempt on the pope?[6] More recently, what mysterious court decision temporarily freed Agca in January 2006 before a public outcry led to his return to prison? As one recent analysis concluded: "Somebody with omnipresent tentacle-like hands that can extend to anywhere—from judiciary to army or security forces or any other institution—within the state makes a plan to kill a journalist, or to kill young students whose ideas they deem to be a threat to the state and that same somebody skillfully protects its bloody pawns from justice."[7] When the author of this book visited Abdullah (Apo) Ocalan, the leader of the PKK[8] in March 1998, moreover, Ocalan spoke often of the "hidden games" all sides in the Kurdish struggle were playing.[9] Although it usually would be judicious to avoid accepting conspiracy theories, one must also remember that even paranoids have enemies.

Given its arcane nature, it is not possible precisely to define and document the Deep State according to normally acceptable scholarly standards. However, if the concept is simply ignored until scholars possess one hundred percent proof, it may be too late to deal with it. Lack of full documentation, therefore, is no excuse for not trying to analyze it.

A useful recent definition found the Deep State to be "made up of elements from the military, security and judicial establishments wedded to a fiercely nationalist, statist ideology who, if need be, are ready to block or even oust a government that does not share their vision."[10] Military and security elements determined to preserve the Kemalist vision of a Turkish nationalist and secular state are the key elements of the Deep State. To some extent, all of these ingredients have long been institutionalized in the *Milli Guvenlik Kurulu* (MGK) or National Security Council. The official job of the MGK was, and still is, to advise the elected government on matters of internal and external security. Until the recent EU reforms mandated by Turkey's EU candidacy supposedly gave civilian authorities more control, the MGK also often served as the ultimate source of authority in Turkey. Before these recent reforms the MGK was clearly under the control of the military. It consisted of ten members: the president and the prime minister of the Republic of Turkey, the chief of the general staff and the four military service chiefs, and the defense, foreign affairs, and interior ministers.

The modern Republic of Turkey, of course, was founded by Mustafa Kemal Ataturk, whose power originally stemmed from his position in the military. Thus, from the beginning, the military played a very important and, it should be noted, very popular role in the defense and, therefore, politics of Turkey. Following the military coup of May 1960, the new constitution, which went into effect in 1961, provided a constitutional role for the military for the first time by establishing the MGK. Over the years, the MGK has gradually extended its power over governmental policy, at times replacing the civilian government as the ultimate center of power over issues of national security. After the "coup by memorandum" in March 1971, for example, the MGK was given the power to give binding, unsolicited advice to the cabinet. After the military coup of September 1980, for a while all power was concentrated in the MGK, chaired by the chief of staff, General Kenan Evren, who later became president from 1982 to 1989. Although the MGK greatly reduced the rampant terrorism in Turkey at that time, a major price was paid in terms of human rights. During the 1990s, the MGK began to exercise virtually total authority over security matters dealing with the Kurdish problem. In his role as chief of staff, General Dogan Gures exercised a particularly strong influence over the elected Turkish government headed by Prime Minister Tansu Ciller to the extent that the phrase "as good as thirty men" was reportedly being used to describe her.[11] The "postmodern coup" in June 1997 toppled Turkey's first Islamist government and was sanctioned by an MGK edict issued a few months earlier.

One important way the MGK exercised its control behind the scenes was through issuing a rather lengthy, and until recently top-secret National Security Policy Document (MGSB) once every four years and updated every two years.[12] The MGSB defined and ranked Turkey's priorities in domestic and international security, and outlined the national strategy to be followed. The precise content of the document was revealed only to the top generals and highest-ranking state administrators. Thus, some referred to the MGSB as "the 'state's secret constitution' or the 'red book' on the basis of which the State is run." In other words, "the real responsibility of running the State is not upon the Cabinet, but actually lies elsewhere [in]...the military [and] other dubious and secret formations involving people either directly from within the institutions of the state or those who are very close to this establishment...defined as 'the Deep State.' "

The most recent MGSB was approved on October 24, 2005, by an MGK expanded to include more civilian members, but only after a dispute between the Turkish military and the new civilian officials of the ruling moderate Islamic AK Party had been settled. This disagreement reportedly dealt with Islamic fundamentalism, especially over women wearing the *turban* or Islamic headscarf as well as the usage of military force versus diplomacy in foreign policy. Separatist terror (the PKK) and radical Islam (Osama bin Laden's al-Qaeda and Hizbullah) were ranked as the top terrorist threats. Other specific issues included water, minorities, and extreme leftist movements. The issue of Greece extending its territorial waters to twelve miles around Greek islands in the Aegean Sea and thus largely shutting it off to Turkey was still referred to as a *casus belli*. An article from the MGSB issued in 1997 concerning the threat of extreme right-wing groups attempting to turn Turkish nationalism into racism and the ultra-nationalist mafia attempting to exploit the situation was dropped in the most recent MGSB. Also deleted, as domestic security concerns, were national education, science, technology, and public administration. In foreign matters, statements on northern Iraq and the Iraqi Kurdish parties as well as Syria were also eliminated from the latest document.

In addition to the MGSB, an MGK Secretariat General bylaw also held great importance in the past, but has now been discontinued due to the EU reforms. This MGK bylaw supposedly had recently defined the Turkish public as "a threat to itself" and spoke of "psychological military operations" against the public to protect the country from that threat. The fact that the contents of these MGK documents have been recently publicized may indicate that they are no longer as important due to the recent formal reforms required by Turkey's EU candidacy. Whether this is true, however, remains to be seen.

In addition to the MGK, other Turkish state security organs that may help institutionalize the Deep State include the *Milli Istihbarat Teshilati* (MIT) or National Intelligence Organization, the *Devlet Guvenlik Mahkemesi* (DGM) or State Security Courts, and the shadowy JITEM[13] or the Gendarmerie Intelligence and Counter Terrorist Service. Officially established in 1965, the MIT combines the functions of internal and external intelligence services. Although in theory reporting to the prime minister, in practice the MIT remains close to the military. Over the years, the MIT has been accused of using extreme rightists to infiltrate and destroy extreme leftist and Kurdish groups. For example, it appears that it was involved in the notorious Susurluk scandal that, among other actions, illegally used criminals to try to destroy the PKK. Indeed criminals carrying out various illegal activities including drug smuggling, murders, and assassinations are also elements of the Deep State. JITEM, for example, reportedly became involved in such extralegal activities as arms and drug smuggling during the war against the PKK.[14] Avni Ozgurel, a journalist well known for his supposed insider knowledge of the Deep State, has argued that "if the PKK conflict granted you unlimited access to confidential funds of the State...and if the Southeast had become a heaven for revenues from the drug trade that would mean that there would certainly be balances supported by all this dirty money."[15]

Each one of the eighteen State Security Courts consisted of two civilian judges, one military judge, and two prosecutors. These courts had legal jurisdiction over civilian cases involving the Anti-Terrorist Law of 1991. This law contained the notorious Article 8 covering membership in illegal organizations and the propagation of ideas banned by law as damaging the indivisible unity of the state. The State Security Courts took a leading role in trying to stifle violent and nonviolent Kurdish activists and in so doing provided a veneer of legality to the state's campaign against Kurdish nationalist demands. Thus, these courts closed down newspapers and narrowly interpreted the right of free speech. Nurset Demiral, the former head of the Ankara State Security Court, became both the symbol and reality of the problem these courts presented to democratic freedoms. For example, Demiral demanded the death penalty for Leyla Zana and the other members of the pro-DEP members of parliament who were accused of supporting the PKK. Later, Demiral joined the ultra-rightist Nationalist Action Party (NAP) led at that time by Alparslan Turkes. Turkey finally abolished the State Security Courts in an attempt to help meet the requirements for membership in the EU.

During the late 1970s, Turkes's notorious *Ulkucus* (Idealists) or Gray Wolves played a leading role in the sectarian violence that raged throughout Turkey. Observers commented on how many members of the gendarmerie's counter guerrilla special teams or *ozel tim* seemed to be associated with Turkes's party. Their attire served to identify them. The three-crescent flag of the Ottoman Empire, a symbol of ultra-Turkish nationalism, decorated the barrels of their guns. Pictures of gray wolves, another ultra-nationalist symbol, were etched on their muzzles. An additional touch was the mustache, which ran down from the corner of their lips. Seemingly contradictory, the Deep State also apparently used extremist Islamic groups in these violent campaigns.[16]

Origins of the Deep State

During the early years of the Cold War, the United States apparently established secret resistance groups within a number of its NATO allies that were intended to fight back against any Soviet occupation. Called *Gladio* (latin for sword), stay-behind organizations, or Special War Department[17] they were small paramilitary units that would supposedly employ guerrilla tactics behind the lines against a Soviet occupation. Working through the U.S. Central Intelligence Agency (CIA) and the Pentagon, such units were apparently formed in Belgium, France, Greece, Italy, the Netherlands, West Germany, and Turkey. The United States continued to fund these organizations into the 1970s.

In Turkey, the secret force worked out of the Joint U.S. Military Aid Team headquarters. It was first known as the Tactical Mobilization Group, and following the military "coup by memorandum" in 1971, the counter guerrilla force or Special Warfare Bureau (*ozel tim*, special team). When the leftist, but nationalist Bulent Ecevit was prime minister in 1974, Chief of Staff General Semih Sancar asked Ecevit for credits from a secret emergency fund. When Ecevit inquired about the nature of this organization he had never heard about, he was told that the United States was terminating its funding and that he should not look too closely at the situation. "There are a certain number of volunteer patriots whose names are kept secret and are engaged for life in this special department. They have hidden arms caches in various parts of the country."[18]

It was apparently around the time that the United States ceased its financing of the *Gladio* organization in the mid-1970s that it began to be used increasingly against perceived domestic leftist opposition to the Turkish government. Ugur Mumcu, the famous leftist journalist whose assassination in 1993 still remains unsolved, wrote how, when he was arrested after the coup in 1971, his torturers told him: "We are the counter guerrilla. Even the president of the republic cannot touch us."[19] A report by the Turkish Parliament's commission for the investigation of the Ugur Mumcu assassination has suggested that the Deep State might have killed him because of his work on the possible MIT–PKK connection he supposedly was working on at the time of his untimely death and then tried to blame it on Iranian-backed Islamists.[20]

During Turkey's domestic, leftist-rightist violence of the 1970s,[21] Turkes's ultra-rightist Gray Wolves operated with the encouragement and even protection of the *ozel tim* or special forces. Some speculate that the *Gladio* or stay-behind organization was behind the notorious 1977 May Day massacre at Taksim Square in Istanbul, when snipers on surrounding rooftops suddenly began firing into a crowd of some 200,000 protesters supporting the radical leftist labor organization DISK.

In 1981, the stay-behind organization may also have been used in the attempt to assassinate Pope John Paul II. Although a well-known extreme rightist who already had been convicted of murdering a leading leftist Turkish journalist (Abdi Ipekci) just two years earlier, in the West Mehmet Ali Agca was painted as a Soviet agent or dupe in an attempt to rid the weakening Soviet communist empire of the meddlesome priest threatening its legitimacy in Poland and, therefore, in the rest of eastern Europe and the Soviet Union itself.[22] Given Agca's extreme rightist sympathies and proven previous acts of murder, however, is it not possible that he really was an agent of extreme rightist forces acting with the help of the stay-behind organization, which was trying to discredit the Soviet Union by connecting it with Agca's attempt on the pope?[23] In Italy, for example, former prime minister Giulio Andreotti admitted that the communists had been blamed for bombings actually perpetrated by *Gladio*. As part of the fallout from the notorious Susurluk scandal, it is also known that Agca had received a false passport from Ibrahim Sahin, a Turkish intelligence operative with links to many of the other Susurluk parties.

From the mid-1980s on, the counter guerrillas were apparently given a new target, the PKK. During the early 1990s, a series of mysterious killings of civilian Kurdish leaders by apparently right-wing government hit squads began. Depending on how one counts, at least 1,000 and probably a lot more died. Not a single one of the slayings of Kurdish leaders or sympathizers resulted in an arrest: "Many of the individual killings still go unexplained amid local claims that certain officials prefer not to pursue such cases."[24] Prominent victims included Musa Anter, seventy-four, one of the more famous Kurdish intellectuals and authors of the twentieth century; and Mehmet Sincar, an ethnic Kurdish member of the Turkish Parliament. Also murdered it should be noted, however, was Major Ahmet Cem Ersever, a leading Turkish nationalist and supposedly a former JITEM or gendarmerie intelligence officer who was an expert on PKK activities. "Executions without verdict" was an expression often used to explain what was occurring.

At the time many argued that the killings were being perpetrated by groups associated with the Islamic Hizbullah (Party of God) and secretly encouraged by the state to protect the unity of the Muslim Turkish state the PKK was threatening to divide.[25] A Turkish parliamentary committee established in 1993 to investigate these murders even concluded: "The state is spawning criminal gangs. The village guards [pro-government Kurds armed to battle the PKK] are involved in many murky events...It must be said that the Gendarmerie Intelligence Organisation (JITEM) is too."[26] For a long time, the government refused to admit that such an organization as Hizbullah even existed. Early in 2000, however, the police began to discover gruesomely tortured bodies buried at hideouts used by the organization.[27]

Susurluk

Although thousands of people are killed each year on Turkey's highways, a fatal car accident near the Turkish city of Susurluk on November 3, 1996, proved unique because of its victims:[28] (1) Huseyin Kocadag, the director of the Istanbul Academy and former deputy director of the National Security Police in Istanbul, who had been driving the speeding Mercedes when it crashed into a truck that had pulled out onto the highway; (2) Abdullah Catli, a notorious international criminal "on the lam" and wanted for multiple murders, drug trafficking, and prison escape; (3) Gonca Us, a gangster's "moll"; and (4) the accident's lone survivor, Sedat Bucak, a member of parliament and the leader of a pro-government Kurdish tribe, who headed a 2,000-strong militia that was deputized as village guards and received more than $1 million a month to battle Kurdish separatists. The obvious question was what was so unlikely an association doing together in the same car? Clearly, Susurluk revealed striking insights into the Deep State and the connections it fostered between the Turkish government's intelligence community and internationally organized criminal activity involving political assassinations, drug trafficking, and political corruption at the highest levels.

What is more, the car's trunk contained a veritable arsenal of five large caliber revolvers, two submachine guns, two silencers, and an abundant quantity of ammunition, as well as a case stuffed with bank notes. Investigators also found on Catli's body a police chief's identity card in the name of Mehmet Ozbay, and a green passport reserved for senior civil servants exempted from visa requirements. Clearly, Catli had been receiving official protection despite being officially sentenced to death in absentia for this role in the massacre of seven leftists in Bahcelievler, Ankara, in 1978. During this unstable period of leftist–rightist violence in Turkey, Catli had been a member of Alparslan Turkes's extreme nationalist NAP and its violent Idealists (*Ulkucus*) militia. In addition, the Turkish police were supposedly seeking Catli for his role in the high-profile murder of the widely known leftist Turkish journalist Abdi Ipekci in 1979 (a crime for which the pope's would-be assassin, Mehmet Ali Agca, was later sentenced), and for organizing Agca's prison escape and the flight to Europe that led to his attempt on the pope's life. Catli was also wanted by Interpol for drug trafficking and having escaped from a Swiss prison.

Mehmet Agar, the Turkish minister of the interior and earlier minister of justice, at first tried to explain Susurluk away by claiming that the police chief, Kocadag, had probably "arrested" Catli and was bringing him into custody. After it became clear that all four occupants of the car had been staying at the same hotel together the previous three nights—where "coincidentally" Agar himself had also been staying—Agar was forced to resign. In the days that immediately followed, Agar virtually admitted his involvement in an illegal, secret organization when he declared: "We have undertook a thousand operations, but they cannot be explained. Their result was the security of the people. Whatever I did, I did for the nation."[29] Both he and Bucak, the crash's lone survivor, who was conveniently suffering from partial amnesia regarding the accident, then claimed parliamentary immunity.

Turkish president Suleyman Demirel seemed to signal the desire of most of the nation's officials to cover up Susurluk's ultimate meaning when he declared that "the incident should be viewed within its limits... Take it as far as it goes... but do not make a sweeping judgment for Turkey."[30] Tansu Ciller (the former prime minister from June 1993 to March 1996 and serving as the deputy prime minister when the Susurluk crash occurred) was already up to her neck in accusations about scandals revolving around her and her husband's finances. Ciller signaled even greater official reluctance to pursue Susurluk when she publicly praised the deceased Catli by saying: "those who fire shots for the state are, for us, as respectable as those who get shot for it."[31] More forthrightly, Alparslan Turkes—known by his extreme right-wing followers as the *Basbug* (chief of chieftains or fuhrer) and a former deputy prime minister in the 1970s—admitted knowing that Catli and the other men traveling in the doomed car had been working with Turkey's intelligence services: "On the basis of my state experience, I admit that Catli has been used by the state in the framework of a secret service working for the good of the state."[32] Turkes's comments constituted a good partial definition of the Deep State itself.

On November 12, 1996, the four main parties in the Turkish Parliament established a special nine-man commission to investigate the circumstances surrounding Susurluk. Mehmet Elkatmis, a member of the senior governing Islamist Refah Party, was elected as its chairman. Early in April 1997, the commission produced a stunted and deeply compromised report that failed to identify any important names.[33] Although it conceded that crimes may have been committed by the state, the report rejected allegations that the state had established the criminal organizations, and dealt with only some of Catli's activities. Nothing was said about the web of other gangs that had spread across the country, nor was there mention of any crimes committed in the war against the PKK in the southeast, or anything about alleged links to gangs in the senior military command. In presenting the report, Elkatmis specifically declared that his commission had been denied access to many government documents on the grounds that they contained state or commercial secrets. The commission also failed to obtain any useful information from Mehmet Agar or Sedat Bucak who continued to claim parliamentary immunity.

In January 1998, Kutlu Savas, the chairman of the prime ministerial investigative committee, handed over the final draft of his report on Susurluk to Prime Minister Mesut Yilmaz. Savas had been working on it as a special prosecutor since shortly after the parliamentary committee investigating the situation had been dissolved in April 1997, and had interviewed the heads of a number of departments in the ministry of the interior as well as the intelligence and security services.

The Savas Report reiterated earlier findings that the special teams had been established with the original duty of fighting the PKK.[34] In time, however, certain individuals working in various organs of the state had formed gangs within the state and, along with figures in organized crime, began to kill businessmen suspected of financing the PKK, such as Behcet Canturk and Savas

Buldan in 1994. These gangs also diverged from their official duties and began to work for their own personal profit, sharing the spoils of drug trafficking and black market operations.

New revelations concerned gangs taking over state banks to finance illegal operations and reap windfall profits. Eyes turned toward former prime minister Tansu Ciller and her husband as being among those who might have directed this foray into criminal banking. In addition, Ilhan Akuzum and Abdulkadir Ates, two former ministers of tourism, were accused of issuing illegal casino licenses. The Savas Report also concluded that arguments over control of illegal activities became so intense that various security organizations even began to kill each other's agents. The death toll from this inter-service rivalry reached fifteen, several of whom were senior officers.

In addition, $50 million had been taken from the prime ministerial slush fund to fight the PKK, but much of it was unaccounted for. The Report also charged that a certain Mahmut Yildirim—codenamed "Yesil" (Green) and an extreme nationalist right-winger—had been one of the main figures used by the MIT in covert operations, and the man who had attacked Prime Minister Mesut Yilmaz himself in a hotel lobby in Budapest in November 1996 for wanting to investigate Susurluk in the first place.

Savas suggested that in the future all security personnel involved in illegal activities be dismissed and the activities of Mehmet Eymur, the former head of counterterrorist operations, be investigated. The special prosecutor further recommended that all the operations of the MIT and the department of security be placed under tighter control, and that the competition between the later two be ended. Finally, he argued for a tough campaign against drug trafficking and recommended that the Istanbul judicial administration be reorganized. In his television address to the nation concerning the Savas

Report, Prime Minister Yilmaz added that immunities should be lifted to permit the prosecution of politicians and public employees and a repentance law enacted to help expose the guilty.

The military, however, was not implicated in any of these matters. Instead, "Yesil," Catli, Agar, Bucak, and the Cillers were blamed for most of them, to the extent that many began to believe that "Yesil" was merely notional,[35] and the remaining five would become convenient scapegoats for others in the military and government who would remain free. Despite his earlier calls for revealing all information regarding Susurluk, Prime Minister Yilmaz now argued that, in the interests of the nation, certain sections of the Savas Report would have to remain secret. These included information about the repression that had followed the military coup of 1980, assassinations of suspected pro-PKK businessmen in the 1990s, and Turkey's role in the failed military coup against Azerbaijan's president Heydar Aliyev in 1995.[36]

Considering the likelihood that so many higher officials were actually involved, and that the judiciary was so heavily influenced by political forces, it seems very unlikely that the Susurluk affair will ever be brought to a satisfactory conclusion. Ten years after the event only a few officials have been sentenced to relatively short prison terms. As Husmettin Cindoruk, the leader of one of the smaller parties in Yilmaz's coalition government at that time, observed: "the state itself is Susurluk."[37] In other words, the Susurluk affair remains one of the best-documented examples of the existence of the Deep State in Turkey.

Semdinli

On November 9, 2005, the small city of Semdinli in the extreme southeastern Turkish province of Hakkari became another excellent example of the Deep State when the Umit [Hope] bookstore owned by Seferi Yilmaz, a former PKK member who had served a fifteen-year term in prison, was bombed.[38] The explosion killed Zahir Korkmaz, a patron of the bookstore, and wounded his brother Metin Korkmaz. Although the bombing was staged to make it appear the work of the PKK exacting revenge for Seferi Yilmaz having left the organization, it instead appears to have been the result of a botched provocation by the Deep State.

Bystanders who had witnessed the attack pursued the bombers and surrounded their car, which turned out to be registered to a gendarmerie unit bearing civilian plates. Two non-commissioned officers of a paramilitary antiterror intelligence squad (Ali Kaya and Ozcan Ildeniz) and a former Kurdish PKK member turned government informer (Veysel Ates) were arrested, but not before one of them had opened fire, killing one bystander and wounding others. The investigating prosecutor found hand grenades, rifles, materials that could be used to make or defuse bombs, a blueprint of the bookstore, a list of 105 other potential targets, and additional evidence.

All three members of the antiterror squad were arrested and held for trial. Turkish Land Forces Commander General Yasar Buyukanit, scheduled to become the new chief of staff in August 2006, strongly rejected any official connections by stating he knew one of the suspects and then praised him as a "good guy."[39] Buyukanit's ludicrous comment appeared to be a warning that the official State should not pursue the matter any further.

Angry citizens protesting what had happened, however, began rioting in several cities throughout the southeast and later in Istanbul itself. (Much more serious rioting broke out in the spring of 2006 following the funerals of fourteen PKK fighters.) Although Prime Minster Recep Tayyip Erdogan promised to get to the bottom of the matter quickly, he soon backed down in the face of military criticism. It was clear that "dark and illegitimate forces with access to legitimate state power were clearly at work again" and that what had occurred "is no conspiracy theory in Turkey."[40] Indeed, the Semdinli bombing was only one of several other unexplained bombing incidents—apparently perpetrated by *cetes* or gangs that many believed were linked to the Turkish military— that had plagued the southeast Kurdish areas of Turkey during the fall of 2005.

When the Van public prosecutor Ferhat Sarikaya sought to indict Buyukanit for setting up an illegal force to create unrest among the Kurds that would undermine Turkey's application to join the EU as well as trying to influence the courts by praising one of the NCOs charged in the Semdinli bombing, the Supreme Board of Prosecutors and Judges (HSYK) sacked him on the grounds of "breach of authority" and the "inclusion of irrelevant claims in the indictment in contravention of the Law on Trial."[41] The government also removed Sabri Uzun, the chief of the Intelligence Department of the General Directorate of Security, who had sought to support Sarikaya. Uzun had told the parliamentary committee investigating Semdinli that it was an insider affair, arguing that there was "no use locking the doors when the thief is indoors."[42] This, of course, implied that the suspected culprits were really in the higher ranks of the military. Seeking to curry favor with the military, Deniz Baykal, the leader of the main opposition Republican People's Party (CHP), declared that there was a "coup attempt against the military."[43]

In July 2006, the Van Third High Criminal Court sentenced Ali Kaya and Ozcan Ildeniz to thirty-nine years and five months in prison. The court also concluded that the two had not acted alone, but must have been following the directives of an organization and carried out their actions with the support of and contributions from the heads of this organization. The court recommended, therefore, that a further investigation should be opened.[44] Following the lead of EU-Turkey Joint Parliamentary Commission Co-chair Joost Lagendijik's "Turkey Report," the European Commission also asked that the Semdinli "hierarchy," that is, those leading the convicted officers, be identified.[45] Shortly afterward, however, the thirty-nine years prison terms of Kaya and Ildeniz were overturned on appeal, and the two were freed. At the present time, therfore, it appeared that no additional action would be taken, thus suggesting a Deep State cover-up.

Given all the theoretical reforms that had occurred as part of Turkey's EU candidacy, Semdinli was a great disappointment and called into question whether Turkey was ready to pursue EU membership. Thus, the official State's ability to solve the Semdinli case might have proved that Turkey could control its Deep State and was fit for EU membership. Indeed, the EU Commission's representative to Turkey, Hans Jorg Kretschmer, said as much when he declared that "shedding light on the Hakkari [Semdinli] events is a test case for Turkey."[46] Instead, concluded one respected source, the "government *prosecuted the prosecutor* and sacked an intelligence officer whose findings supported the prosecutor; and in doing so dismissing a historic chance to shed light on covert and behind-the-scenes operations which for many decades have been the biggest obstacle for the truly democratic Turkey of tomorrow."[47]

For its part, the parliamentary commission investigating the Semdinli affair concluded that the accusations against the military were "legal fantasy" and that "our commission has come up with no evidence pointing to such an illegal set up within the gendarmerie."[48] Instead the commission's report actually warned that the Iraqi Kurdish leader Massoud Barzani was trying to gain influence in the region and that he could be more dangerous than the PKK itself. The report also exonerated the ruling AKP government from any blame.

In an interview on NTV television shortly after the Semdinli bombing, Suleyman Demirel, the former president (1993–2000) and several times prime minister of Turkey, declared that "there are two states. There is the state and there is the deep state... When a small difficulty occurs, the civilian state steps back and the deep state becomes the generator [of decisions]"[49] Several months earlier, Demirel, who had been removed as prime minister twice in the past by military coups, had replied to the query "What do you mean by 'deep state'?" that it was the Turkish Armed Forces (TSK).[50] The general who had headed the coup that removed Demirel the second time and succeeded him as president from 1982 to 1989, Kenan Evren, agreed: "Demirel tells the truth. When the state is weakened we take it over. We are the deep state."[51] Bulent Ecevit, another former prime minister, also recently concurred with these sentiments.[52]

Other Countries

To a certain extent, many other countries have their own versions of a Deep State. Thorough historical and sociological studies of any state and government will illustrate how political notables and other influentials can sway and sometimes even dominate the visible official government from behind the scenes. In Britain, for example, the public school and Oxbridge educated establishment supposedly constitutes a social elite that monopolizes politics. In France, the *grandes ecoles* or grand schools train the brightest and most motivated youths in the practical matters of running the country and then place them in top civil service or managerial positions. Indeed, the *Ecole Nationale d'Administration* (ENA), the grandest of the grand schools, has its *enarchs* or graduates dominating the cabinet. In the former Soviet Union, the *nomenklatura* was a secret list of sensitive positions and people eligible to fill them. It clearly constituted the Soviet elite behind the façade of both the Communist Party and the Soviet government. In post-Communist Russia, on the other hand, the so-called mafia—ranging from local strong-arm rackets to the oligarchs, egregiously greedy characters who have bought up state-owned firms at giveaway prices when Russia privatized ("piratized" one might exclaim) after the fall of Communism—sometimes seems to dominate affairs behind the formal state. Few mafia members get caught because most people in high office are in on the deals. In Iran, a more visible theorcracy headed by the *velayat-e faqih* or guardianship of the religious jurist exists parallel to the official state government and is manifested as constituting the ultimate authority.

Finally, in the United States itself, C. Wright Mills discerned a socioeconomic power elite "in command of the major hierarchies and organizations of modern society. They rule the big corporations. They run the machinery of the state and claim its prerogatives. They direct the military establishment."[53] A few years later, in his famous farewell address to the nation, President Dwight D. Eisenhower warned against the baleful effects of what he termed the military–industrial complex. By this he meant that many corporations providing the goods and services necessary for military consumption employ retired military officers at influential executive levels and thus gain unwarranted influence over politics and the economy.

President Woodrow Wilson had his confidential advisor Colonel Edward House alongside his official secretary of state Robert Lansing. President Franklin D. Roosevelt had his Harry Hopkins parallel to Secretary of State Cordell Hull, and President Richard M. Nixon had Henry Kissinger behind Secretary of State William Rogers. The current U.S. president George W. Bush had Karl Rove to take care of confidential matters. All through history many other state leaders also have had their private advisors.

Further, in the United States, the U.S. Senate Select Intelligence Committee (Church Committee) in 1975 documented illegal activities of the CIA, including attempted assassinations against such leaders of other states as Fidel Castro (Cuba), Patrice Lumumba (Congo), Rafael Trujilo (Dominican Republic), Ngo Dinh Diem (South Vietnam), Abdul Karim Kassem (Iraq), and Chilean general Rene Schneider.[54] Although the committee's chairman Senator Frank Church concluded that the CIA had become "a rogue elephant rampaging out of control"[55] it is clear that the president—despite plausible deniability—not only knew what was occurring, but initiated it.

A decade later, the Iran-Contra scandal revealed how Oliver North, a mere marine lieutenant colonel on the staff of the National Security Council (NSC), covertly ran an illegal parallel foreign policy during the administration of President Ronald Reagan. This clandestine operation used profits from secret arms sales to Iran to illegally fund the Nicaraguan Contras in defiance of a congressional ban on such usage. Once again, however, it was also clear that President Reagan not only knew what was going on, but also directed the entire operation to be established in the first place.[56]

In most cases, however, one must conclude that these arcane activities or organizations in other states were much less powerful and only occasionally challenged or gave background direction to the official State government. These other organizations were not like the one in Turkey where the Deep State is said to be the ultimate power, officially sanctioned but also officially denied.

Conclusion

The Deep State is probably *not* a specific organization with a specific leader, both of which can be identified. Rather, it is a *mentality* concerning what Turkey should be, namely strongly nationalist, statist, secular, and right-wing; not Islamist, reformist, and/or a member of the EU. Members of the military and intelligence branches of the Turkish government in particular, but also those from any other agencies of the government such as the cabinet, parliament, judiciary, bureaucracy, and the like, or for that matter outside the government such as business interests, and even religious figures or criminals—anyone who would be motivated by the vision of an ultra-nationalist state and the need to protect it even at the cost of violating the technical laws of the official State can become a member of the Deep State for particular purposes. Indeed, sometimes someone who might be motivated mostly by pure financial gain such as criminals can become a member. Then when the purpose is completed, that person simply returns to working for the official State or whatever other organization he previously served. Or one could simultaneously "serve" the Deep State for a particular purpose, while at the same time work for the official State in other more mundane capacities.

In this sense of being a subjective, psychological mentality rather than an objective organization that can be specifically identified, the Deep State is even deeper than most have thought because it is in the minds of people. Thus, the only way to dismantle the Deep State would be to convince or reeducate its "members" that Turkey is not the object of some imperialist conspiracy plot to control and even dismember it, that the vision of a genuinely pluralistic democratic Turkey for all its citizens is legitimate and should be defended and promoted according to the laws of the official State. When such a pluralistic democratic mentality genuinely pervades the official Turkish State, the Deep State will have been dismantled, the Kurdish problem on its way to being solved, and Turkey a fit candidate for membership in the EU. This is proving a difficult task, but the process is irrevocably established, as the tremendous AK Party electoral victory on July 22, 2007 over determined military opposition illustrates.

CHAPTER 7

THE OTHER KURDS IN IRAN AND SYRIA

Iran

A lthough twice as many Kurds live in Iran as do in Iraq, the Kurdish national movement in Iran historically enjoyed much less success due in part to the relatively greater long-term strength of the Iranian governments. (More recently, of course, the Kurds in Iran have not benefited from the positive developments their co-nationals have experienced in Iraq and Turkey.) This, however, did not prevent Ismail Agha Simko from leading major Kurdish revolts in the 1920s, which only ended when the Iranian government treacherously assassinated him under false pretenses of negotiation in 1930.[1]

This Iranian technique of solving its Kurdish problem was used again on July 13, 1989, when Iranian agents assassinated the leader of the KDPI, Abdul Rahman Ghassemlou, in Vienna, Austria, while supposedly negotiating with him. On September 17, 1992, Iranian agents also assassinated Ghassemlou's successor, Sadegh Sharafkandi, while he was dining at the Mykonos Restaurant in Berlin, Germany. Mustafa Hejri became the new KDPI leader and has remained so into 2007.

Earlier, the KDPI's revolt against the Ayatollah Ruhollah Khomeini's new government had been completely smashed by 1981. Armed KDPI remnants, however, continued to shelter in northern Iraq. Their goal was "autonomy for Kurdistan, democracy for Iran."[2] Fighting, however, broke out between the more moderate KDPI and the more radical Marxist Komala in 1985. Hundreds died in this intra-Kurdish bloodletting. Further divisions occurred among the Iranian Kurds in 2006. As of the beginning of 2007, the splintered KDPI continues to shelter in the KRG just west of Sulaymaniya. Komala also maintains an armed militia in the area.

Although neither the KDPI nor Komala is currently active militarily in Iran, some have argued that the United States would like to use them to overthrow the present Iranian regime.[3] In 2006, top KDPI and Komala leaders such as KDPI head Mustafa Hejri visited Washington to meet with middle-level U.S. State Department and intelligence officials. Hejri made it clear that though he would accept U.S. financial aid, he opposed U.S. military attacks against Iran as being counterproductive. On the other hand, Komala declared that it neither opposed nor supported such attacks.

Despite these problems, the Iranian Kurds are famous among their Kurdish brethren for having established the only Kurdish state in the twentieth century, the short-lived Mahabad Republic of Kurdistan (January–December 1946). When this rump Kurdish state was destroyed, however, its president, Qazi Muhammad, was summarily hanged on March 31, 1947, a blow from which the Iranian Kurds still have not completely recovered.[4]

Unlike the Arabs and the Turks, the Persians are closely related to the Kurds. This ethnic affinity at times has probably served to moderate Kurdish national demands in Iran. Iran also received large numbers of Kurdish refugees from Iraq after the failed Iraqi

Kurdish revolts in 1975 and 1991. Unlike the Azeris, however, the Kurds have been barred from high levels of power in Iran. Many Iranian Kurds supported reformist Mohammad Khatami when he was elected president of Iran in May 1997.[5] Khatami appointed Abdullah Ramazanzadeh, a Shiite Kurd, as the first governor general of Iranian Kurdistan. In turn, Ramazanzadeh appointed a number of Sunni Kurds to important governmental positions. Khatami's reformist movement, however, proved too weak to stand up against the hard-liners. In April 2001, Ramazanzadeh was accused of libelous statements against the powerful watchdog body, the Council of Guardians, for objecting to the nullification of the Majlis votes in two Kurdish cities. A non-Kurd succeeded him. During the same year, several legislators from the Kurdish provinces resigned from the Majlis, accusing the government of discrimination. The situation continued to deteriorate when over half of the Kurdish members of the Majlis were prevented from participating in the February 2004 elections. As a result, more than seventy percent of the Kurds boycotted the election and civil unrest occurred in several Kurdish cities.

Many Kurds also boycotted the election of hard-line Mahmoud Ahmadinejad, who was elected president of Iran in June 2005. Only twenty-five percent of those eligible voted in the decisive second round of the June 2005 presidential elections in Kordestan province. Even fewer Kurds voted in other provinces. This compared with a national turnout of more than sixty percent and would seemingly be indicative of Kurdish alienation from the current Iranian political system.[6] Ahmadinejad immediately rebuked Kurdish appeals to place qualified Kurds in his new administration. Indeed, some Kurdish sources claimed that Ahmadinejad had been behind the assassination of the Iranian Kurdish leader Ghassemlou in 1989.[7]

The creation of a de facto state of Kurdistan in northern Iraq, in general, and the inauguration of Massoud Barzani in June 2005 as its president, in specific, also have influenced the neighboring Iranian Kurds to demand changes. On July 9, 2005, Iranian troops killed Shivan Qadiri, a young Kurdish leader, and dragged his body through the streets. The government claimed that Qadiri had organized the destruction of ballots in three voting centers in the recent elections that had resulted in Mahmoud Ahmadinejad winning the presidency. Thousands of Iranian Kurds launched protests in Mahabad, the unofficial capital of Iranian Kurdistan, as well as in Sanandaj, Sardasht, Oshnavieh, Divandareh, Baneh, Sinne, Bokan, and Saqqez, among others.[8] The Iranian government had to respond with a state of de facto martial law and deploy large numbers of security forces. A number of deaths were reported on both sides. Further Kurdish demonstrations in protest against a death sentence handed down for the July unrest occurred in Mahabad at the end of October 2005.

Moreover, during 2005, the PJAK, a new Iranian Kurdish party cooperating with the PKK, was reported to be engaging in various military operations against government troops in the Merivan region along the border with Iraq. Along with the PKK, the PJAK was based in the Kandil Mountains of the KRG and along the Iranian border. From this base, the PJAK was able to launch occasional raids into Iran. The PJAK has also welcomed possible U.S. attacks against Iran as a way to topple the regime. On February 16, 2007, the anniversary of Abdullah Ocalan's capture, large demonstrations and mass meetings were held in Iranian Kurdistan. They led to three deaths and hundreds of detentions. These events served as a reminder to the Iranian authorities that they still had a volatile Kurdish problem.

Syria

Approximately a million Kurds live in Syria, a much smaller number than in Turkey, Iraq, and Iran.[9] Although the largest minority in Syria, the Kurds in Syria live in three non-contiguous areas and have been much less successfully organized and developed than in the other three states. For many years the repressive Syrian government of Hafez Assad sought to maintain an Arab belt between its Kurds and those in Turkey and Iraq. This Arab belt uprooted many Syrian Kurds and deprived them of their livelihoods.

Many Kurds in Syria have even been denied Syrian citizenship. In 1962, Law 93 classified some 160,000 Kurds as *ajanib* or foreigners who could not vote, own property, or work in government jobs.[10] Some 75,000 other Syrian Kurds are known as *maktoumeen* or concealed. As such, they have virtually no civil rights. A government decree in September 1992 prohibited the registration of children with Kurdish first names. Kurdish cultural centers, bookshops, and similar activities have also been banned. Indeed, some have suspected that in return for giving the PKK sanctuary in Syria for many years, the PKK kept the lid on Syrian Kurdish unrest. For all these reasons, therefore, little was heard about the Kurds in Syria.

Events in Kurdistan of Iraq, however, helped begin to change this situation. In March 2004, Kurdish rioting broke out at a football match in Qamishli. Since then, the atmosphere has remained tense. Renewed rioting occurred a year later in Aleppo following the killing of Maashouq al-Haznawi, an outspoken Kurdish cleric critical of the regime. Within days of becoming the president of Kurdistan in Iraq in June 2005, Massoud Barzani demanded that the Syrian Kurds be granted their rights peacefully. On October 16, 2005, an emboldened domestic opposition consisting of such disparate groups as the Muslim Brotherhood and the communists issued a "Damascus Declaration for Democratic National Change." Among many other points, the Declaration called for "a just democratic solution to the Kurdish issue in Syria, in a manner that guarantees the complete equality of Syrian Kurdish citizens, with regard to nationality rights, culture, learning the national language, and other constitutional... rights."[11]

The forced Syrian troop withdrawal from Lebanon following the assassination of the former Lebanese prime minister, Rafiq Hariri, in February 2005, a strong UN Security Council response to apparent Syrian involvement in the affair, and the U.S. occupation of neighboring Iraq have also presented grave international challenges to the Syrian regime. Bashar Assad—who had succeeded his father when he died in 2000—indicated that he was willing to entertain reforms, but has not offered any specific timetable. Thus, as of the beginning of 2007, the Syrian Kurds are showing increased signs of national awareness due to the developments in the KRG, but remain much less successful implementing them than do their brethren in Iraq and Turkey.

CHAPTER 8

THE KRG'S DELICATE BALANCE

Introduction

Since the fall of Saddam Hussein in 2003, the KRG has maintained a cautiously optimistic, but delicate balance to maintain its existence amidst perilous surroundings. The first and, of course, most immediate dimension of this delicate balance is the KRG's precarious relationship with the Iraqi central government in Baghdad. This situation was put on hold due to the inconclusive Iraqi national elections of March 7, 2010, and the resulting hung parliament.[1] However, even though the Kurds eventually prove to be one of the kingmakers in this electoral imbroglio,[2] once a new central government emerged in Baghdad, the inherently more powerful Arab majority will again begin pressuring the Kurds for concessions.[3] This situation will be analyzed more fully below.

The second dimension of the KRG's delicate balance is the relationship with Turkey, a situation that has improved dramatically since the initial days following Saddam Hussein's fall of Turkish "red lines" drawn against so-called Kurdish war lords. Thriving economic relations between the two, however, gradually led to better political relations.[4] In May 2009 the new Turkish foreign

minister Ahmet Davutoglu announced his state's innovative foreign policy of zero problems with its neighbors.[5] Among many
other issues, this means that instead of viewing the Iraqi Kurds as
an existential enemy threatening its territorial integrity, Turkey
now views the KRG through less hostile, potentially cooperative
lenses. In October 2009, Davutoglu brought this new policy home
by actually visiting Irbil. Then in March 2010, Turkey opened a
high-powered consulate in Irbil that serves as a de facto embassy.[6]
Finally in June 2010, KRG president Massoud Barzani successfully
returned Davutoglu's earlier visit, by journeying to Ankara where
he was most significantly received with his official title of KRG
president.[7] Although the issues of Kirkuk[8] and the PKK still remain
to cloud relations, it is now practical to envision Turkey as a possible friend or even protector if the KRG's relationships with
Baghdad deteriorated.[9]

The third dimension of the KRG's delicate balance concerns its
relationship with the United States, the KRG's creator and ultimate protector. However, as the United States begins to wind
down its mission in Iraq and assume a noncombat, background
role, one wonders what this means for the KRG's long-term future.[10] Many Kurds hope that their position is now strong enough
and a residual U.S. presence in the form of U.S. troops training
Iraqi soldiers and shepherding joint Iraqi-KRG troop patrols (so-
called Combined Security Mechanisms [CSMs]) on their dividing
line in the disputed areas capable enough to successfully maintain
this delicate balance.[11] In January 2010, Barzani himself visited
Washington, D.C., met with U.S. president Barack Obama and
other senior officials, and received assurances of continuing U.S.
support.[12] The KRG maintains a liaison office just nine blocks
north of the White House. Qubad Talabani, the son of the Iraqi

president, continues as the young and dynamic head of this office and KRG representative in the United States. In May 2010, the U.S. House of Representatives approved Resolution 873 calling for a U.S. consulate in Irbil.[13] At the end of August 2010, Fuad Hussein, the chief of staff to KRG president Barzani, conducted a week of meetings with U.S. government officials, members of Congress, and the staffs of the Senate foreign relations committee and the House foreign affairs committee.[14]

The fourth dimension of the KRG's delicate balance concerns its own internal situation. The KRG has been ruled by the so-called Kurdistani List, an alliance of the Kurdistan Democratic Party (KDP) and the Patriotic Union of Kurdistan (PUK), since the fall of Saddam Hussein and actually earlier once the two main Kurdish parties settled their civil war that had raged from 1994 to 1998. Although this alliance was necessary to avoid further internal strife between the two and was, therefore, welcomed, the Kurdistani List also reminds one of the criticisms of the Grand Coalitions in Germany during 1966–1969 and then again from 2005 to 2009. Both times these Grand Coalitions performed adequately, but impaired German democracy because they left only small parties to oppose and criticize. Thus, they made citizens feel that no one could seriously criticize the government, that politics was a game manipulated by the powerful, and that democracy was simply a facade. A good democracy requires a lively interplay between the "ins" and the "outs," rather than complicity between them. Thus, as soon as a more normal majority was achieved in a subsequent election, the German Grand Coalitions were dissolved. Similarly, the all-party British electoral coalitions in both world wars were disbanded as soon as the fighting stopped. Indeed, at the height of his power in July 1945, British prime minister Winston Churchill was summarily dismissed by the electorate. The Kurdistani List, however, has demonstrated no inclination to follow suit.

Thus, the rise but uncertain future of Nowshirwan Mustafa's (Amin) *Gorran* (Change) Party at the expense of the PUK creates novel possibilities and uncertainties for the KRG, giving it for the first time a real opposition in its parliament of 111 seats. Rancor and even shootouts between PUK and *Gorran* supporters, however, serve as an ominous reminder of bloody past intra-Kurdish struggles.[15] This new party won an impressive twenty-five seats in the KRG parliamentary elections of July 25, 2009,[16] but only a disappointing eight in the Iraqi national elections held on March 7, 2010. Subsequently, to maintain a necessary united Kurdish front against Baghdad, *Gorran* agreed to cooperate with the Kurdistani List but then withdrew this support because of disagreements over its share in the new Iraqi government announced in December 2010. Thus, despite all the initial hopes it aroused, the *Gorran* Party seems destined to be little more than a flash party a la the Poujadists in France during the late 1950s.

An aging Jalal Talabani (born 1933) finally managed to win reelection as president of Iraq and also continued as secretary-general of the PUK. One wondered, however, how much longer he could remain active. Does this mean that Massoud Barzani's KDP will soon institute one-party dominance over the KRG? Although only time will tell, it is difficult to see how the PUK can regain its former equal position with the KDP. The PUK's longtime leader Jalal Talabani has visibly aged and is nearing eighty, while its two long-serving deputy leaders are in effect gone. Nowshirwan Mustafa (Amin) quit the PUK to head the *Gorran* Party and Kosrat Rasul has long been ailing. Barham Salih, the current KRG prime minister and PUK politburo member, is bright and capable, but lacks deep roots within the party as he was only brought from abroad and installed by Talabani in 2001. In October 2010, Barham Salih vouched how closely he has been able to work with Massoud Barzani, the longtime leader of the KDP.[17] In February 2010, however, when Massoud Barzani journeyed to Washington, D.C., to visit President Obama and other U.S. officials, U.S. sources criticized Massoud Barzani for leaving out Barham Salih but bringing along his nephew Nechirvan Barzani and son Masrour Barzani.[18]

What does all this mean for already existing problems regarding corruption, nepotism, transparency, and civil liberties?[19] These problems can only grow worse unless the KRG authorities manifest a renewed determination to follow the rule of law. In May 2010, for example, Sardasht Osman, a twenty-three-year-old journalist who had been critical of the KRG, KDP, and Barzani family was kidnapped in broad daylight in front of the College of Arts in Irbil and then murdered. After a few months the KDP lamely announced that its secret investigation found that Osman had been killed by an insurgent group because he had refused to work with them. These dubious findings "have seriously undermined the authority of the KRG"[20] by illustrating how it is willing to cover up crime and operate outside of the purview of any independent judiciary.

On February 17, 2011, violent demonstrations against the KDP and PUK broke out in Sulaymaniya and, as this book went to press, were continuing early in March 2011. During the first few days at least three protestors were killed and scores wounded. Most of the demonstrators were protesting against corruption, nepotism, and the lack of effective services such as jobs and electricity. Intellectuals and journalists also protested against limitations against speech and press as well as daily harassment. Among all there was a deep anger against the Barzani's KDP and Talabani's PUK family domination over society and government. There were even calls for the resignation of President Massoud Barzani and Prime Minister Barham Salih.

Despite the supposedly unified KRG, the interior, peshmerga, and finance ministries are still divided into separate KDP and PUK branches. Also still split are the intelligence agencies: the KDP's *Asayesh* [Security] and *Parastin* [Protection] headed by Masrour Barzani (Massoud Barzani's son) and the PUK's *Zanyari* (Information) headed by Bafel Talabani (Jalal Talabani's elder son). The judiciary was also partisan. Most of the press too was not neutral, *Livin* magazine and *Awane* newspaper being two rare independent exceptions.

Gunmen attached to the KDP initially responded to the demonstrations by opening fire on the protestors and set fire to the offices of the opposition *Gorran* Party. PUK loyalists burned down an independent television station to prevent further coverage of the events. Although the KRG parliament met and issued a seventeen-point set of recommendations for grassroots reforms, broadened freedoms, and improved living conditions, the demonstrations continued. At the least they constituted a serious wake up call that all was not well with the KRG and potentially held momentous consequences for the future.[21]

In addition, what about the continuing existence of the PKK and PJAK ensconced in the Kandil Mountains, a situation that leads to constant threats of Turkish and Iranian cross-border shellings and even interventions?[22] Although this state of affairs will remain an irritant, the PKK and PJAK presences in Iraqi Kurdistan are not likely to escalate into KRG-threatening scenarios as none of those involved would benefit. Turkey and Iran seek to balance each other in the region; neither would accept the other becoming dominant over the KRG. For its part the KRG will never flagrantly support these two insurgent groups enough to draw in Turkey and/ or Iran fully because to do so would threaten the KRG's existence. In addition, as long as the KRG remains part of Iraq, that state's recognized territorial integrity will prevent Turkey and/or Iran from seeking to permanently incorporate the KRG. Of course, if Iraq collapses, all bets are off.

The future of Kirkuk also remains a crucial internal threat to the KRG's delicate balance.[23] In addition, what do the Islamic elements in the KRG portend for its future? In the KRG parliamentary elections of July 25, 2009, the Kurdistan Islamic Union led by Salahaddin Bahauddin won 5 seats in the 111-seat parliament, while Ali Bapir's Kurdistan Islamic Group garnered 4 seats. Although Islamic groups will continue to exist, they seem too splintered and weak to constitute a major threat.[24]

Finally, other threats to the KRG's delicate balance concern its position in the regional Middle Eastern arena where a potentially hostile Arab world still regards the KRG existence as a threat to the regional Arab patrimony. The larger Arab region, however, is too divided and full of its own problems to threaten the KRG in any major manner. In addition, as just mentioned, as long as the KRG remains a federal state within Iraq, that state's territorial integrity offers the KRG protection. Finally, both the EU and UN look favorably upon the KRG, but are unlikely to affect its delicate balance in any meaningful way because both are not immediately involved with the situation and have much more important problems with which to deal.

KRG-Baghdad Relations

As noted in Chapter 3, the Iraqi Kurds now not only possess their most powerful regional government since the creation of Iraq following World War I (the Kurdistan Regional Government or KRG), but also play a very prominent role in the Iraqi government in Baghdad including holding the posts of president (Jalal Talabani), (until August 2009 when he resigned in preparation to become prime minister of the KRG) deputy prime minister (Barham Salih), foreign minister (Hoshyar Zebari), and several other cabinet positions. After a great deal of wrangling, the Kurds managed to maintain their strong position in the new al-Maliki government finally cobbled together in December 2010. This dual governmental role stood in mark contrast to the situation that existed before the events of 1991 and 2003, when the Kurds were treated as second class citizens and worse. The ultimate question, of course, is for how long this unique Kurdish position of strength will last. Many Arabs still resent the Kurdish claims to autonomy as a challenge to the Arab patrimony and a federal state for the Iraqi Kurds within Iraq as simply a prelude to secession that was forced upon the Arabs at a moment of temporary weakness following the war in 2003. Indeed, most Kurds would quickly opt for independence when they perceive the time as ripe. When will the Iraqi Arabs get their act together and start trying to reduce the Kurds again?

This chapter argues that the time for this to happen has arrived. As the [2010] "Annual Threat Assessment of the US Intelligence Community" pointed out in its otherwise largely positive assessment of Iraqi security needs,

Arab-Kurd tensions have [the] potential to derail Iraq's generally positive security trajectory, including triggering conflict among Iraq's ethnosectarian groups. Many of the drivers of Arab-Kurd tensions—disputed territories, revenue sharing and control of oil resources, and integration of peshmerga forces—still need to be worked out, and miscalculations or misperceptions on either side risk an inadvertent escalation of violence.[25]

Although their current role in Baghdad has been a hedge against renewed Arab chauvinism, it is likely that the Kurds will gradually play a reduced role in the new al-Maliki government eventually formed in December 2010 after protracted negotiations.

What can the KRG do to halt this gradual decline in its position? First, as already mentioned, one must query whether the Kurdish house itself is in order to meet this impending struggle. The long conflict for ultimate power in Iraqi Kurdistan between Massoud Barzani's KDP and Jalal Talabani's PUK—a contest that led to a bloody civil war between the two as recently as the mid-1990s and even saw Barzani call upon Saddam Hussein for help in 1996—was put on hold by ceding Barzani the presidency of the KRG while Talabani assumed the largely ceremonial presidency of Iraq. Although one might wonder what will follow once Talabani retires from the Iraqi presidency, the KDP-PUK compromise continues to hold as Barham Sahih from the PUK became the new KRG prime minister despite significant PUK loses to Nowshirwan Mustafa's *Gorran* or Change Party following the KRG elections held on July 25, 2009. The KDP-PUK also continued their joint electoral slate for the Iraqi parliamentary elections held on March 7, 2010, and in which the *Gorran* Party fell short of its expectations. Nevertheless, the *Gorran* Party still has the potential to divide the Kurds.

The Iraqi Constitution approved by a hotly contested referendum on October 15, 2005, established a federal structure for Iraq that grants significant powers to the regions.[26] Indeed, for the first time ever most Kurds now think of their government in Irbil, not the one in Baghdad, when the concept of government is broached. The actual division of power between the Iraqi government and the KRG, however, remains in potential dispute. As noted above, these contested powers include the ownership of natural resources and the control of the revenues flowing from them, the role of the KRG army or peshmerga (militia), and the final status of Kirkuk (see below) as well as several other disputed territories such as Sinjar and Makhmur, among others. Mosul, Iraq's third largest city, has a big Kurdish population in its eastern part and is also being contested.

Oil

As noted above, Dr. Ashti A. Hawrami, the KRG minister for Natural Resources and a well-known former international oil executive, addressed the issue of natural resource ownership in a wide-ranging interview in the KRG capital of Irbil on June 14, 2006.[27] He argued strongly that Article 115 of the new Iraqi Constitution "states the supremacy of regional laws over federal laws, and can be invoked if no agreement is reached on the management of oil and gas resources and the distribution of proceeds." He also argued that Article 112 of the Constitution only permits the Iraqi Government "an administrative role confined to the handling, i.e., exporting and marketing, of the extracted oil and gas from existing producing fields.... The elected authorities of the regions and producing governorates are now entitled to administer and supervise the extraction process; in other words local oilfield managers are answerable to the local authorities." Hawrami went on to maintain that since the new Constitution was silent on undeveloped fields or any new fields, "the regions and governorates will have all the controls." Although he stated that the KRG and the government in Baghdad would be able to cooperate, heated verbal conflict over the issue of natural resources has been occurring.

Since Hawrami's speech, several apparent compromises on a Hydrocarbons law have fallen through. In June 2009, for example, the KRG actually signed several contracts with foreign companies to extract oil from the Taq Taq and Tawke fields in the KRG region, including one with Norway's DNO as well as Canada's Addax Petroleum (acquired by China Petrochemical) and Turkey's Genel Enerji International.[28] At the time, this development was hailed as an important breakthrough for KRG-Iraq relations as the Kurds said they could produce 200,000 barrels a day by the end of 2010, about 10 percent of Iraq's current output and up from a maximum of 100,000 barrels daily the previous year. However, the deal fell through over who should pay the foreign oil firms developing fields in the KRG region. Nouri al-Maliki's government in Baghdad labeled the deals illicit and declared that the KRG would pay the firms from its percentage of the annual national budget. The KRG declined to go along with this interpretation. In October 2009, the Kurds suspended exports, and the KRG's output subsequently slumped to 20,000 barrels a day.

Nevertheless, in February 2010, Hussain al-Shahristani, the Iraqi oil minister and the Kurds' nemesis on this situation, announced that Iraq expected to resume oil exports from the Kurdistan region "in the near future."[29] However, the fate of the earlier disputed deals between the KRG and foreign companies remained unclear. Al-Shahristani claimed that the resumption of oil exports had no connection with finding a solution to the problem of the earlier KRG contracts. Hawrami inexplicably declared that the KRG was "happy about this development... but we have not received any official reply from the central government about accepting our proposals or allowing us to resume exports."[30] In other words, the impasse remained.

The new al-Maliki government finally cobbled together in December 2010, appointed Al-Shahristani deputy prime minister with overall responsibilities in the energy sector. His increased prominence might bode ill for the Kurds. On the other hand, Abdul-Karim Luaibi, the new Iraqi Oil Minister, has had less antagonistic relations with Irbil in the past, while acting as the main intermediary in talks between the KRG and Baghdad.

The Current Situation

At the present time the relationship between Irbil and Baghdad "is characterized by suspicion, animosity and brinkmanship"[31] that "threaten the stability of the [Iraqi] state at a far deeper political level."[32] As the Baghdad government of al-Maliki grew in strength and confidence, it naturally began to seek to reimpose its authority over the northern Kurdish part of the state. The 2005 constitution that guaranteed real federalism and thus semi-independence for the KRG was now challenged as having been imposed at a moment of weakness. Many (but not all[33]) Shiite and Sunni Arabs now seek to return to what they see as the rightful situation of a more centralized state that will need to alter the constitution. Indeed, this is a position that offers al-Maliki or any Arab successor a strong arguing point as he seeks to rebuild Iraq and end the sectarian violence between Shiite and Sunni Arabs. Given the inherent demographics and overall assets of the two sides, there is a sense that time is on Baghdad's side. The inability to form a new government for more than nine months after the national elections of March 7, 2010, only postponed this situation. As the new al-Maliki government takes hold in 2011, however, the Arab position relative to the Kurds will continue to strengthen.

For example, in the local elections of January 2009, the Kurds lost their artificial majority in the Nineveh provincial government because the Sunnis participated instead of boycotting as they had done in the previous elections. The national parliamentary elections in March 2010 seemed to highlight the tensions as politicians on both sides complained of harassment of candidates, pressure on parties, and violence when they campaigned on the opposite side. The new parliament will include thirty-one members from Nineveh and the Kurds expected to win only ten this time, their estimated percentage of the population in Nineveh. In actuality, they only won eight. Khasro Goran, a leading local Kurdish official, put it succinctly: "First ethnicity, second political party."[34] Accordingly, there are those in the KRG who think it would be best to confront Baghdad militarily sooner rather than later when the power equation between the two would be less favorable to the Kurds.

For the past three years, Barzani and al-Maliki have been locked in a bitter on again/off-again verbal struggle over the situation. During a tense meeting in Baghdad in November 2008, for example, Barzani told al-Maliki "you smell like a dictator"[35] and also declared that the Iraqi prime minister was "playing with fire."[36] In August 2008, these semantic fireworks nearly resulted in open hostilities over the disputed city of Khanaqin situated in Diyala province some ninety miles north of Baghdad on their de facto internal border often referred to as the "trigger line." Here the Kurdish peshmerga ignored an ultimatum by the Iraqi Security Forces (ISF) to withdraw within twenty-four hours. After some very tense brinkmanship, the two sides each withdrew some fifteen miles north and south of the city leaving security within Khanaqin to be handled by the police.

The two sides have come close to fighting on several subsequent occasions, usually outside of the urban areas where military commanders are more prone to act on their own. In 2009, however, Baghdad troops entered the disputed but mainly Kurdish town of Altun Kupri. When the residents supported by the peshmerga began to demonstrate, the Baghdad troops were told to shoot to kill. Only the presence of U.S. troops stationed nearby prevented bloodshed.[37] Since late January 2010, the then-U.S. commander in Iraq General Raymond Odierno and his successor have been trying to build trust between the two sides by using them in joint patrols (called CSMs) and manning checkpoints together. In a few places they even sleep and eat together. Some 450 peshmerga are involved in these joint patrols working in the three provinces of Diyala, Kirkuk, and Nineveh. Barham Salih, the KRG prime minister, has called these sorts of measures "Band-Aids to build confidence and generate stability."[38] However, what will happen when the U.S. troops are withdrawn in the near future? Salih has confided that "I think as the Americans are leaving I am very, very concerned." Even with the Americans still present, for example, the two sides dispute over who actually commands the joint patrols. In addition, it is highly unlikely that the fortifications along the line in Kalar and Kifri, northwest of Khanaqin, will be dismantled soon or the landmines removed.

In February 2010, just before the hotly contested national elections, yet another close encounter occurred in the town of Takleef, a Kurdish controlled settlement in the province of Nineveh.[39] U.S. forces had escorted Atheel al-Nujaifi, the controversial Arab governor of Mosul, into Takleff, after Barzani had already referred to al-Nujaifi as a criminal and declared that a warrant would be issued for this arrest due to a previous incident. The result was the governor alleging an assassination attempt, his troops arresting Kurdish troops, retaliatory arrests of Iraqi troops by the Kurds, and a temporary suspension of the joint patrols and checkpoints throughout the entire province. The United States finally was able to restore order, but how many times can such incidents occur without exploding into actual violence?

Oil-rich and strategically located Kirkuk, of course, represents the center of these Irbil-Baghdad tensions. It "is a classic divided city...over which people are prepared to fight and die....The numbers of actors involved, resource dimensions, and international involvement—add...layers of complexity that are matched by few other disputes over territorial 'ownership.'"[40] From a position of initial strength that appeared to be ready to hand Kirkuk to the KRG under the provisions of Article 140 of the 2005 Iraqi constitution, the contested city and province now seem the proverbial bridge too far for the Kurds to take. Kirkuk also represents the opposing constitutional positions with the Kurds maintaining that the Iraqi constitution (including Article 140) must be implemented, while Baghdad has become increasingly critical of the constitution in general and particularly Article 140 as being part of a constitution written for a now dated situation.

Ironically, however, many Arabs fall back on the constitution by pointing to Article 142, which implements the promise to the Sunnis to review the document by allowing amendments agreed to by a parliamentary majority to be passed together as one bloc.[41] Indeed an Iraqi Constitutional Review Committee has been at work since the adoption of the constitution in 2005. Maybe its most important work has been to try to define the constitutional definition of federalism as it would be implemented in a manner acceptable to all Iraqi parties.

To buttress his position, al-Maliki has established so-called *Isnad* (support) councils in Mosul, similar in scope and purpose to the earlier *Sahwat* (awakening) councils in the center and south of Iraq. He also ordered the Baghdad ministry of interior to assume direct responsibility for security in Mosul in November 2008, and transferred away those units of the Iraqi Security Forces (ISF) dominated by Kurds. Earlier the Iraqi prime minister had also replaced Kurdish officers in (ISF) units stationed in the provinces of Nineveh, Diyala, and Salahadin.

The Future

How then will ties between the KRG and Baghdad play out?[42] Clearly, their political future remains in doubt. Whether Iraq will remain truly federal as the KRG demands or federal in name only as the Arabs recentralize the state remains to be seen. However, KRG president Massoud Barzani has unequivocally warned: "We will not allow the Kurdish people's achievements to be wrecked by the Iraqi parliament. Iraq will fall apart if the Iraqi constitution is violated."[43] In addition, as Stansfield and Anderson concluded, "A government founded on Arab nationalism, devoid of Kurdish representation and dedicated to eliminating meaningful Kurdish autonomy in the north, would spell the beginning of the end for the territorial integrity of Iraq."[44] As suggested above—despite the long governmental impasse that followed the national elections of March 7, 2010—time seems to be on the side of Baghdad. Does this mean that the KRG might be tempted to strike before it is too late? So far, the KRG leadership has shown a wisdom and maturity that argues against any such rash action. Violence and even civil war, if they come, are more likely to eventuate inadvertently.

A shaky Iraqi political order currently exists in which the Sunnis have recently begun to participate, extremist sectarian violence constrained, and effective central government instituted. Within this order the Kurds have been major participants. They also have a proven track record of instituting their own successful government, the KRG, protected by some 75,000 peshmerga, increasing acceptance from Turkey, and a tenuous U.S. guarantee of protection, which, however, will become increasingly problematic as U.S. forces begin to withdraw. As this occurs, violence between Irbil and Baghdad could result.[45]

If the Sunnis continue to participate in Iraq's new order, they gradually may replace the Kurds in Iraq's governing coalition with the Shiites. Indeed, many thought that the Kurds would lose their hold on the Iraqi presidency following the national elections of March 7, 2010. Such a development would have stimulated Kurdish marginalization from the Iraqi state and made ethnic violence between the Kurds and Arabs more probable. Although this did not happen, the belief that it might have illustrated the Kurds' perceived vulnerability. For the time being the Kurds' position in Baghdad remained tenable. On the other hand, if the Sunnis are effectively excluded from the next Iraqi government or perceive their role as unfairly minimized, there might be a return to full-scale sectarian civil war. Either way one side or the other is likely to become deeply dissatisfied and fearful about its future. The continuing uncertainty over the future of Iraq's rich oil reserves would certainly fuel any such struggle. The broadly based government consisting of all Iraq's contending elements that was finally cobbled together in December 2010 may prove too cumbersome to be effective.

Others, however, argue that despite these signs of Arab impatience with the Kurdish gains and continuing demands, there is

still a general consensus to accept the Kurdish federal state given
the realities of post–Saddam Hussein Iraq. On the basis of his
lengthy experience, for example, Zalmay Khalilzad, the former
U.S. ambassador in Iraq, made just this point in March 2010.[46]
What is required then is a wisdom and maturity that lead both sides
to compromise their extreme visions in order to implement a federalism satisfactory to both.

CHAPTER 9

TURKEY'S KURDISH INITIATIVE

Astrong case can be made that ever since the Sheikh Said rebellion was crushed in 1925,[1] the Kurdish question in Turkey has been one of the main factors preventing it from becoming a complete democracy. The Kurds have been viewed as threatening the very foundational rationale for Turkey's existence as a unitary state in which ethnicity is supposedly an irrelevant criterion in the public and political sphere.[2] As a result, Turkey has largely opted for "securitization"[3] rather than democratization to deal with the problem. In other words, the Kurdish question has impeded the development of democracy in Turkey itself. Accordingly, a democratic resolution of the Kurdish problem could open the door to the full development of democracy in Turkey and would go a long way toward making Turkey eligible for admission into the European Union (EU). The purpose of this chapter is to analyze Turkey's tortured road toward a Kurdish Initiative or Democratic Opening following the AK Party's enormous electoral victory in July 2007.

New Kurdish Dawn in Turkey

Given recent democratic developments, the legal and political condition of the Turkish Kurds is changing dramatically.[4] Long gone are the days of their being dismissed as mere "Mountain Turks" and the very term "Kurd" being treated as a four-letter word. The Turkish Kurds no longer scare so easily and feel freer to express themselves. They have a new openness and even boldness. For example, in 2008, the Diyarbakir Bar Association even mulled over hauling General Yasar Buyukanit, the outspoken, ultra-nationalist Turkish Chief of Staff, before the courts for his actions and statements against the Kurds. There is a new self-esteem in being ethnic Kurdish citizens of the Republic of Turkey and desire to prosper as such.

What has given rise to this new dawn awakening? Despite the Kurdistan Workers Party (PKK) being labeled as a terrorist group by Turkey, the United States, and the EU, a recent trip to Diyarbakir, the unofficial capital of Turkish Kurdistan, found few Kurds wanting to criticize the rebel PKK and its imprisoned leader Abdullah Ocalan. Rather, there is pride that the PKK was a formidable force that came close to successfully challenging the Turkish state. In more recent years, the belief is that since the PKK has repeatedly shown a willingness to engage peacefully in the political process, the onus is now on the Turkish state to respond positively. Indeed some have argued that the PKK attacks against Turkish targets in the fall of 2007 were provoked by earlier Turkish offensive strikes seeking clashes with the PKK that then could be used as an excuse to invade northern Iraq and eliminate the Kurdistan Regional Government (KRG) as well as to gain leverage over the AK Party Government.[5] Others have further maintained that some of the reputed PKK attacks actually were provocations by hardline, rogue

PKK elements opposed to peace or even Turkish "false-flag operations" similarly opposed to peace and masquerading as the PKK. The Beytussebap assault that killed thirteen civilians, early in October 2007, an attack against a gendarmerie team in Tokat's Resadiye district that killed seven soldiers in May 2009, and the Hakkari roadside bombing that left nine civilians dead in September 2010 are some of the examples.[6]

Effectively barred from entry into the Turkish parliament by the 10 percent threshold, the then-legal pro-Kurdish party called the Democratic Society Party (DTP) still managed to gain seats in the national elections of July 22, 2007, by having twenty of its candidates elected as independents. Thus, for the first time since the Democracy Party (DEP) was expelled from the Turkish Parliament in March 1994, an avowed Kurdish party had entered the national legislature.

More importantly perhaps, the ruling AK Party of Prime Minister Recep Tayyip Erdogan—with its roots in Islamic politics—garnered even more votes from Turkey's ethnic Kurds by stressing its economic reforms and conservative values. The DTP seemingly erred by focusing more on political and ideological demands, but ignoring more immediately important bread and butter socioeconomic issues. The AK Party, on the other hand, has come to represent a convergence of moderate, popular Islam with liberal economics, secularism, and moderate nationalism, that is a modern democratic Turkey comfortable with its Islamic heritage and seriously working to become fit to join the EU.[7]

The result was a 180-degree turnabout in Turkish politics. In an attempt to preserve their privileged position, the secularist Kemalists, as well as the military, have adopted a reactionary anti-Western position and are now skeptical about Turkey's EU candidacy. On the other hand, the AK Party (despite its Islamic roots) has become progressive supporters of the EU and the West, in part, admittedly to protect itself against any new state crackdown as had occurred against previous Islamic parties.

Further, one might even argue that both the Turkish military and the PKK have a vested interest in keeping their struggle going or else both will become increasingly irrelevant politically. On the other hand, it was the AK Party, which had come to represent the best hope for ending the struggle with a democratic political solution that integrated the Kurds into Turkey's political system.[8]

Continuing Turkish Hostility

Metin Heper (a distinguished Turkish professor of politics and the recipient of some very impressive academic honors) has written an important book—not so much for the accuracy of its basic theme that the Turkish Republic has not sought to promote Turkish ethnic nationalism that would assimilate its ethnic Kurdish population—but because of how it illustrates the continuing Turkish hostility toward its ethnic Kurdish population.[9] Heper rejects what he terms "the received wisdom" (p. 181) or "the present paradigm of the assimilation-resistance-assimilation model in respect to ethnic conflict" (p. 2) to explain the Kurdish question in Turkey. In so doing he seemingly rejects the position of practically everyone who has written on the Kurdish issue including the present author and even such prominent Turkish scholars as Kemal Kirisci[10] and M. Hakan Yavuz[11] whom he also takes to task by name. In rejecting the model of ethnic conflict to analyze the Kurdish problem in Turkey, Heper calls for "a paradigmatic shift" (p. 8) to an "alternative paradigm" (p. 11) that he terms "the *acculturation-concern for de-acculturation-non-recognition paradigm*" (p. 181).

Heper maintains: "The [Turkish] state has not resorted to forceful assimilation of the Kurds, because the founders of the state had been of the opinion that for long centuries, both Turks and Kurds in Turkey, particularly the latter, had gone through a process of *acculturation*, or steady disappearance of cultural distinctiveness as a consequence of a process of *voluntary*, or rather *unconscious*, assimilation" (p. 6).

He goes on to explain that "when the Kurds rebelled, for reasons that the state thought could not be ethnic, the state reversed its earlier policy of recognizing the distinct Kurdish ethnicity, and pursued a new strategy of the *non-recognition* of the ethnic distinctiveness of the Kurds in the hope that... it could arrest a de-acculturation process on the part of the Kurds, and reactivate the earlier acculturation process" (ibid.). In other words, "the rationale behind non-recognition [of the Kurds] is that of trying to hinder the de-acculturation of the already acculturated, not that of assimilating people who are non-acculturated" (pp. 6–7). However, what is really so different about Heper's alternative paradigm? As he admits: "acculturation [is]... *unconscious* assimilation" (p. 6).

As proof of the validity of his "alternative paradigm," Heper accurately points out how the Kurds as Muslims supported the Turks during the Turkish War of Independence that followed World War I. He declares that this is a "critical question that the students of ethnic conflict in Turkey subscribers to the present paradigm [of ethnic conflict and differentiation] would be hard pressed to answer in a persuasive manner" (p. 5). What Heper omits, however, is the fact that the idea of their Kurdish identity superseding their Ottoman and Islamic identity struck the Kurds late. This point has been well documented by Hakan Ozoglu, whose book[12] Heper fails to mention although he does credit Ozoglu's earlier article in his bibliography. Certainly most advocates of what Heper terms the present paradigm of ethnic conflict recognize that Kurdish ethnic awareness and a sense of nationalism largely began to develop only after World War I and the collapse of the Ottoman Empire. They do not argue, as Heper claims they do, that "the Turks and Kurds in that country [Turkey] had always had a deep ethnic cleavage between them" (p. 7).

Almost missed in all this is what might be called Heper's escape clause: "The present essay does *not* address itself to the question of whether or not the state's perception of the 'Kurdish question' did fit the empirical reality. After all, what shapes thought and action is the *perception* of the empirical reality, and not the objective empirical reality" (p. 12). In other words Heper is simply maintaining that the Turkish state authorities think that Turkey has not tried to assimilate its Kurds, but instead believe that it only has tried to prevent their de-acculturation.

The remaining chapters constitute an attempt to fit the facts into Heper's alternative paradigm, and although they are not without heuristic value for the present purposes are mainly interesting for what they show about current Turkish scholarship and its hostility toward the Kurds. Chapter 2 illustrates how the Ottomans had a tradition of not trying to assimilate people under their suzerainty. "In contrast to the Habsburg and Romanov Empires, the Ottoman Empire lacked an ethnic 'core'. Islam-created categories of Muslim and non-Muslims, which constituted the dominant status groups in society, [and] transcended ethnicity" (p. 23). Chapter 3 traces relations between the Ottomans and the Kurds, and argues that "the Ottomans' policy towards the Kurds was not one of 'divide and rule,' but one of 'revive, unite, and, to the extent feasible, let them rule themselves'" (p. 38). Heper further argues that "'indigenization,' or providing uncalled for benefits to an ethnic group, in this case the Kurds" (p. 52) was amicably employed.

Although Heper mentions Sharaf Khan's *Sharafnama* as "an important piece of Kurdish history, penned in 1597" (p. 54) he fails to add that this work regards a number of historical Kurdish dynasties as exercising the status of royalty or in effect statehood. Instead Heper argues that these Kurdish emirates "could not have developed into what may be called proper independent states" (p. 45), and dismisses their *mirs* or rulers as mere "chieftains" (p. 38). In an attempt to illustrate the Ottomans' benevolent attitude toward rebellious Kurds, Heper writes about how "Kor Ahmed Pasha of Revanduz...surrendered on conditions of honourable treatment...[and how] the Ottoman government kept its word and sent him and his family and tribesmen to no other place than Istanbul" (pp. 51–52). Heper neglects to tell his readers, however, that during his return from Istanbul Kor Ahmed Pasha (also known as Miri Kor or the blind *mir* because of an eye affliction) simply disappeared, probably treacherously executed on the orders of the Sultan. Heper also fails to mention Ahmad-i Khani's *Mem u Zin*, a seventeenth-century work universally considered to be the Kurdish national epic because its introductory parts contain an obvious reference to Kurdish nationalist beliefs.

Chapter 4 examines how the Ottomans reacted to rising nationalism during the nineteenth century and maintains that they did not "resort to ethnic management strategies" (p. 81). The following three chapters "investigate whether or not the Republican state drifted from the said Ottoman tradition vis-à-vis its Kurds in any significant extent" (p. 82). Employing rather difficult arguments, Heper denies that the notorious Turkish History Thesis, Sun-Language Theory, and Turanism represented "different incarnations of the presumed ethnic nationalist policies pursued by the state in the early Republican Period" (p. 99), but instead argues that "not surprisingly, in the constitutions, which the Republic adopted in later decades, there was also a studious avoidance of references to nationalism in an ethnic sense" (p. 93). He also cites numerous conciliatory statements concerning the Kurds made by Kemal Ataturk, Celal Bayar, Suleyman Demirel, Ismet and Erdal Inonu, Turgut Ozal, and others. Only at the end does he admit "that the policies formulated by politicians on [the] Kurdish problem were not always approved by the military" (p. 138), that "in some instances those measures bordered on and, at times, turned out to be outright human rights violations" (p. 140).

In his final chapter Heper examines what he euphemistically calls the "Times of Troubles" during "1925–1938 and 1984–1999" (p. 116)—that is the major Kurdish rebellions since the creation of the Turkish Republic—neglecting to add the renewal of the "Troubles" since 2005. He goes so far as to have even Devlet Bahceli, the leader of the extreme Turkish nationalist *Milliyetci Hareket Partisi* (MHP) or Nationalist Action Party supposedly showing "his balanced approach towards primary [Turkish] and secondary [Kurdish cultural] identities" (p. 130). Summing up the causes for Kurdish unrest, Heper points to "the religious impetus [in reaction to the secular state] and foreign complicity... [as well as] the Kurds' displeasure with the emerging centralized state system, [and] individual restlessness and discomfort due to hostile and harsh acts towards them by agents of government" (p. 154). He blames the radical left for the rise of the Kurdistan Workers Party (PKK), but incredulously concludes that this organization "itself has had even less support among the Kurds" (p. 115). Heper's arguments and Turkey's EU reforms notwithstanding, as recently as June 2007, the Turkish government demonstrated its continuing hostility toward the Kurds when it summarily dismissed Abdullah

Demirbas (the mayor of the Sur district in Diyarbakir) because he had provided municipal services to his largely Kurdish-speaking constituency in Kurdish as well as Turkish.[13]

The AK Party (AKP)

As previously noted, Recep Tayyip Erdogan's *Adalet ve Kalkinma Partisi* (AK Party or Justice and Development Party) with its roots in Islamic politics[14] first swept to victory in November 2002 on the promise of economic achievement, honest government, and pursuit of EU membership, which implied a solution to Turkey' longstanding Kurdish problem as well as further democratization of the state. As progressive Islamists, the AK Party was increasingly opposed by the reactionary Kemalist establishment including Turkey's influential military fearful of losing their long held privilege positions.[15] This situation eventually led to the crisis of 2007 over the election of the AK Party's Abdullah Gul as Turkey's new president. Although the AK Party seemingly triumphed in this struggle by winning an enormous electoral victory on July 22, 2007, and then electing Gul as president, the party was soon put on the defensive by a nearly successful attempt in the Constitutional Court to ban it as a threat to Turkey's secular order.[16] Having survived this threat to its very existence,[17] the AK Party seemingly lost its reformist zeal and became a party of the status quo that has forsaken reform and the Kurdish issue.[18] A detailed analysis of these developments will throw more light on the current situation.

Initial Hope. When it first rose to power, the AK Party had a unique opportunity to change Turkish politics by pursuing EU membership and a solution to the Kurdish problem, among numerous other initiatives.[19] Instead of being a traditional Islamic party seeking to install an Islamic political order, the AK Party seemed to be endeavoring to improve the political, social, cultural, and economic opportunities of Muslims by democratizing the state. Seeking EU membership became both a catalyst and a result of this democratization process. In harmonizing Turkish laws with the EU *acquis communautaire* (in effect the existing EU law), the AK Party implemented a series of important democratic reforms, including the reduction of military influence over politics, abolishment of the death penalty and the State Security Courts, and improvements in freedom of the press and speech, among numerous other initiatives such as economic improvements. These steps had the side effect of creating a Turkey more tolerant and supportive of its ethnic Kurdish population.[20] Indeed, as noted above, in August 2005, Erdogan journeyed to Diyarbakir, the largest city in Turkey's southeast and long considered the unofficial capital of the historic Kurdish provinces in Turkey, to declare that Turkey has a "Kurdish problem," had made "grave mistakes" in the past, and now needed "more democracy to solve the problem."[21] Never before had a Turkish leader so explicitly addressed the Kurdish problem and seemingly promised to try to solve it. As a result of these achievements, the EU decided that Turkey had met the required Copenhagen Criteria[22] for membership and initiated accession negotiations with Turkey on October 3, 2005. Indeed, the AK Party actually polled more votes in the southeast in the elections of July 2007 than the explicitly pro-Kurdish *Demokratik Toplum Partisi* (DTP) or Democratic Society Party.

Retrenchment. The EU accession process, however, has introduced divisive issues into Turkish domestic politics that have led to sharp debates between the AK Party and its secular Kemalist opposition, which includes the still politically powerful military. During the crisis over electing the AK Party's Gul president in 2007, for example, the military famously posted on its web site the so-called e-memorandum (*e-muhtira*) warning against the threat posed by some groups aiming to destroy Turkey's secular system under the cover of religion, read the AK Party.[23] As recently as 1997, the military had forced Necemettin Erbakan's Islamist Refah Party (RP) to resign.[24] In 2004, the military apparently considered yet another coup.[25]

During the fall of 2008, the continuing Ergenekon trial of ultranationalists and retired military officers charged with planning violent campaigns to destabilize the AK Party government continued.[26] Indeed, the massive indictment of 2,455 pages described an incredible plot connecting some 86 military, mafia, ultra-nationalists, lawyers, and academic figures supposedly attempting to weaken the country's administration and justify an illegal intervention against the AK Party government. Erdogan himself was said to be on the alleged hit list. Critics, however, accused the AK Party of simply taking revenge on its Kemalist opponents with all these charges.[27]

Unfortunately, therefore, the AK Party has not succeeded in countering the hostile political atmosphere. "The dilemma the JDP [AK Party] faces is that it can only reform the system by solving the deeply rooted political tensions emanating from the undemocratic management of identity claims in Turkey without upsetting the status quo. This dilemma necessitates consensus-building between the JDP, the Republican People's Party (CHP or RPP) and the secularist establishment, which is not happening."[28] The Kemalist establishment still considers demands for changes to its strict interpretation of secularism as a security threat. Although at first the cultural and identity dimensions of the Kurdish issue could be debated, for example, by 2008 the AK Party had been forced to shift back to a mere economic and security agenda a la the Ecevit days before 2003.

Following its tremendous electoral victory in July 2007, the AK Party apparently committed an error by trying to amend Turkey's secular constitution to allow the headscarf to be worn in universities. Not only did this attempt place Kurdish reforms on the back burner, but it also presented the Kemalist establishment the ammunition it needed to attack the AK Party as an Islamic threat to secularism. Soon, the AK Party was battling for its very life against the attempt by the Constitutional Court to ban it. Although Erdogan's party managed to survive this attempt at a "judicial coup" by one lone vote in July 2008, the AK Party seemingly emerged from the ordeal significantly chastised. Many believe that it was at that point that Erdogan struck an informal compromise with the military to drop his reformist agenda in return for being allowed to remain in power. According to Yavuz Baydar, a columnist for *Today's Zaman*, the result was "a new, sort of confused, aimless AKP."[29] Thus, accession talks with the EU began to drift, while preexisting Kemalist constitutionalism trumped parliamentary sovereignty. Plans for writing a new constitution were shelved. On top of this, the AK Party itself began to show problems with being publicly criticized and increasingly resorted to the language of democracy only in selective ways. At the same time, the military managed to recoup its political influence despite the EU harmonization laws that sought to limit it. New strategies such as press briefings on political developments in the country as well as activities intended to further popular support were employed.

The AK Party's retrenchment on the Kurdish issue was amply illustrated when Erdogan journeyed to the southeast in the fall of

2008 to campaign for the local elections scheduled to be held in March 2009. As noted above, the AK Party had already shocked observers by slightly outpolling the pro-Kurdish DTP in the southeast during the July 2007 elections. At that time the AK Party's stress on improving economic conditions for the locals had seemingly resonated more with them than with the DTP's Kurdish nationalist stance. Thus, when Erdogan arrived in the fall of 2008, the pro-Kurdish DTP reacted strongly against the attempt to seize what its mayor in Diyarbakir Osman Baydemir called its "castle," by orchestrating the closure of shops, stone throwing, and running street battles. Erdogan responded with a call to his Kurdish opponents "to love it [Turkey] or leave it."[30] Nothing more strikingly could contrast the newly security-oriented prime minister of 2008 with the one who had called for more democracy to solve the Kurdish problem in 2005. "These are not the words of a reformer," declared Yasemin Congar, the deputy editor in chief of *Taraf*, a liberal newspaper.[31] Hasan Cemal, a columnist for the daily newspaper *Milliyet*, added: "Erdogan changed the whole discourse. This is the kind of disillusionment we have been having." Cemal also confessed that he was now having doubts about "whether Erdogan is still sincere about Turkey's membership accession to E.U."

At the same time, another significant event of the AK Party's new Turkish nationalist, security-oriented position occurred with the resignation of Dengir Mir Mehmet Firat as the deputy chairman of the party. Firat had been known for being a relative of a former Kurdish rebel and, to be more specific, for his progressive opinions on the Kurdish issue, EU membership, and writing a new constitution. He had recently ruffled Kemalist feathers by joining some DTP leaders for lunch in Istanbul. Thus, his resignation announced on November 7, 2008, not only seemed forced, but also in protest against his party's new hardened attitude toward the Kurds. He was replaced by former Interior Minister Abdulkadir Aksu who, although of Kurdish origins, has always had positive relations with the state security forces.[32] The annual EU Progress Reports on Turkey and U.S. State Department Country Reports on Human Rights practices in Turkey offer detailed analyses of the altered situation.

EU Progress Reports on Turkey

The European Commission (EC)—the EU's executive organ— released its annual Progress Report on Turkey on November 5, 2008.[33] The Report did not criticize Turkey's ruling AK Party as harshly as it might have probably due to its near death experience with the Constitutional Court during the year in review. Nevertheless, the Report made it clear that the EU was not satisfied with the lack of reforms on issues ranging from human rights and the protection of minorities, democracy and the rule of law, corruption, and the role of the military, among others. Little was new in all this, except for the first time the EU Report referred specifically to *the Kurdish issue* on several occasions. For example, in its section on "civil and political rights," the Report observed how "Articles... of the Turkish Criminal Code, that ciminalise offences against public order, and the Anti-Terror law have been applied to prosecute and convict those expressing non-violent opinions on *Kurdish issues... and Kurdish-related issues*" (p. 16, italics added.) This, declared the Report, "is not in line with the ECtHR [European Court of Human Rights] case law on freedom of expression and implies in particular a lack of differentiation between violent and non-violent opinions" (ibid.).

The Report also cited "the case against 53 DTP mayors for sending a letter to the Danish Prime Minister requesting that [the pro-Kurdish] Roj TV not be closed" and mentioned that the case "was finalized in April 2008. The [Turkish] Court sentenced the defendants to 2 months and 15 days imprisonment, which was commuted to a fine" (ibid.). The Report also stated that "overall, Turkey has made no progress on ensuring cultural diversity and promoting respect for and protection of minorities in accordance with European standards" (p. 26). The Report did note that amendments to the relevant law had supposedly allowed broadcasts "nationally all day long in languages other than Turkish," while "a new local radio channel, Mus FM, has received authorization to broadcast in Kurdish" (ibid.). (This positive development climaxed on January 1, 2009, with the start up of TRT-6, a 24/7 Turkish television channel broadcasting in Kurdish.)

The Report also took issue with Turkey's continuing approach to the rights of minority ethnic groups, which—with the exception of such non-Muslim groups as Greeks, Armenians, and Jews who are protected as minority groups by the Treaty of Lausanne (1923)—grants rights only to individuals, not groups. "This should not prevent Turkey, in accordance with European standards, from granting specific rights to certain Turkish citizens on the grounds of their ethnic origin, religion or language, so that they can preserve their identity" (p. 25) concluded the Report. Although "Turkey is a party to the UN International Covenant on Civil and Political Rights, . . . its reservation regarding the rights of minorities and its reservation concerning the UN Covenant on Economic, Social and Cultural Rights . . . regarding the right to education are causes for concern" (ibid.). Finally, the Report also noted that "Turkey has not signed the Council of Europe Framework

Convention for the Protection of National Minorities or the European Charter for Regional or Minority Languages" (ibid.).

The Report also listed a number of other points specifically concerning the Kurds: (1) "The Kurdish *Newroz* Spring celebrations in March 2008 resulted in violence against demonstrators in several provinces" (p. 17); (2) "No steps have been taken to abolish the system of village guards" (p. 28) long seen by many as an instrument of official state repression; (3) "The 'temporary security zones' established in June 2007 in the provinces of Sirnak, Siirt and Hakkari close to the Iraqi border remain operational" (p. 27). These "temporary security zones" were suggestive of the former emergency rule provinces that had been seen as another arm of state repression but had been finally abolished in 2002. In all fairness to Turkey, however, the Report explained that "terrorist attacks by the PKK, which is on the EU list of terrorist organizations, [not only] continued in the South-East, but also throughout the country and claimed many lives" (ibid.). In addition, "landmines remain a security concern for both military personnel and civilians. The government reported ongoing use of anti-personnel mines by the PKK/KONGRAGEL" (ibid.).

The continuing attempt to ban the DTP for allegedly "engaging in activities against the unity and integrity of the country" (p. 6) also merited concern: The Report noted that the Chief Public Prosecutor had applied to the Constitutional Court requesting "that 221 former and present members of the party be banned from being member[s] of a political party for five years" (ibid.). This would preclude these DTP members from simply joining a new pro-Kurdish party as previously had occurred when the earlier one had been banned. The Report concluded that "the closure cases against the AKP and the DTP...illustrate that the current legal provisions applicable to political parties do not provide political actors with an adequate level of protection from the state's interference in their freedom of association and freedom of expression" (p. 18). This statement was to prove prophetic when on December 11, 2009, the Turkish Constitutional Court finally did ban the DTP, a move that many saw as the kiss of death to the Kurdish (Democratic) Initiative Opening that had so auspiciously started earlier that summer (see below).

Regarding the new constitution for Turkey "aligning Turkey with international standards on fundamental rights" (p. 6) and promised by the AK Party following its great electoral triumph in July 2007, "no draft has been presented either to the public or to parliament, and no clear timetable has been set for discussing it" (ibid.). Rather, the government spent its energies on trying to constitutionally lift "the headscarf ban for university students" (ibid.). Furthermore, "the armed forces have continued to exercise significant political influence via formal and informal mechanisms. Senior members of the armed forces have expressed their opinion on domestic and foreign policy issues going beyond their remit, including...the South East" (p. 9). The Report also added that "no progress has been made on strengthening parliamentary oversight of the military budget and expenditure" (ibid.).[34] In addition, the Semdinli case was transferred to a military court and the accused released "pending trial" (p. 10). The Semdinli case involved a bombing in November 2005 that killed one person and injured others in this southeastern town. This bombing was apparently carried out with covert military approval to provoke the Kurdish nationalists and had been covered up.[35]

On a more positive note, the Report mentioned that the Turkish government had announced an economic plan of development for the Southeast in May 2008. This proposal would fund 14 billion euros to complete the Southeast Anatolia Project (GAP). "The four pillars of the action plan are: economic development, social development, infrastructure development and institutional strengthening. Most investments will concentrate on the energy and agriculture sectors" (p. 27). Unfortunately, as of 2011, little evidence of such an economic plan for the Southeast was evident, a continuation of a pattern of unfulfilled promises

In conclusion, although "the government expressed its commitment to the EU accession process and to political reforms, ... despite its strong political mandate, the government did not put forward a consistent and comprehensive programme of political reforms" (p. 7). "Further efforts are needed in order to create the conditions for the predominantly Kurdish population to enjoy full rights and freedoms" (p. 28). A motion on behalf of the EU Parliament's Committee on Foreign Affairs regarding the Report called "on the Turkish government to launch as a matter of priority a political initiative favouring a lasting settlement of the Kurdish issue, which initiative needs to address the economic and social opportunities of citizens of Kurdish origin."[36] The Kurdish Human Rights Project (KHRP) in London, a major watchdog for Kurdish rights, concurred, arguing that the EU Progress Report "underlines the failure of the Turkish authorities to press ahead with earlier human rights reforms."[37] The KHRP added that it was also "disappointing" that the Report had not addressed "the human rights impact of Turkish cross-border military operations in northern Iraq, and the impact of hydro-electric projects in south-eastern Turkey on local populations."

Others were not so diplomatic. A report in *Today's Zaman*, a newspaper usually sympathetic to the AK Party, concluded that "the European Union is simmering with anger and discontent about…Erdogan's performance since his last election victory in July 2007.…Erdogan is about to lose his once-immense respect among EU officials."[38] According to this report, "many diplomats and other high-level bureaucrats in Brussels…think Erdogan is leaning towards 'old-style Ankara politics,' where all the energy is focused on winning elections and smearing rival politicians, but not reforming the country." More specifically, "EU officials think that Erdogan pushed all the wrong buttons in the wake of his enormous election victory by shelving the proposed constitutional reform and focusing on the specific issue of the headscarf ban at universities, committing a massive strategic mistake." One high-level EU source concluded that "Erdogan has no strategy at all with what to do with the EU. The perception we have is that he has shelved all EU-related reform and, more seriously, many think that he could not care less about Turkey-EU relations." As for the Kurdish issue specifically, "Erdogan's latest remarks calling on 'those who do not want to live in Turkey to leave' have created waves of shock in the diplomatic center of Europe." On the other hand, Erdogan's supporters claimed that his government's inertia had more to do with the upcoming municipal elections scheduled to be held in March 2009. "Once the elections are over, you'll see the old AK,"[39] declared Abdurrahman Kurt, an AK Party MP from Diyarbakir. This speculation was to prove accurate. First, however, it will be useful to review what the U.S. State Department Country Report on Turkey had to say about the Kurdish issue.

U.S. State Department Country Report on Turkey

Although the United States and Turkey have had an alliance for more than half a century, in recent years it has been challenged by the Kurdish issue, among other factors.[40] Thus, the U.S. State Department Country Reports on Human Rights Practices—2007 offers another highly placed evaluation of Turkey's progress in those areas that most concern its Kurdish problem and a valuable confirmation of the EU Progress Report on Turkey.[41] The most recent Country Report, for example, found that "serious [human rights] problems remained in several areas," and cited "a rise in cases of torture, beating, and abuse by security forces... [who] committed unlawful killings" (p. 2). The Report also noted "the overly close relationship of judges and prosecutors [which] continued to hinder the right to a fair trial" (ibid.). Finally, "the government limited freedom of expression through the use of constitutional restrictions and numerous laws, including articles of the penal code prohibiting insults to the government, the state, 'Turkishness,' or the institution and symbols of the republic" (ibid.). On the other hand, a respected Turkish newspaper revealed how a recent decision by the High Court of Appeals in effect incited ultra-Turkish nationalists to kill pro-Kurdish DTP members and concluded: "In this country, you cannot say 'Happy Bayram' in Kurdish. But you can say 'cleanse the Kurdish microbes' in Turkish."[42]

Regarding the Kurdish issue in particular, the Country Report noted how in November 2007, the Diyarbakir prosecutor "investigated 14 children, ages 12 to 17 for 'promulgating propaganda on behalf of an illegal organization [the PKK]' after they sang a Kurdish folk song also utilized as the anthem of Iraq's Kurdistan Regional Government at the San Francisco International Music Festival, held during the last week in October [2007]" (p. 12). Although "at year's end the prosecutor had not formally indicted the participants" (ibid.) the mere threat such an indictment represented obviously placed a chilling effect over Kurdish cultural rights and freedom of speech in Turkey.

The Country Report also mentioned how "throughout the year, law enforcement and the judiciary increased pressure on members of the pro-Kurdish DTP. The most common tactic used was investigation and prosecution of DTP leaders for speaking in the Kurdish language or making statements critical of the government" (ibid.). The Country Report noted how a court in Ankara "sentenced DTP co-chairs Ahmet Turk and Aysel Tugluk to 18 month's imprisonment for violating the Political Parties Law by printing and delivering Kurdish-language handouts on the occasion of World Women's Day in March 2006" (pp. 12–13). "On March 8, [2007] a Kars court ordered police to seize *Nevruz* (Kurdish New Year) invitations and posters from DTP's Kars office because they used the letter 'w,' which occurs in Kurdish but not Turkish" (p. 13). Less than two weeks later, "a Van heavy penal court sentenced Hakkari DTP Mayor Metin Tekce to 10 months in prison for 'making propaganda on behalf of a terror organization,' for his comment in March 2007...that the PKK was not a terrorist organization" (ibid.).

The Country Report also stressed how on June 14, 2007 a Council of State court, following a request from the Ministry of Interior, "decided to dissolve the Sur Municipality of Diyarbakir and dismiss its mayor, Abdullah Demirbas, after the municipality attempted to institute a program to offer multilingual services to its citizens, 72 percent of whom the municipality stated spoke Kurdish as a first language" (ibid.). On October 19, 2007, the Grand Chamber of the Council of State upheld this decision. In addition, "prosecutors opened 15 cases against Diyarbakir Mayor Osman Baydemir during the year, bringing the total number of cases against him to 24.... He faces a total of 280 years' imprisonment if convicted on all charges in the remaining 20 cases" (ibid.). The Country Report also noted how "the prosecution continued at year's end against DTP mayor of Batman Huseyin Kalkan for his remarks on the PKK and Kurdish sentiments in the *Los Angeles Times* in May 2006" (ibid.). Furthermore, "on February 14, 2007, an Ankara court sentenced 13 officials of the pro-Kurdish Hak-Par for speaking Kurdish at, and distributing Kurdish-language invitations to, the 2004 party convention" (ibid.). In addition, "there was no new information available regarding the appeal of the 2005 conviction of DEHAP [an earlier pro-Kurdish party since merged into the DTP] official Ahmet Dagtekin for illegal speech for using Kurdish language and symbolism during a 2004 campaign event" (ibid.).

Finally, it should be noted that in December 2008, Leyla Zana, one of the most prominent symbols of Turkish repression of Kurdish cultural rights, again was sentenced for her comments regarding the Kurdish situation in Turkey.[43] The Turkish court ruled that she had violated the penal code and the antiterror law in nine different speeches by stating that Abdullah Ocalan was one of three Kurdish leaders. Previously, of course, Zana, a former MP in the Turkish Parliament, had served a lengthy ten-year prison term for earlier remarks she had made about Kurdish rights. Her new prison term reminded one of what the French sighed about the Bourbons: "They learned nothing and they forgot nothing." Nevertheless, Zana continues nonviolently to demand recognition for the Kurdish language, Kurdish identity, and freedom of speech as well as political and cultural rights while her new prison sentence is on appeal.

The Kurdish Opening Begins

In December 2008, the Turkish Economic and Social Studies Foundation (TESEV) released an important report on how to solve Turkey's Kurdish problem peacefully.[44] The TESEV Report called for a new Turkish constitution that would be more inclusive of the state's various ethnicities and a declaration of unconditional general amnesty for members of the PKK, among other recommendations. Since the Report was based on the opinions of thirty-five individuals of various ideological and political backgrounds representing the Kurdish community as well as interviews with residents, local governors and administrators in Turkey's Kurdish region, it presumably reflected the wishes and demands of Turkey's ethnic Kurdish community and those government officials most closely attuned to the situation. The Report also found similar demands from distinct groups on such issues as language rights, the village guards, clearing of mines planted by the Turkish military, and positive discrimination. Dilek Kurban, TESEV's Democratization Program director, emphasized that the Kurdish problem was essentially a matter of human rights, not security as seen by the government. The state's policy of denial and assimilation of Kurdish identity was the main reason behind the Kurdish problem. Although the PKK had committed some violations of human rights, most violations were the result of state actions. She also declared that all parties should protect the right of the DTP to remain in politics. Economic reform that favored investments in the Kurdish region should go along with political reforms. Can Paker, TESEV's president, declared that unless Turkey solved its Kurdish problem, societal peace and Turkey's hopes to join the EU would be unattainable. This new TESEV Report quickly met with a more favorable audience than the earlier

much-maligned, but largely accurate TOBB Report[45] authored by
Dogu Ergil in 1995, and may, therefore, be seen as a harbinger to
Turkey's Kurdish Initiative (Opening) in 2009.

In May 2009, Turkish president Abdullah Gul declared that "the
biggest problem of Turkey is the Kurdish question" and that "there
is an opportunity [to solve it] and it should not be missed."[46] Then
in July 2009, Turkish prime minister Recep Tayyip Erdogan
announced a much publicized and promising Kurdish Initiative,
later broadened to be called the Democratic Opening and then
National Unity Project.[47] He followed up with an emotional call
for support, asking: "If Turkey had not spent its energy, budget,
peace and young people on [combating] terrorism, if Turkey had
not spent the last 25 years in conflict, where would we be today?"[48]
Besir Atalay, the interior minister, met with the opposition political parties, unions, and business associations in an effort to drum
up support. Even General Ilker Basbug, the chief of staff, declared
that the Kurdish problem was a test of Turkey's modernization,
while the *Milli Guvenlik Kurulu* (MGK) or National Security
Council gave its cautious approval for Kurdish reforms.

The Kurdish Initiative also dovetailed logically with the new
Turkish foreign minister Ahmet Davutoglu's policy of zero problems with neighbors and emphasis on Turkey's soft democratic and
economic power, instead of the conventional siege mentality view
that Turkey was surrounded by enemies against whom it should be
prepared to defend itself. Thus, by August 2009, the AK Party government had begun a Kurdish Initiative with the announced inten-
tion of helping to solve the Kurdish problem. For a brief period,
optimism ran rampant.

Problems. It soon became evident, however, that the AK Party
had not thought out its Kurdish Initiative very well and then

proved rather inept in trying to implement it. For example, although there was much speculation about changes to laws regarding human rights violations, permitting the use of formerly Kurdish titles for districts, eliminating legal barriers for speaking Kurdish during prison visits and establishing Kurdish language and literature departments at various universities, specific proposals were lacking. In addition, although it may have been well intended, Abdullah Ocalan's attempt to submit a 160-page "roadmap to peace" probably backfired by associating the Kurdish Initiative with being soft on the PKK. Despite AK Party appeals to support its Kurdish Initiative, all three of the parliamentary opposition parties declined. Indeed, the CHP (Kemalists) accused the AK Party of "separatism, cowing to the goals of the terrorist PKK, violating the Constitution, causing fratricide and/or ethnic polarization between Kurds and Turks, being an agent of foreign states, and even betraying the country,"[49] while the MHP (Turkish Nationalists) "declared AKP to be dangerous and accused it of treason and weakness."[50] Even the pro-Kurdish DTP failed to be engaged because it declined to condemn the PKK as the AK Party government had demanded.[51]

Given this lack of a responsible and engaged opposition, the election on May 22, 2010, of Kemal Kilicdaroglu as the new leader of the CHP offered some hope that he could revitalize the hidebound party and make it into a viable opposition to the AKP. Kilicdaroglu is known for his opposition to corruption in government and is an Alevi of Kurdish or Dimili (Zaza) origin and Armenian ancestry born in the southeastern province of Tunceli (Dersim) in 1948. All of this might indicate that he would understand and even be sympathetic to the necessity of Kurdish reforms. So far, however, he has given little indication that he understands the ethnic dimension of the Kurdish problem; instead he considered it a mere extension of economic difficulties.

The PKK's "peace group" gambit on October 18, 2009, to return home to Turkey, twenty-six people from its Mahmur Refugee Camp in Northern Iraq and another eight from its military headquarters in the Kandil Mountains of Northern Iraq also backfired badly when these Kurdish expatriates were met by huge welcoming receptions at the Habur Border Crossing with Turkey and later in Diyarbakir. These celebrations were broadcast throughout Turkey and proved too provocative for even moderate Turks who perceived the affair as some sort of PKK victory parade. The Peace Group affair seemed to prove that the government had not thought out the implications of its Kurdish Initiative and could not manage its implementation, let along consequences.

Then on December 11, 2009, the Constitutional Court, after mulling over the issue for more than two years, suddenly banned the DTP because of its close association with the PKK. Although the *Baris ve Demokrasi Partisi* (BDP) or Peace and Democracy Party quickly took the DTP's place, coming when it did, the state-ordered banning of the pro-Kurdish DTP could have not come at a worse time and put the kiss of death to the Kurdish Initiative. In short, more than 1,000 BDP and other Kurdish notables were placed under arrest for their supposed support of the PKK, yet another body blow to the Kurdish Initiative.[52] Soon the entire country was ablaze from the fury that had arisen, and the Kurdish Opening seemed closed. The mountain had not even given birth to a mouse, and the entire Kurdish question seemed to have been set back to square one.[53]

In May 2010, the Kurdistan National Congress (KNK), an arm of the PKK, charged that since April 2009, more than 1500 politicians, human rights advocates, writers, artisans, and leaders of civil society organizations had been arrested. In addition, 4000 children had been taken to court and 400 of them imprisoned for participating in demonstrations. Osman Baydemir, the popular ethnic Kurdish mayor of Diyarbakir, was scheduled to go to court on charges of "membership in a terror organization," while Muharrem Erbey, the vice chairman of Turkey's largest human rights organization the Human Rights Association (IHD), had already been imprisoned. Jake Hess, an American freelance journalist, had been deported for reporting critically on human rights abuses against the Kurds.[54] Although the PKK had declared a cease-fire as of March 2009, sporadic fighting continued. Umit Firat, a Kurdish intellectual, concluded that "the PKK is being led by hawks at the moment," while Turkish Prime Minister Erdogan's language also turned hawkish as he threatened to "drown the insurgents in their own blood."[55] On May 31, 2010, from his prison cell on Imrali Island in the Bosporus, Ocalan announced that the cease-fire was over and he had stepped aside from attempting dialogue with the government.

Renewed Hope

Although the Kurdish Initiative had clearly failed, new developments soon made it possible to argue that since reaching a solution to the Kurdish problem is a process, not a discrete occurrence, a second Kurdish or Democratic Initiative could be built on the experiences of the first one. Early in 2011, a perceptive report noted how "many Turks are ready to make at least some concessions to the Kurds.... Behind the scenes, it [the AK Party] has been reaching out to Kurdish activists to find common ground on which to build a viable solution."[56] Once again TESEV stepped forward with new recommendations.[57] (1) The references to Turkish identity and Turkishness in many laws and the Turkish constitution do not comply with the multiethnic structure of Turkish society. These constitutional references should be changed despite the dictum in Article 4 of the current constitution that they "cannot be changed; changing them cannot even be suggested." (2) Laws regarding political parties and the ways deputies are elected need to be altered as they are "incompatible with the principles of democracy and the state of law." (3) Article 301 of the Turkish Penal law on "insulting Turkishness" and Article 318 regarding criticism of the military prevent freedom of speech in Turkey and need to be deleted. (4) The Anti-Terror Law (TMY) protects the security of the state at the expense of freedom and security of individuals. This too should be corrected. (5) The education law needs to be changed because it presently reflects "the ideological and monist education understanding of the state." (6) The law on provincial governance has been the basis of changing the Kurdish names of many locations. In addition, the laws on surnames and the alphabet prevent Kurds from using their language freely.

The AK Party government, of course, supposedly had been considering writing a new constitution for Turkey along similar lines for many years. The success of its referendum on several constitutional amendments held on September 12, 2010, reinvigorated this process.[58] Since the far-right nationalist MHP had strongly opposed the constitutional referendum, the AKP victory might now relieve the AKP from nationalist pressures and encourage it to take bold new initiatives on the Kurdish question. In addition, given the AKP referendum victory, it now seemed all the more likely that it would win the national elections scheduled for June 2011 and remain in power until 2015. If this did indeed occur, the AKP would then be in a position to lead the process of writing a new, more democratic constitution. It might also be poised to strike some type of meaningful deal with Turkey's ethnic Kurds that would include a Parliamentary Truth Commission to investigate not only the state's past mistakes but also those of the PKK. Such a process might help understand the past and resolve future problems as has already occurred in South Africa. The current 10 percent electoral threshold that makes it so difficult for pro-Kurdish political parties to win any seats in the Turkish parliament should also be lowered in line with current EU standards. In addition, the government should accept mother-tongue education and usage in courts, and drop its prosecution of the 151 Kurdish politicians, lawyers, and civil society leaders (the so-called KCK trials) that were continuing into 2011. Finally, the government should consider ending its military operations to match the PKK's cease-fire as a military process was not going to solve the continuing Kurdish political problem. Unfortunately, many but not all Kurdish voters had complied with orders from the BDP to boycott the successful constitutional amendment referendum of September 12, 2010, on the grounds that it failed to address its demands for greater political and cultural autonomy for the Kurds. On the other hand, Ocalan had recommended that Kurdish voters support the referendum. Obviously, the Kurds themselves were divided on how to proceed.

The constitutional referendum aside, the main problem now, of course, was with whom to talk. Although even Turkish observers recognized that "Ocalan and the PKK have legitimacy among a considerable portion of the Kurds despite all the state's efforts to discredit them,"[59] it was not possible for the state formally and

openly to negotiate with them given how the state had always defined them as mere terrorists. However, this problem could be finessed and indeed by the fall of 2010 it apparently was. These talks
with Ocalan appeared to cover such important issues as a cessation
of military operations, the release of KCK detainees, an initiative
for a new constitution, and a review of the 10 percent electoral
threshold that made it so difficult for regional pro-Kurdish parties
to win seats in the Turkish parliament.[60] Although it was not clear
exactly what elements of the Turkish government were involved in
these secretive contacts, they were enough to lead the PKK to extend its cease-fire until June 2011 when the next national elections
were scheduled. Therefore, it would be useful to conclude this
chapter with the proposals submitted by the PKK and what is in
effect its legal voice, the BDP.

Ocalan's Proposals. Although Ocalan's 160-page roadmap for
solving the Kurdish problem was confiscated by the Turkish authorities in August 2009 and, therefore, never even submitted, its
contents are basically known based on his earlier testimony at his
trial for treason in 1999[61] and subsequent statements over the years.[62]
In essence, the imprisoned PKK leader has proposed a democratization and decentralization of the Turkish state into what he has
termed at various times a democratic republic, democratic confederalism, democratic nation, or democratic homeland. State citizenship would be decoupled from Turkish ethno-nationalism into a
nonethnic civic nationalism in which all ethnic groups in Turkey
would participate on an equal nonethnic basis. Kurds also would
gain some form of autonomy through local self-government. Cemil
Bayik, a longtime associate of Ocalan, has described Ocalan's proposals as "a model that aims to mobilize the Kurdish people to make
their own decisions and have their own governing institutions...to

organize Kurdish people in the political, social, cultural, economic and security areas and solve their own problems through their free will."[63]

The BDP, which is in effect the legal political arm of the PKK, elaborated on Ocalan's autonomy proposals with its own call for democratic autonomy.[64] This would include the establishment of regional parliaments with real political and economic power as well as their own flags and symbols. Such autonomy would be based on the guidelines already listed in the European Charter of Local Self-Government adopted in 1985 and presently ratified by forty-one states including—with numerous important conditions, however—Turkey, and the European Charter of Regional Self-Government, which is still only in draft form. Thus, one might actually argue that these BDP proposals would be bringing Turkey into conformity with EU guidelines by giving the Kurds local self-government.

However, the AK Party was appalled when the Kurdish Democratic Society Congress (DTK)—a new formation that is close to the PKK and BDP—met in Diyarbakir in mid-December 2010 and outlined its solution for democratic autonomy that envisaged Kurdish as a second official language, a separate flag, and a Marxist-style organizational model for Kurdish society. The DTK's draft also broached the vague idea of "self-defense forces" that would be used not only against external forces but also against the subjects of the so-called democratic autonomy initiative who were not participating in what was called the "struggle."[65]

Although the AK Party has already granted some small concessions for local administrations in an administrative and financial sense, the Turkish Republic created by Ataturk in 1923 has always been a strongly centralized state. Radical decentralization as proposed by the BDP and Ocalan goes against this strong mindset and would be most problematic. "The charters the BDP's demands are based on have been developed in line with Europe's socio-economic circumstances. Turkey has its own circumstances,"[66] declared Saffet Ozdemir of the Turkish Association of Local Authorities. On the other hand, many states such as Britain and France, famous for their centralized unitary structure, have recently rolled back centuries of constitutional forms in favor of what they saw as necessary decentralization. Far from leading to their breakup as states, this decentralization has satisfied local particularisms and checked possible demands for future independence. Thus, far from threatening national unity, decentralization might help preserve it.

Indeed, the ruling AK Party made several unsuccessful attempts to pass a comprehensive law concerning decentralization when it first came to power in 2002, but has since settled for piecemeal laws that have gradually devolved some authority to municipalities and local administrations. Given its new position of strength alluded to above, the AK Party government may now be in a position to move toward bolder models of state decentralization if it wins a new electoral mandate in the national elections scheduled for June 2011. When he addressed the Turkish parliament in September 2010, for example, Turkish president Abdullah Gul declared that a new constitution has to be prepared that is "plural, democratic and civil" while meeting the needs and demands of every segment of society.[67] Specifically addressing the Kurdish issue, the Turkish president added that "our past problems are here today because we did not solve them in time. More democracy and more pluralism is a method to solve political issues...We have to separate the [Kurdish] issue from terror [in order to reach] a solution." In apparent response, the PKK extended its no-action period that had begun on August 13, 2010, noting that the state's dialogue with Ocalan "revealed a valuable chance for a solution."[68] Demonstrating his continuing efforts to reach out to Turkey's Kurds, Gul made his third trip as president to Turkey's Kurdish region in January 2011. Despite such suggestions for reform Turkey still seems far from the radical changes that would seem necessary to satisfy many of its ethnic Kurds. Nevertheless, the AK Party has come a long way along the road of reform. Given how more than half of Turkey's ethnic Kurdish population does not even live in its historic southeastern Anatolian homeland but is scattered throughout the country especially in such cities as Istanbul as well as the fact that a sizeable number of Turkey's ethnic Kurds have mostly assimilated into a larger Turkish civic identity; radical decentralization that would be incompatible with modern Turkey's heritage may not be necessary. What is needed, however, is for the state to begin seriously talking with the most important, genuine representatives of its disaffected Kurdish minority. This, of course, means the PKK.

To the extent that direct open negotiations are not possible at the present time, this problem, as mentioned above, could be finessed, in part, by also talking to the BDP, the legal pro-Kurdish voice of the PKK, as Britain did in the 1990s when it negotiated successfully with Sinn Fein, the legal arm of the illegal IRA terrorists. As Ihsan Dagi, a prescient Turkish scholar and friend of the AK party has noted: "There could be deals with the PKK and Ocalan, but any deal can only be sold to the Turks via the agency of the BDP. If BDP leaders really want a solution they should take their responsibility in mediating a settlement."[69]

However, now that the Turkish government has begun apparently negotiating with Ocalan, the time must surely come for

Turkey to cease terming the PKK a terrorist organization. This terrorism appellation not only prevents the two main parties to the problem from fully negotiating with each other, but also impedes the European Union from playing a stronger role in achieving peace and in the case of the United States from permitting its citizens even to advise the PKK to opt for peace as illustrated by the case of retired U.S. administrative judge Ralph Fertig. This prominent U.S. citizen has run afoul of his country's new laws on terrorism because he advised the PKK to disarm and use peaceful means to achieve its political goals. In June 2010, however, the U.S. Supreme Court ruled by a vote of 6–3 that national security trumped Fertig's first amendment rights of free speech and made him liable under provisions of the USA Patriot Act for giving illegal "material support" to terrorists.[70] Unless the PKK is removed from the U.S. terrorism list, it is only a matter of time before other legitimate academic scholars will also find themselves in legal problems. This unfortunate situation would cease once Turkey no longer brands the PKK as terrorist and begins negotiating with it, since then both the United States and the European Union would probably drop the PKK from their terrorist lists. Therefore, as a logical step towards a final fair solution to the Kurdish problem in Turkey, that state should remove the PKK from its terrorist list and challenge it to live up to its claims for wanting peace. Even if this should occur, however, the road remains long and difficult. Nevertheless, so much has already been covered that the continuing process seems irresistible.

NOTES

1 Historical Overview

1. Possibly the two best studies of the Kurds in English remain Bruinessen, *Agha, Shaikh and State*; and McDowall, *A Modern History of the Kurds*. More recently, see Romano, *The Kurdish Nationalist Movement*; and Natali, *The Kurds and the State*. Portions of this chapter originally appeared in other articles and chapters I have published including "The Kurdish Problem in International Politics," in Joseph, *Turkey and the European Union*, pp. 96–121.

2. For further discussions of the size of the Kurdish population, see McDowall, *Modern History of the Kurds*, pp. 3–5; Bruinessen, *Agha, Shaikh and State*, pp. 14–15; and Izady, *The Kurds*, pp. 111–20. For a detailed analysis that lists considerably smaller figures for Turkey, see Mutlu, "Ethnic Kurds in Turkey," pp. 517–41.

3. For a solid study of the Sheikh Said revolt, see Olson, *The Emergence of Kurdish Nationalism*.

4. For a recent detailed analysis of the Kurdish problem in Turkey, see Ozcan, *Turkey's Kurds*.

5. "The Sun also Rises in the South East," pp. 1–2.

6. For a meticulous analysis of the many problems involved, see Yildiz, *The Kurds in Turkey*, as well as my analysis in chapter 5 of this book.

7. "Ozkok: Biggest Crisis of Trust with US" *Turkish Daily News*, July 7, 2003; and Nicholas Kralev, "U.S. Warns Turkey against Operations in Northern Iraq." *Washington Times*, July 8, 2003.

8. For recent detailed analysis of the Kurdish problem in Iraq, see Stansfield, *Iraqi Kurdistan*.

9. For Henry Kissinger's exact words, see "The CIA Report the President Doesn't Want You to Read," *The Village Voice*, February 16, 1976, pp. 70–92. This article contains the U.S. Congress House of Representatives Pike Committee Report, which investigated the CIA in the mid-1970s. The part dealing with the Kurds is entitled "Case 2: Arms Support," and appears on pp. 85 and 87–88. Many years latter, Kissinger explained his position more thoroughly in *Years of Renewal*, pp. 576–96.

10. Galbraith, "What Went Wrong," in O'Leary et al., *The Future of Kurdistan in Iraq*, p. 242. In other words, given that Iraq has proved to be a failed state, its inhabitants simply reject further identification with it, identifying instead with their ethnic and/ or sectarian groups. In addition to the series of articles in the O'Leary collection cited here, see Ahmed and Gunter, *The Kurdish Question and the 2003 Iraqi War*, for background analysis of the results of the 2003 War in Kurdistan in Iraq.

11. For a copy of the TAL, see <http://www.cpa-iraq.org/ government/TAL.html>.

12. Article 61 (c) of the TAL—the so-called "Kurdish veto"— declared that "the general referendum will be successful and the draft constitution ratified if a majority of the voters in Iraq approve and if two-thirds of the voters in three or more governorates do not reject it." Since Iraqi Kurdistan consists of three governorates, this provision gave the Kurds an effective veto over the final constitution. Iraq's Sunni Arabs also came close to using it successfully to block approval of the permanent constitution in the referendum held on October 15, 2005.

13. Cited in Daniel Williams, "Iraqi Kurdish Leader Demands Guarantees: Minority Seeks Autonomous Region, Expulsion of Arabs under New Government," *Washington Post*, January 18, 2004.

14. Cited in "Turkey's Growing Uneasiness over Iraqi Kurds' Federalist Aspirations," *Briefing* (Ankara), January 19, 2004.

15. What Barzani and Talabani probably really meant was that to declare independence now would be premature.

16. For details see Richard Boudreaux, "Iraq Charter Ratified by Big Margin in Final Tally," *Los Angeles Times*, October 26, 2005.

2 The Iraqi Kurds' Federalism Imperative

1. An anonymous young Kurdish minister in Irbil speaking on April 6, 2004, cited in Karna Eklund, Brendan O'Leary, and Paul R. Williams, "Negotiating a Federation in Iraq," in O'Leary et al., *The Future of Kurdistan in Iraq*, p. 138. For further background, see Natali, *The Kurds and the State*. I previously published portions of this chapter as "The Iraqi Kurds' Federalism Imperative," *Journal of South Asian and Middle Eastern Studies* 29 (Winter 2006), pp. 1–10.

2. For background, see Elazar, *Exploring Federalism*; King, *Federalism and Federation*; Riker, *Federalism: Origin, Operation, Significance*; and Watts, *Comparing Federal Systems*. The work of Brendan O'Leary on federalism is particularly important for the current situation in Iraq. See his "Power-Sharing, Pluralist Federation, and Federacy," in O'Leary et al., *Future of Kurdistan in Iraq*, pp. 47–91.

3. Kanan Makiya, "A Model for Post-Saddam Iraq," October 3, 2002, accessed on the Internet at <http://www.benadorassociates. com/article/140>; and Dawisha and Dawisha, "How to Build a Democratic Iraq," pp. 36–50.

4. Horowitz, *Ethnic Groups in Conflict*, pp. 563–652.

5. Donald L. Horowitz, "Constitutional Design: An Oxymoron," in Shapiro and Macedo, *Designing Democratic Institutions*, p. 259.

6. Brancati, "Is Federalism a Panacea for Post-Saddam Iraq?" pp. 7–21.

7. Wimmer, "Democracy and Ethno-Religious Conflict in Iraq," pp. 111–34.

8. Yavuz, "*Provincial* not *Ethnic* Federalism in Iraq," pp. 126–31.

9. The Shiites, of course, are far from being totally united.

10. For details, see Gunter, "Kurdish Future in a Post-Saddam Iraq," pp. 9–23.

11. In the following section on Quebec and the Canadian federal system, I owe a great debt to the lucid arguments made by John McGarry, "Canadian Lessons for Iraq," in O'Leary et al., *Future of Kurdistan in Iraq*, pp. 92–115.

12. Although as recently as 1995, the Quebec separatists came within a single percentage point of winning a referendum on sovereignty, a

special type of self-government for the province has not led to the break-up of Canada and the separatists are now in retreat. Indeed, the federal government in Ottawa finally passed a law that would require Quebec's approval before any constitutional change could be enacted in Canada. Since this Quebec veto could be rescinded by a mere majority vote, however, it still does not completely satisfy Quebec's demand for recognition as a "distinct society" as the failed Meech Lake Accord in 1990 would have granted. The Kurds certainly would want their own Meech Lake Accord in the Iraqi Constitution that would grant them a veto over any future constitutional amendment they would consider fundamental to their existence.

13. For background to the concept of consociational politics, see the writings of Lijphart: *The Politics of Accommodation*; "Consociational Democracy," pp. 207–25; and *Democracy in Plural Societies*.

14. For background, see Noel, *Patrons, Clients, Brokers*.

15. Recently, however, significant deposits of oil and natural gas have been verified in the Sunni area in a line that runs from Ninewa province in the north through Anbar province west of Baghdad and near the Syrian border all the way to the frontier with Saudi Arabia in the south. This development has the potential to change the Sunni disillusionment about their future in a decentralized Iraq. It would take years, however, before these new deposits could be tapped. See Glanz, "Iraqi Sunni Lands Show New Oil and Gas Promise."

16. See, for example, Galbraith, *The End of Iraq*; and Cockburn, "Kurdistan: Birth of a Nation?"

17. See, for example, U.N. General Assembly Resolutions 2672 C (XXV), in *UN Chronicle*, 1971, no. 1, 46; 3236 (XXIX), in *UN Chronicle*, 1974, no. 11, 36–74; and 33/23, in *UN Chronicle*, 1978, nos. 11, 80.

18. See, for example, U.N. General Assembly Resolutions 2396 (XXIII), in *UN Chronicle*, 1969, no. 1, 94; and 31/61, in *UN Chronicle*, 1976, no. 1, 79.

19. For an analysis of Ozal's initiatives, see Gunter, *The Kurds and the Future of Turkey*, pp. 61–79.

20. Stansfield, *Iraqi Kurdistan*, p. 6. Also see Gareth R.V. Stansfield, "Governing Kurdistan: The Strengths of Division," in O'Leary et al., *Future of Kurdistan in Iraq*, pp. 195–218.

3   The Changing Dynamics in the Kurdistan Regional Government of Iraq

1. Two useful recent studies of the Kurds are Natali, *The Kurds and the State*; and Romano, *The Kurdish Nationalist Movement*. I published portions of this following chapter earlier as "The Changing Dynamics in the Kurdistan Regional Government (KRG) of Iraq," *Journal of South Asian and Middle Eastern Studies* 30 (Fall 2006), pp. 1–14.
2. For an interesting and revealing profile of Jalal Talabani, see Jon Lee Anderson, "Mr. Big," *The New Yorker*, February 5, 2007, pp. 46–57.
3. For a list, see "Ministers of the New Unified Cabinet," <KRG. org>, May 7, 2006.
4. For further analysis, see chapter 2, in this book.
5. The following data and citations are taken from "Iraq: Oil and Gas Rights of Regions and Governorates," <KurdishMedia>, June 14, 2006. With an estimated 1.5 million inhabitants, Irbil is the largest city in the KRG.
6. Vvienne Walt, "A New Oil Plan for Iraq," <www.time.com>, January 12, 2007; and Glanz, "Draft Law Keeps Central Control over Oil in Iraq."
7. See <www.Kurdishmedia.com>, May 2, 2006.
8. See the *Turkish Daily News*, January 23, 2006.
9. The following data and citation are taken from "Kurds Approve Foreigner-Friendly Investment Law."
10. The following information is largely based on "Foreign Investors See Northern Iraq as Gateway to Rest of Country." For further background to business opportunities in Iraqi Kurdistan, see Kurdistan Development Corporation (KDC), *Iraqi Kurdistan Business & Investment, 2004*; and Gunter, "Kurdistan's Revival," pp. 32–34. The KDC website is <www.kurdistancorporation. com>.

11. Cited in Fayad, "Interview with Kurdistan Region President Masoud Barzani."
12. Cited in Goudsouzian, "Prime Minister: Kurdistan Open for Business," as cited in <KurdishMedia.org>, June 17, 2006.
13. Cited in "Kurds Declare Right to Have Their Own Armed Forces."
14. "Visiting Iraqi Prime Minister Pledges to Strengthen Regional-Federal Relations," KRG, July 12, 2006.
15. "Al Maliki: We Will Respect the Result of Referendum on Kirkuk," <KurdishMedia.com>, July 13, 2006.
16. Directorate of Population, Ministry of Interior, *Iraq's General Statistical Census for 1957*.
17. On these points, see Gunter, *The Kurds of Iraq*, pp. 17 and 28.
18. Talabany, *Mantikat Kirkuk Wa Muhawalat Taghyeer Wakiiha Al-Kawmy*, p. 81.
19. "Talabani Accuses Al-Ja'fari of Assaulting the Kurds' Rights," *Al-Hayat*, July 11, 2005.
20. "Military Issues Dire Warning on Iraq," *Briefing* (Ankara), November 8, 2004, p. 11.
21. Baker and Hamilton, *The Iraqi Study Group Report*.
22. Mohammed A. Salih and Jamal Ekhtiar, "Kurds Warn White House Not To Adopt Baker-Hamilton Report," *The Kurdish Globe*, December 12, 2006.
23. For a report, see Worth, "Memorial Gathering in Iraqi Kurdistan Turns to Violence."
24. These citations were garnered from "AFP Account of the Halabja Events," AFP, March 17, 2006.
25. "Senior Kurdish Official Proposes Mass Resignations," IWPR, April 26, 2006.
26. Cited in "Barzani: Kurds Are Entitled to a State but in Due Time."
27. This information and citation were gathered from Ari Anwar, "The Voice of the People, *Soma* (Irbil), August 25–September 7, 2006, p. 5.
28. Amnesty International, "Prosecutions Threaten Freedom of Expression in Kurdistan-Northern Iraq," March 29, 2006.
29. Butters, "Trouble in Kurdistan."

30. Cited in "Barzani: Kurds Are Entitled."
31. Cited in Fazil Najib, "Black Market Thrives as Fuel Crisis Continues," *The Kurdish Globe* (Irbil), September 5, 2006, p. 4.
32. Cited in Awat Abdullah, "Kurdish Economy on Downward Spiral," *Soma*, August 25–September 7, 2006, p. 15.
33. Natali, *The Kurdish Quasi-State.*
34. The following information and citation were taken from Brandon, "Pro-US Kurds Eye Nascent Islamic Parties."
35. Louis Meixler, "Turkey Prepared to Start 2nd Iraq War with Kurds," Associated Press, July 19, 2006.
36. Cevik, "Burning the Qandil at Both Ends," p. 4.
37. Cited in "Nechirvan Barzani: Iraq Will Not Be Used as a Base for Attacking Neighbouring States," *The Globe*, July 22, 2006.
38. Mizgin Yilmaz, "Lockheed Martin, Joseph Ralston and the PKK," <KurdishMedia.com>, October 4, 2006.
39. Stansfield, "Governing Kurdistan: The Strengths of Division," in O'Leary et al., *The Future of Kurdistan in Iraq*, pp. 195–218.
40. These figures, however, are somewhat fluid, and slight changes in minority representation have occurred.
41. For further analysis, see Fatah, "Unification of Administrations."
42. Stansfield, "Can Iraq's Kurds Transcend Persistent Factionalism?"
43. Galbraith, *The End of Iraq.*

4 After Ocalan's Capture

1. For background, see Barkey and Fuller, *Turkey's Kurdish Question*; Gunter, *The Kurds and the Future of Turkey*; Kirisci and Winrow, *The Kurdish Question and Turkey*; White, *Primitive Rebels or Revolutionary Modernizers?*; and Ozcan, *Turkey's Kurds.* Also see Imset, The PKK; and Imset, "The PKK: Terrorists or Freedom Fighters?" pp. 45–100. I published an earlier version of this chapter as "The Continuing Kurdish Problem in Turkey after Ocalan's Capture," *Third World Quarterly* 21 (October 2000), pp. 849–69.
2. For details, see the statement by Dylan Semsi Kilic—a close associate of Ocalan's and an eyewitness to his capture—broadcast

over the PKK's MED-TV and accessed over the Internet, February 21, 1999; Weiner, "U.S. Helped Turkey Find and Capture Kurd Rebel"; Gee, "The Odyssey of a Kurdish Hot Potato"; Helena Smith, Chris Morris, and Ed Vulliamy, "Global Plot that Lured Kurds' Hero into Trap," *Observer* (London), February 21, 1999; and Berkan, "The Story of Apo's Capture." Turkish prime minister Bulent Ecevit declined to elaborate on any of the details, and merely cited a Turkish proverb: "Let us eat the grape and not ask where it came from."

3. "Osman Ocalan's Statement about the Arrest," February 18, 1999, accessed over the Internet.

4. "MED TV Reports More on PKK Statement on Congress Results," London MED TV Television in Turkish, 1900 GMT, March 4, 1999, as cited in *Foreign Broadcast Information Service—Near East/South Asia.* Hereafter cited as *FBIS-WEU.*

5. "PKK Members on Mountains Pitted against Those in Europe," *Hurriyet* (Istanbul), March 14, 1999, as cited in *FBIS-WEU-1999-0314*, March 14, 1999.

6. "Experts: Execution Possible in PKK Member's Disappearance," Ankara Anatolia in Turkish, 0826 GMT, March 18, 1999, as cited in *FBIS-WEU-1999-0318*, March 18, 1999. Yet another report claimed that Cemil Bayik had been named the "highest authority in the organization." "Ocalan Removed, Bayik Tasked," *Hurriyet*, March 3, 1999, p. 14, as cited in *FBIS-WEU-1999-0303*, March 3, 1999.

7. "Presidency Council Replaces Apo," *Milliyet* (Istanbul), February 27, 1999, as cited in *FBIS-WEU-1999-0228*, February 27, 1999.

8. *FBIS-WEU-1999-0318.* See note 6 above for the full citation. In February 2006, Yilmaz was assassinated in Sulaymaniya northern Iraq by a car bombing apparently as a result of intra-PKK animosities.

9. "Turks vs. Kurds: Turning Point?" *New York Times*, February 21, 1999, p. 8.

10. "Statement from PKK Leader Abdullah Ocalan," released via his lawyers, March 18, 1999, accessed over the Internet.

11. "Sezer: 'Thought Crimes' Have No Place in a Democracy," *Briefing* (Ankara), May 3, 1999, pp. 10–12. For further comments on these problems in Turkey, see "Human Rights in the Republic of Turkey: Testimony of the Honorable Harold Hongju Koh Assistant Secretary for Democracy, Human Rights and Labor Before the Commission on Security and Cooperation in Europe" (mimeographed), March 18, 1999.

12. "They Called It another Earthquake," *Briefing*, September 13, 1999, pp. 9–12.

13. Turgut, "Kurd Rebels See Turkish Change of Tack," Reuters, September 7, 1999, accessed over the Internet.

14. Michael M. Gunter, "Interview: Abdullah Ocalan, Head of the PKK," *Middle East Quarterly*, 5 (June 1988): 79–85. In this interview, Ocalan broached in embryonic form many of the ideas he more fully developed during his trial in June 1999 and analyzed below.

15. Kinnane, The Kurds and Kurdistan, pp. 32–33; and Besikci, Kurdistan & Turkish Colonialism, p. 34.

16. For background, see Lewis, *The Emergence of Modern Turkey*; and Shaw and Shaw, *History of the Ottoman Empire and Modern Turkey*, Vol. II: *Reform, Revolution, and Republic*.

17. This and the following citation were taken from Kamran Qurrah Daghi, "Ocalan Explains Peace Overtures," *Al-Hayah*, March 17, 1993, pp. 1, 4, as cited in *FBIS-WEU*, March 22, 1993, p. 42.

18. Gunter, "Susurluk: The Connection between Turkey's Intelligence Community and Organized Crime," pp. 119–41.

19. Ocalan, Declaration on the Democratic Solution of the Kurdish Question, p. 85.

20. Stephen Kinzer, "Turkish Premier Hints at New Approach if Rebel Kurds End Violence," *New York Times*, February 22, 1999, accessed over the Internet.

21. Kurdistan Information Centre (London), "Press Statement issued by the PKK Presidential Council on 2 June 1999 on the Trial of Kurdish National Leader Abdullah Ocalan."

22. PKK Executive [Presidential] Council, "Statement to the Press and General Public, 29 June 1999," accessed over the Internet.

23. "PKK Presidential Council Statement," July 6, 1999, accessed over the Internet.

24. "Interview with PKK Commander Duran Kalkan," Kurdish Media, July 19, 1999, accessed over the Internet.

25. This and the following citations were taken from Birand, "Turkish Public Opinion Is Softening toward the Kurds."

26. "Ocalan Urges Kurd Rebel Peace as Clashes Rage," Reuters, August 4, 1999, accessed over the Internet. September 1 is observed as World Peace Day in many places around the world.

27. Elif Unal, "Turk PM Says 'Time Will Tell' on Ocalan Call," Reuters, August 4, 1999, accessed over the Internet.

28. "PKK: Defeat and Retreat or Master Stroke?" *Briefing*, August 9, 1999, p. 11.

29. The following citations were taken from "Opening Statement of Harold Hongju Koh," Press conference at U.S. Embassy, Ankara, Turkey, August 5, 1999, accessed over the Internet.

30. "PKK: Defeat and Retreat or Master Stroke?" p. 12.

31. For background on the trials and tribulations of some legal Kurdish parties in Turkey, see Nicole F. Watts, "Allies and Enemies: Pro-Kurdish Parties in Turkish Politics, 1990–94," *International Journal of Middle East Studies* 31 (November 1999): 631–56.

32. The following citations were taken from Ilnur Cevik, "Military Not Mellowing on Kurdish Rights," *Turkish Daily News*, September 10, 1999, accessed over the Internet.

33. Pelin Turgut, "Kurd Rebels See Turkish Change of Tack," Reuters, September 7, 1999, accessed over the Internet.

34. This and the following citation were taken from "Kurdish Rebels Hail Turkish General's Words as Goodwill Gesture," Agence France-Presse, September 6, 1999.

35. This and the following citation were taken from "Top General's Remarks Misinterpreted, General Staff Says," Agence France-Presse, September 11, 1999, accessed over the Internet.

36. "PKK Rejects Turkish Call for Surrender, Rules Out Further Concessions," Agence France-Presse, September 29, 1999, accessed over the Internet.

37. PKK Presidential Council, "Press Release," September 26, 1999, accessed over the Internet.

38. "Rights-Turkey: Media Is Latest Venue for Talks on the Kurds," Inter-Press Service, September 13, 1999, accessed over the Internet.

39. "Army Launches Cross Border Operation and Rejects PKK Peace Call," *Turkey Update*, October 1, 1999, accessed over the Internet.

40. The following citations were taken from the "Letter from the PKK Central Committee to the President of the Republic of Turkey, Suleyman Demirel on 1 October 1999," accessed over the Internet. The letter was dated "20 September 1999."

41. The following citations were taken from PKK Presidential Council, "Letter to the OSCE and the International Public," November 15, 1999, accessed over the Internet.

42. Abdullah Ocalan, "Letter to the Presidency of the OSCE," November 18, 1999, accessed over the Internet.

43. "No Plans to Execute Ocalan, but Still Trying to Come Out on Top in the Situation," *Briefing*, December 6, 1999, p. 8.

44. This and the following citation were taken from "11 December 1999 PKK Presidential Council Statement," accessed over the Internet.

45. This and the following citations were taken from "Yilmaz: Road to EU Passes through Diyarbakir," *Turkish Daily News*, December 17, 1999, accessed over the Internet. Diyarbakir is the largest city in Turkey's southeast and has long been considered the unofficial capital of the Kurdish provinces in Turkey.

46. "The Road to the EU," *Briefing*, December 20, 1999, p. 11.

47. This and the following citation were taken from "Interview with PKK's Murat Karayilan," *Kurdish Observer/Ozgur Politika*, January 11, 2000, accessed over the Internet.

48. Ertugrul Ozkok, "Let Us Try Not Hanging," *Hurriyet*, January 11, 2000, accessed over the Internet.

49. Amberin Zaman, "Turks Find It in Nation's Interest to Befriend Foe," *Los Angeles Times*, January 14, 2000, accessed over the Internet.

50. This and the following citations were taken from Ismet Berkan, "Peace Would Be Threatened," *Radikal*, January 11, 2000, accessed over the Internet.

51. Stephen Kinzer, "Turkey Delays the Execution of Rebel Kurd," *New York Times*, January 13, 2000, accessed over the Internet.

52. "Kurdish Rebel Leader Ocalan at the Mercy of the PKK," Agence France-Presse, January 13, 2000, accessed over the Internet.

53. This and the following citations were taken from "Abdullah Ocalan's Public Statement: Press Release 16 January 2000," accessed over the Internet.

54. This and the following citations were taken from "PKK Central Committee Pledges Support," January 14, 2000, accessed over the Internet.

55. Stephen Kinzer, "Government Refuses to Deal with Ocalan on Kurdish Issue," *New York Times*, January 18, 2000, accessed over the Internet.

56. Cited in Steve Bryant, "Turkey's Demirel Hails Ocalan Decision," Reuters, January 13, 2000, accessed over the Internet.

57. This and the following citations were taken from "Do Not Create Chaos," *Kurdish Observer/Ozgur Politika*, January 11, 2000, accessed over the Internet.

58. "Brief Statement on PKK 'Peace Project,'" released by the Kurdish Information Centre (London), April 4, 2000, accessed over the Internet.

59. For a discussion of some of the following points, see Brandon, "The Evolution of the PKK."

60. For background, see Ocalan, Prison Writings.

61. Cited in "The Sun also Rises in the South East."

62. "Cannot Advance with Rigid Nationalism, Says Coup Leader," *Turkish Daily News*, March 5, 2007.

5   Turkey's EU Promise

1. For background analyses on Turkey, see Ahmad, *The Making of Modern Turkey*; Lewis, *The Emergence of Modern Turkey*; and Zurcher, *Turkey: A Modern History*. I earlier published portions of the following chapter as "Turkey's Floundering EU Candidacy

and Its Kurdish Problem," *Middle East Policy* 14 (Spring 2007), pp. 117–23.

2. For background analyses of the Kurdish problem in Turkey, see Barkey and Fuller, *Turkey's Kurdish Question*; Gunter, *The Kurds and the Future of Turkey*; Kirisci and Winrow, *The Kurdish Question and Turkey*; and White, *Primitive Rebels or Revolutionary Modernizers?*. Also see McDowall, *A Modern History of the Kurds*, pp. 395–444.

3. For background analyses of Turkey's EU candidacy, see Arikan, *Turkey and the EU*; Lake, *The EU & Turkey*; and Laciner et al., *European Union with Turkey*. Also see John K. Cooley, "Turkey Belongs in the European Union," *Christian Science Monitor*, October 2, 2006.

4. Mango, *Ataturk*, pp. 219, 479, 527, and 538.

5. This term was coined by Huntington, "The Clash of Civilizations?" pp. 22–49. Also see his further elaboration, *The Clash of Civilizations and the Remaking of World Order*.

6. Yildiz, *The Kurds in Turkey*. Also see the background papers for the second and third international conferences sponsored by the EU Turkey Civic Commission (EUTCC) on "The EU, Turkey, and the Kurds," European Parliament, Brussels, September 19–20, 2005, by Hans Branscheidt, "Turkish Accession to the European Union: Human Rights and the Kurds"; and by Kerim Yildiz et al., "Third International Conference on EU, Turkey and the Kurds," European Parliament, Brussels, October 16–17, 2006.

7. Yildiz, *Kurds in Turkey*, p. 20.

8. Ibid.

9. "Kurdish Reality Recognized," Ankara Anatolia in English, 1505 GMT, December 8, 1991, as cited in *Foreign Broadcast Information Service—West Europe*, December 9, 1991, p. 55.

10. Barkey and Fuller, *Turkey's Kurdish Question*, p. 137.

11. "Yilmaz: Road to EU Passes through Diyarbakir."

12. "The Sun also Rises in the South East."

13. Eliot [Odysseus], *Turkey in Europe*, p. 130.

14. The following discussion is largely based on "Heading for a Crisis in Turkish-EU Ties?" pp. 7–14.

15. In 2004, the Turkish Cypriots had supported a UN plan to end the long-standing Cyprus dispute, but the Greek Cypriots had refused. Nevertheless, the EU had gone ahead by rewarding the Greek Cypriots with EU membership, while the Turkish Cypriots remained economically isolated and ostracized. Turkey argued that the situation had resulted in a biased and hypocritically unfair situation.

16. Commission of the European Community, *Commission Staff Working Document: Turkey 2006 Progress Report* (Com (2006) 649 final), November 11, 2006.

17. Simon Hooper, "Turkey Caught at a Crossroads," CNN, October 25, 2006.

18. "Turks' Optimism for EU Defies Current Troubles," *Turkish Daily News*, December 19, 2006.

19. "New Anti-Terror Law: End of the Timid Democratisation," *Info Turk*, No. 333, May 2006, citing *New Anatolian* and other media, April 19, 2006 <http://www.info-turk.be/index.html#Activists>.

20. *Ibid.*

21. O. Korket, "Anti-Terror Schemes May Encourage Torture," *BIA News Center*, April 26, 2006, as cited in *Info Turk*, No. 333, May 2006 <http://www.info-turk.be/index.html#Activists>.

22. On the first major Kurdish rebellion in the Republic of Turkey, see Olson, *The Emergence of Kurdish Nationalism and the Sheikh Said Rebellion, 1880–1925.*

23. "Prosperity Party Leader Interviewed," Ankara Show Television in Turkish, 2030 GMT, January 31, 1994, as cited in *Foreign Broadcast Information Service—West Europe*, February 3, 1994, p. 41.

24. The following citations and discussion are largely based on "EU, Buyukanit Clash on Ethnic Identity."

25. See Gunter, "Abdullah Ocalan," p. 81. In his writings published since his capture, Ocalan has continued to argue similarly, much to the chagrin of most of his followers and surprise of his enemies, who are probably too narrow-minded to appreciate the possibilities in such a position.

26. The following citations were taken from "Opening Statement of Harold Hongju Koh," Press conference at U.S. Embassy, Ankara, Turkey, August 5, 1999, accessed over the Internet.

27. Fraser, "Turkey Thanks United States for Helping Ankara Open EU Entry Talks."
28. Cited in Steven A. Cook and Elizabeth D. Sherwood-Randall, "Generating Momentum for a New Era in U.S.–Turkey Relations," report issued by The Council on Foreign Relations, June 22, 2006.
29. "Turkey: US Ambassador Discusses EU Support, Investment Complaints," *IPR Strategic Business Information Database*, October 27, 2004.
30. "EU/Turkey: US Openly Calls for Turkey's Accession," p. 509.
31. Taylor, "Turkey Thanks United States for Helping Ankara Open EU Entry Talks."
32. "EU/Turkey: US Openly Call for Turkey's Accession."
33. "Turkey: Politics: US Warned to Stay Out of Turkey's EU Entry Talks," *Economist Intelligence Unit: Country Views Wire*, April 22, 2003.
34. For an analysis of this doubly ironic situation, see Michael M. Gunter, "Kurdish Prospects in Post-Saddam Iraq," in Ahmed and Gunter, *The Kurdish Question and the 2003 Iraqi War*, pp. 71–96.
35. On the historic racial situation in the United States, see C. Vann Woodward, *The Strange Career of Jim Crow* (New York: Oxford University Press, 1957).
36. Mark Kesselman, "France," in Kesselman, Krieger, et al., *European Politics in Transition*, p. 246.
37. Christopher S. Allen, "Germany," in Kesselman, Krieger, et al., *European Politics in Transition,*, p. 323.

6 Taming Turkey's Deep State

1. On the development of the modern Republic of Turkey, see Lewis, *The Emergence of Modern Turkey*; Ahmad, *The Making of Modern Turkey*; and Zurcher, *Turkey: A Modern History*. I earlier published portions of the following chapter as "Deep State: The Arcane Parallel State in Turkey," *Orient* 47, 3 (2006): 334–48.
2. "Government and Opposition United Over the Semdinli Affair," p. 2.

3. For background, see Muller et al., *International Conference on Turkey, the Kurds and the EU*.

4. The Copenhagen Criteria require that EU candidates should have achieved "the stability of institutions guaranteeing democracy, the rule of law, human rights and respect for and protection of minorities."

5. For an analysis of conspiracy theories in the Middle East, see Pipes, *The Hidden Hand*.

6. On Agca's attempt to assassinate the pope and the supposed Soviet hand behind it, see Sterling, *The Time of the Assassins*; and Henze, *The Plot to Assassinate the Pope*. For a conflicting opinion, see Herman and Brodhead, *The Rise and Fall of the Bulgarian Connection*. Stephen E. Tabachnick has written an insightful critique of all three of these books in "Dedefining Reality," *American Book Review*, January/February 1987, pp. 9–10. Some even see the hand of the U.S. Central Intelligence Agency (CIA) working surreptitiously to blacken the Soviet image.

7. Cited in "The Man Who Shot [the] Pope and Other Men Who Shot Other Men," *Briefing*, January 23, 2006, p. 4.

8. For background on the Kurdish problem in Turkey and the PKK, see Ozcan, *Turkey's Kurds*; White, *Primitive Rebels or Revolutionary Modernizers?*; Barkey and Fuller, *Turkey's Kurdish Question*; Gunter, *The Kurds and the Future of Turkey*; and Kirisci and Winrow, *The Kurdish Question and Turkey*.

9. Gunter, "We Are Fighting Turks Everywhere," pp. 79–85. Some have even argued that the PKK itself is part of the Deep State. See, for example, from among numerous sources, "Dark Forces Hidden behind the State?" p. 9. Although it is likely that the Turkish state and PKK have had to bargain indirectly over the years, given the bitterness of their conflict and the strict way Ocalan has been imprisoned since his capture in February 1999, the present author finds suggestions of Deep State–PKK cooperation misleading and even ludicrous.

10. Jones, "Bombing Throws Spotlight on Turkey."

11. Cited in "Government Adopts Military Thinking Despite Spattering of Appeals for Common Sense," *Briefing* (Turkey), November 15, 1993, p. 6.

12. The following discussion and citations are taken from "Turkey's National Security Policy under Debate," pp. 9–11.

13. Although JITEM was supposedly established in the mid-1970s to implement covert operations against terrorist organizations, the Turkish government still officially denies its existence. A court in Diyarbakir, Turkey, however, recently mentioned JITEM in relationship to 10 ex-PKK informers, and thus seemingly confirmed its existence. Former Gendarmerie commander, General Teoman Koman, however, claimed that certain people simply use JITEM as a cover for their illegal activities. "Judiciary Say 'JITEM' Aloud for the First Time."

14. See Martin van Bruinessen, "Turkey's Death Squads," *Middle East Report* no. 199 (April–June 1996), p. 22.

15. See the interview with Avni Ozgurel, *Radikal* (Turkey), October 27, 2003.

16. For background, see Ismet G. Imset, "News Analysis: Who Really Controls the Kurdish Hezbollah?" *Turkish Daily News*, September 7, 1993; and Ismet G. Imset, "Is There a 'Nationalist' Connection to the Killings?" *Turkish Daily News*, September 8, 1993.

17. The following discussion is largely based on Komisar, "CIA Legacy Lives On." pp. 24–27; an editorial published in the Turkish daily *Milliyet* (Turkey), November 8, 1996; and "Government and Opposition United over the Semdinli Affair," p. 3.

18. Cited in Komisar, "CIA Legacy Lives On."

19. Cited in *ibid*.

20. "Semdinli: The Burning Flame of Suspicion," p. 11.

21. For background, see Gunter, "Political Instability in Turkey during the 1970s," pp. 63–77.

22. On the supposed Soviet hand behind the attempt to assassinate the pope, see Henze, *Plot to Kill the Pope*; and Sterling, *Time of the Assassins*, cited above in note 6.

23. For a well-reasoned analysis that paramilitary organizations affiliated with extreme right-wing groups in Turkey actually made the attempt on the pope, see Bale, "The Ultranationalist Right in Turkey and the Attempted Assassination of Pope John Paul II," pp. 1–63.

24. Ismet G. Imset, "Terrorist Acts in Southeast Detailed," *Turkish Daily News*, May 27, 1992.

25. In addition to the two Imset articles cited in note 16 above, see Bruinessen, "Turkey's Death Squads," pp. 20–23.

26. Cited in "The Southeast on a Hidden Agenda," *Briefing*, November 25, 1996, p. 8.

27. Stephen Kinzer, "Turkey Accused of Arming Terrorist Group," *New York Times*, February 15, 2000; and Yahya Kocoglu, "Hizbullah: The Susurluk of the Southeast," *Turkish Daily News*, January 27, 2000.

28. For a fuller analysis of Susurluk, see Gunter, "The Connection between Turkey's Intelligence Community and Organized Crime," pp. 119–41. The following, much briefer discussion is largely based on this earlier source.

29. Cited in "Susurluk: A Year of Fading Dreams," *Briefing*, October 27, 1997, p. 5.

30. Cited in "Demirel: Probe Links but Go Easy on State," *Turkish Daily News*, November 8, 1996.

31. Cited in Kelly Couturier, "Turkish Scandal Exposes Links between Crime, State Officials," *Washington Post*, January 1, 1997, p. A21.

32. Cited in Stephen Kinzer, "Turkish Car Crash Yields Debris of Death and Terror," *New York Times*, December 10, 1996, p. A1. In April 1997, Turkes died of a stroke at the age of eighty.

33. The following data are largely based on "Susurluk Back on the Street," *Briefing*, April 7, 1997, pp. 1, 3; M. Akif Beki, "Whose Report Is This?" *Turkish Daily News*, April 4, 1997; and Stephen Kinzer, "Turkish Panel Links Killings to Authorities," *New York Times*, April 8, 1997.

34. The following data were largely taken from "Susurluk Report Set to Protect Not Reveal," *Briefing*, January 19, 1998, pp. 7–8; Kemal Bal, "Gangs Almost Got Hold of State," *Turkish Daily News*, January 24, 1998; and Stephen Kinzer, "Former Turkish Governments Linked to Assassinations," *New York Times*, January 26, 1998.

35. However, a recent report indicated that "Yesil" might still be alive, and that his son, Murat Yildirim, had been apprehended.

"Bearded," "Terminator," and "Mehmet Kirmizi" were other names "Yesil" supposedly used. "Police Say 'Yesil' Still Alive," *New Anatolian*, February 19, 2006.

36. Heydar Aliyev, a former member of the politburo of the Communist Party of the Soviet Union, was reputedly targeted by Catli and his associates because he opposed a drug smuggling route through Baku to the West. The coup against Aliyev was foiled only when Turkish president Suleyman Demirel tipped him off. Hugh Pope, "Turkish Probe Links Old Government to Death Squads," *Wall Street Journal*, January 26, 1998.

37. Cited in "Susurluk: Yilmaz Hopes Not Reflected," *Briefing*, October 20, 1997, p. 4.

38. For some of the following details, see Jon Gorvett, "Turkey's 'Deep State' Surfaces in Former President's Words, Deeds in Kurdish Town," *Washington Report on Middle East Affairs* (MRMEA), February 7, 2006.

39. Cited in "Semdinli Proves Tougher than Meets the Eye," *Briefing*, December 5, 2005, p. 11. Buyukanit had served as the chief commander in the region from 1997 to 2000.

40. "Government and Opposition United over the Semdinli Affair," p. 2.

41. "Semdinli Investigation Leads to Nowhere," *Briefing*, April 3, 2006, p. 10. Also see Pelin Turgut, "Senior General Stoked Kurdish Conflict To Keep Turkey Out of EU," *The Independent* (UK), March 8, 2006.

42. Cited in "Government Suffers Humiliating Defeat in Putting the Semdinli Probe on the Right Course," p. 2.

43. Cited in *Hurriyet* (Turkey), March 8, 2006.

44. The following data were taken from, Yildiz, "Semdinli Gang Protected by Top Officers," <zaman.com>, July 20, 2006.

45. "European Commission Hints at 'Semdinli Hierarchy,'" *Briefing*, June 26, 2006, p. 4.

46. "EU on Turkey's Case in Semdinli," *Briefing*, November 28, 2005, p. 8.

47. Cited in "Semdinli Investigation Leads to Nowhere."

48. Cited in "Semdinli Commission's Report on the Turkish 9/11 Aims to Shelve the Case for the Time Being," *Briefing*, April 17, 2006, p. 2.

49. Cited in Jones, "Bombing Throws Spotlight on Turkey's 'Deep State.'"
50. "My Name Is State, Deep State," *New Anatolian*, April 19, 2005.
51. Cited in "Former President Says There Are Two States in Turkey."
52. "Government and Opposition United over the Semdinli Affair," p. 2.
53. Mills, *The Power Elite*. Mills's classic study was first published in 1956.
54. For a fascinating analysis of these events, see Powers, *The Man Who Kept the Secrets*, pp. 149–80.
55. Cited in *ibid.*, p. 165.
56. For a detailed account of these events by its chief investigator in the U.S. government, see Walsh, *Firewall*.

7   The Other Kurds in Iran and Syria

1. For further background on the Kurds in Iran, see Yildiz and Taysi, *The Kurds in Iran*; Koohi-Kamali, *The Political Development of the Kurds in Iran*; Nader Entessar, "The Kurdish National Movement in Iran Since the Islamic Revolution of 1979," in Ahmed and Gunter, *The Evolution of Kurdish Nationalism*, pp. 260–75; and A.R. Ghassemlou, "Kurdistan in Iran," in Chaliand, *A People without a Country*, pp. 95–121. I originally published portions of this chapter in "The Kurdish Problem in International Politics," in Joseph, *Turkey and the European Union*, pp. 113–16.
2. In 2005, this motto was changed to "Kurdish national rights within the context of a democratic and federal Iran."
3. The following data were largely taken from Erlich, *The Iran Agenda*.
4. On the Mahabad Republic of Kurdistan, see Eagleton, Jr., *The Kurdish Republic of 1946*; Roosevelt, Jr., "The Kurdish Republic of Mahabad," pp. 247–69; and the special issue of *International Journal of Kurdish Studies* 11, nos. 1–2 (1997), entitled "The Republic of Kurdistan: Fifty Years Later."
5. For further analysis, see Nader Entessar, "The Impact of the Iraq War on the Future of the Kurds in Iran," in Ahmed and Gunter, *The Kurdish Question and the 2003 Iraqi War*, pp. 174–91.

6. These figures were taken from Bill Samii, "Iran: Country Faces Agitated Kurdish Population," Radio Free Europe/RL, July 23, 2005.

7. These data and the following were taken from "Iran Puts Pressure on Kurdish Cities in East Kurdistan," <KurdishMedia.com>, July 15, 2005.

8. Michael Howard, "Iran Sends in Troops to Crush Border Unrest." *Guardian*, August 5, 2005.

9. For further background on the Kurds in Syria, see Yildiz, *The Kurds in Syria*; Amnesty International, *Amnesty International Report: Kurds in the Syrian Arab Republic One Year after the March 2004 Events*, 2005; Ismet Cheriff Vanly, "The Oppression of the Kurdish People in Syria," in Ahmed and Gunter, *Kurdish Exodus*, pp. 49–61; and Robert Lowe, "Kurdish Nationalism in Syria," in Ahmed and Gunter, *Evolution of Kurdish Nationalism*, pp. 287–308.

10. Some of the following information is based on Bashdar Ismaeel, "Kurdish Expectations Will Test Assad." *Daily Star* (Beirut), July 11, 2005.

11. Cited in "Politics & Policies: Pressure for Change Mounts in Syria." United Press International, October 3, 2005.

8   The KRG's Delicate Balance

1. Ned Parker, "In Iraq, Political Negotiation is a Blood Sport," *Los Angeles Times*, October 10, 2010. Http://www.latimes. com/news/nationalworld/world/la-fg-iraq-politics, accessed October 12, 2010. I originally published parts of this chapter as "Kurdish-Arab Tensions and Irbil-Baghdad Relations," *Journal of South Asian and Middle Eastern Studies* 33 (Spring 2010), pp. 40–47.

2. Leila Fadel, "Iraq's Kurds Set to Be Kingmakers Again," *Washington Post Foreign Service*, October 16, 2010. Http:/ www. washingtonpost.com/wp-dyn/content/article/2010/10/15, accessed October 18, 2010. On November 11, 2010 KRG

president Massoud Barzani's roundtable initiative in Baghdad played an important role in establishing the new al-Maliki government that was finally announced one month later.

3. See, for example, the report in October 2010 that the United States has proposed selling $4.2 billion worth of arms to Iraq to strengthen its military. The package includes eighteen Lockheed Martin F-16 strike jets, Raytheon AIM-9 Sidewinder air-to-air heat-seeking missiles, laser-guided bombs and reconnaissance equipment. The KRG would have nothing to match this. "U.S. Plans $4.2 billion Arms Sale to Iraq," *Space War: Your World at War*, October 1, 2010. Http://www.spacewar.com/reports/US _plans_42-billion_arms_sale_to_Iraq_999.html. Given this overall situation, KRG president Massoud Barzani asked the 13th Congress of his Kurdistan Democratic Party (KDP) that convened in December 2010 to analyze the Kurdish right to self-determination. "Kurdish Self-Determination Call Sparks Iraqi Ire," Agence France Press, December 13, 2010. Http://www.hurriyetdaily-news.com, accessed December 16, 2010.

4. For background, see Chapter 3.

5. For further background, see Ahmet Davutoglu, "Turkey's Foreign Policy Vision: An Assessment of 2007," *Insight Turkey* 10:1 (2008), pp. 77–96.

6. Alihan Hasanoglu, "Turkey Starts Preliminary Work for Arbil Consulate," *Today's Zaman*, February 17, 2010. Http://www. todayszaman.com/tz-web/detaylar.do?load=detay&link=201755, accessed February 20, 2010.

7. Veysel Ayhan, "An Analysis of Massoud Barzani's Visit to Turkey," *Today's Zaman*, July 6, 2010. Http://www.todaysza-man.com/tz-web/news-215263-an-analysis-...., accessed July 9, 2010.

8. For background, see Liam Anderson and Gareth Stansfield, *Crisis in Kirkuk: The Ethnopolitics of Conflict and Compromise* (Philadelphia: University of Pennsylvania Press, 2009); and Chapter 3 above.

9. Anthony Shadid, "Resurgent Turkey Flexes Its Muscles around Iraq," *New York Times*, January 4, 2011.

10. Anthony H. Cordesman and Charles Loi, Iraq; *The Realities of U.S. "Withdrawal of Combat Forces" and the Challenges of Strategic Partnership* (Washington, D. C.: The Center for Strategic and International Studies: 2010). Http://csis.org/publication/iraq-realities-us-withdrawal-combat-forces-and-challenges-strategic-partnership-O, accessed October 4, 2010.

11. Colin H. Kahl, "Breaking Dawn: Building a Long-Term Strategic Partnership with Iraq," *Foreign Policy*, August 31, 2010. Http://mideast.foreignpolicy.com/posts/2010/08/31/breaking_dawn, accessed September 4, 2010.

12. Kurdistan Regional Government (KRG), "Statement on President Barzani's Meeting with President Obama," January 25, 2010. Http://www.krg.org/articles/detail.asp?smap=02010100&lngnr=12&rnr=223&anr=33539.

13. There already were seventeen other states that had some sort of diplomatic representation to the KRG.

14. Kurdistan Regional Government, "Top KRG Officials Visit U.S.," *[KRG] U.S. Liaison Office Newsletter*, September 2010. www.knowkurdistan.com, accessed October 6, 2010.

15. Leila Fadel, "Clashes in Iraq's North Underscore Fierce Political Rivalry among Kurds," *Washington Post Foreign Service*, March 5, 2010. Http://www.washingtonpost.com/wp-dyn/content/article/2010/03/04/AR2010030405153, accessed March 12, 2010. I analyzed this situation in general earlier in *The Kurdish Predicament in Iraq; A Political Analysis* (New York: St. Martin's Press, 1999), pp. 67–109.

16. David Romano, "The Gorran Movement—A Change in the Iraqi Kurdish Political Landscape," Vol. 8, No. 13, *Terrorism Monitor* (Jamestown Foundation), April 2, 2010.

17. "Kurdistan's PM Rules Out Having Disputes with Massoud Barzani," *Kurd Net*, October 18, 2010. Http://www.ekurd.net

/mismas/articles/misc2010/10/state4294.htm, accessed October 22, 2010.

18. "US Displeased by Absence [of] Barham Salih," *Kurd Net*, February 14, 2010. Http://www.ekurd.net/mismas/articles/misc2010/2/independentstate3516.htm.

19. For background, see Michel Rubin "The Middle East's Real Bane: Corruption," *Daily Star* (Beirut), November 18, 2005. Http://www.michaelrubin.org/959/the-middle-easts-real-bane-corruption, accessed November 21, 2010; and Michael Rubin, "Dissident Watch: Kamal Sayid Qadir," *Middle East Quarterly* 13 (Spring 2006), pp. 95–96.

20. Rebwar Fatah, "The Quest for Civil Society in Kurdistan: Sardasht Osman's Enquiry," *Kurdishmedia.com*, October 18, 2010. www.kurdishmedia.com/article.aspx?id=16511, accessed October 21, 2010.

21. Kamal Chomani and Jake Hess, "Pro-Democracy Demonstrations in Northern Iraq/South Kurdistan," March 2, 2011. Http://www.mesop.de/2011/03/02/pro-democracy...., accessed March 3, 2011; Michael Rubin, "Saddam in Kurdistan," *Commentary Magazine*, February 23, 2011. Http://www.mesop.de/2011/02/25/saddam-in-kurdistan-michael-rubin/, accessed February 25, 2011; and Karzan Kardozi, "Sulaimaniya: Day Fifteen of Protest, A Brighter Day," Http://www.mesop.de/2011/03/03/sulaimaniya-a-day-fifteen-of-protest-a-brighter-day/, accessed March 3, 2011.

22. See, for example, Jonathan Spyer, "Kurds in the Middle: Caught between Iran and Turkey, with Nowhere To Hide," *WeeklyStandard.com*, October 25, 2010. Http://www.weeklystandard.com/print/articles/kurds-middle_508829.html, accessed October 29, 2010; and "Iraq: Turkish, Iranian Shelling Displaces Villagers in North," *IRIN* (A Project of the UN Office for the

Coordination of Humanitarian Affairs), July 5, 2010. Http://
www.irinnews.org/subscriberlogin.aspx, accessed July 9, 2010.

23. See endnote 8.

24. For background, see David Romano, "An Outline of Kurdish
Islamist Groups in Iraq." *Jamestown Occasional Papers Series*,
September 17, 2007. Http://www.jamestown.org/uploads
/media/Jamestown-RomanoIraqiKurds_01.pdf, accessed July
11, 2010. However, see also Michael Rubin, "The Islamist
Threat from Iraqi Kurdistan," *Middle East Intelligence Bulletin*,
December 2001. Http://www.michaelrubin.org/1208/the-
islamist-threat-from-iraqi-kurdistan, accessed July 11, 2010.

25. Dennis C. Blair (Director of National Intelligence), "Annual Threat
Assessment of the US Intelligence Community for the Senate Select
Committee on Intelligence," February 2, 2010, p. 23.

26. For background, see Brendan O'Leary, John McGarry, and
Khaled Salih, eds., *The Future of Kurdistan in Iraq* (Philadelphia:
University of Pennsylvania Press, 2005). For a more recent
analysis, see Denise Natali, *The Kurdish Quasi-State: Development
and Dependency in Post-Gulf War Iraq* (Syracuse, NY: Syracuse
University Press, 2010).

27. The following data and citations were taken from "Iraq: Oil and
Gas Rights of Regions and Governorates," <KurdishMedia>,
June 14, 2006. With an estimated 1.1 million inhabitants, Irbil is
the largest city in the KRG.

28. The following data were taken from Ben Holland, "An Oil
Boomtown in Iraqi Kurdistan: Erbil is Prospering, but Tensions
with Baghdad are Increasing," *BusinessWeek*, January 21, 2010.

29. This citation and the following data were garnered from "Iraq to
Resume Kurdish Oil Exports Soon," February 9, 2010. Http://
medyanews.com/english/?p=747, accessed February 12, 2010.

30. Cited in ibid.

31. For a lucid analysis, see Gareth Stansfield and Liam Anderson, "Kurds in Iraq: The Struggle between Baghdad and Erbil," *Middle East Policy* 16 (Spring 2009), pp. 134–45. This penetrating article sums up very well the current dilemma.

32. Ibid., p. 135.

33. The Shiite Islamic Supreme Council of Iraq (ISCI) agrees with the Kurds about maintaining real federalism in Iraq. Although influential in Basra, the ISCI lost considerable electoral support in the local Iraqi elections held in January 2009. It came in a stronger third in the national elections held on March 7, 2010, winning seventy seats. Ayyad Allawi's Iraqiya Alliance (largely Sunni supported) came in first with ninety-one seats and Nouri al-Maliki's State of Law (Shiite) List came in a very close second with eighty-nine seats. The Kurdistani List (KDP-PUK alliance) came in fourth with forty-three. When *Gorran* and the Kurdish Islamists are added to the Kurdistani List, the Kurds have fifty-seven seats in the Iraqi Parliament that was elected on March 7, 2010.

34. Steven Lee Myers, "In Northern Iraq, a Vote Seems Likely to Split," *The New York Times*, February 9, 2010.

35. Cited in "Iraq: Is It Really Coming Right?" *The Economist*, November 27, 2008.

36. Cited in Ernesto Londono, "Kurds in Northern Iraq Receive Arms from Bulgaria," *The Washington Post*, November 23, 2008.

37. The following narrative is largely based on "Too Late to Keep the Peace? The Americans Are Trying Again to Keep the Peace between Arabs and Kurds," *The Economist*, February 11, 2010.

38. This and the following were cited in Sam Dagher, "Iraqi Elections: The View from Kurdistan," *The New York Times*, February 10, 2010.

39. The following data were taken from Jane Arraf, "Before Iraq Election, Arab and Kurd Tensions Soar in the North," *Christian*

Science Monitor, March 1, 2010. Http://www.csmonitor.com /World/Middle-East/2010/0301, accessed March 4, 2010.

40. Anderson and Stansfield, *Crisis in Kirkuk*, p. 9.

41. The following discussion is largely based on Haider Hamoudi and Chibil Mallat, "Iraq at a Crossroads: Constitutional Review Committee Fills in Crucial Gaps," *The Daily Star* (Beirut), November 19, 2009.

42. For a recent analysis, see Rand National Defense Research Institute, *Security in Iraq: A Framework for Analyzing Emerging Threats as U.S. Forces Leave* (Santa Monica: Rand, 2010).

43. Kurdistan Regional Government, "President Barzani: Iraq Will Fall Apart If Constitution Violated," KRG Press Release, August 7, 2008. Http://www.krg.org/articles/detail.aspsmap=02010100 &lngnr=12&anr=25113&rnr=223, accessed March 7, 2010.

44. Stansfield and Anderson, "Kurds in Iraq: The Struggle between Baghdad and Erbil," p. 144.

45. On the other hand, as the recent U.S. Intelligence Threat Assessment noted: "We judge the Sunni Arab insurgency will weaken without the US presence as a common motivating factor." "Annual Threat Assessment," p. 22.

46. Zalmay Khalilzad, remarks made at the conference sponsored by the Jamestown Foundation on "The Iraqi Elections & the Changing Politico-Security Environment in Iraq," Carnegie Endowment for International Peace, Washington, D.C., March 4, 2010.

9 Turkey's Kurdish Initiative

1. On the Sheik Said Rebellion, see Robert Olson, *The Emergence of Kurdish Nationalism and the Sheikh Said Rebellion, 1880–1925* (Austin, TX: University of Texas Press, 1989). I previously published portions of this chapter in "The Kurdish Road to

Turkish Democracy," *Journal of South Asian and Middle Eastern Studies* 31 (Winter 2008), pp. 1–12; and "Navigating the EU Shoals: Turkey's AK Party and the Kurds," *Journal of South Asian and Middle Eastern Studies* 32 (Winter 2009), pp. 19–37.

2. On this point and its consequences, see Asa Lundgren, *The Unwelcome Neighbour: Turkey's Kurdish Policy* (London and New York: I.B. Tauris, 2007).

3. For further analysis of this situation, see Chapter 6 above: "Taming Turkey's Deep State." Also see the chapter entitled "The Authoritarian Tradition in the Republic of Turkey" by Michael M. Gunter, *The Kurds and the Future of Turkey* (New York: St. Martin's Press, 1997), pp. 3–21; and Michael M. Gunter, "The Connection between Turkey's Intelligence Community and Organized Crime," *International Journal of Intelligence and CounterIntelligence* 11 (Summer 1998), pp. 119–141.

4. Sabrina Tavernise, "As Kurds' Status Improves, Support for Militants Erodes in Turkey," *New York Times*, November 2, 2007.

5. Andrew McGregor, "Tactical and Strategic Factors in Turkey's Offensive Against the PKK," *Terrorism Focus* (The Jamestown Foundation) 4 (October 2, 2007); and Deborah Haynes, "We Will Fight to the Death, Kurdish Rebel Leader Vows from His Hideout," *Times of London* (UK), October 18, 2007.

6. "HPG [PKK] Statement on Beytussebap Massacre," http://rastibini.blogspot.com/, October 2, 2007; and Ercan Yavuz, "Government Moves to End Terror Raise Cautious Optimism," *Today's Zaman*, September 28, 2010.

7. For background analysis, see Michael M. Gunter and M. Hakan Yavuz, "Turkish Paradox: Progressive Islamists versus Reactionary Secularists," *Critique: Critical Middle Eastern Studies* 16 (Fall 2007), pp. 289–301; M. Hakan Yavuz and Nihat Ali Ozcan, "Crisis in Turkey: The Conflict of Political Languages," *Middle East Policy* 14

(Fall 2007), pp. 118–135; and Omer Taspinar, "The Old Turks Revolt," *Foreign Affairs* 86 (November/January 2007), pp. 114–30.

8. For further development of these points, see the following articles by Ihsan Dagi, "The Future of Kemalism and the Istanbul Biennial," *Today's Zaman*, October, 1, 2007; "Is Kemalism Compatible with Democracy?" *Today's Zaman*, October 4, 2007; "Is the PKK Trying to Provoke a Cross-Border Operation?" *Today's Zaman*, October 22, 2007; and "Rights and Wrongs in the Fight against the PKK," *Today's Zaman*, November 1, 2007. For a more optimistic view of the role of the Turkish military, see Ersel Aydinli, Nihat Ali Ozcan, and Dogan Akyaz, "The Turkish Military's March Toward Europe," *Foreign Affairs* 85 (January/February 2006), pp. 77–90.

9. Metin Heper, *The State and Kurds in Turkey: The Question of Assimilation* (Houndmills, UK and New York: Palgrave Macmillan, 2007). The following citations from Heper's book are listed in the text in parentheses.

   For additional recent analyses of how the official Kemalist ideology in Turkey has inhibited a realistic attitude toward Turkey's Kurdish problem, see Levent Koker, "A Key to the 'Democratic Opening': Rethinking Citizenship, Ethnicity and Turkish Nation-State," *Insight Turkey* 12 (Spring 2010), pp. 49–69; Kivanc Ulusoy, "The 'Democratic Opening' in Turkey: A Historical/Comparative Perspective," *Insight Turkey* 12 (Spring 2010), pp. 71–90; and Murat Somer, "Defensive and Liberal Nationalisms: The Kurdish Question and Modernization/Democratization," in E. F. Keyman, ed., *Remaking Turkey: Globalization, Alternative Modernities, and Democracy* (Oxford: Lexington Books, 2007), pp. 103–35.

10. See Kemal Kirisci and Gareth M. Winrow, *The Kurdish Question and Turkey: An Example of a Trans-State Ethnic Conflict* (London: Frank Cass, 1997).

11. See M. Hakan Yavuz, "Five Stages of the Construction of Kurdish Nationalism in Turkey," *Nationalism & Ethnic Politics* 7 (Autumn 2001), pp. 1–24.

12. Hakan Ozoglu, *Kurdish Notables and the Ottoman State: Evolving Identities, Competing Loyalties, and Shifting Boundaries* (Albany, NY: State University of New York Press, 2004).

13. Minority Rights Group International, "Minority Rights Group Deplores Actions against Local Authorities Providing Services in Languages Other Than Turkish," July 4, 2007, http://www.minorityrights.org/?lid=622&s=91. Also see "Multilingual Sur Municipality under Investigation," *Turkish Daily News*, January 6, 2007.

14. M. Hakan Yavuz, ed., *The Emergence of a New Turkey: Democracy and the AK Parti* (Salt Lake City: The University of Utah Press, 2006); and M. Hakan Yavuz, *Secularism and Muslim Democracy in Turkey* (New York: Cambridge University Press, 2009).

15. For a collection of trenchant articles, see Marlies Casier and Joost Jongerden, eds. *Nationalisms and Politics in Turkey: Political Islam, Kemalism and the Kurdish Issue* (London and New York: Routledge, 2011).

16. Hasan Kosebalaban, "The AK Party Closure Case: Domestic Situation and International Reactions," *SETA*, Policy Brief No. 10, April 2008; Ihsan Dagi, "The Kurdish Question and Current Political Crisis," *Today's Zaman*, March 31, 2008; and Morton Abramowitz and Henri J. Barkey, *"Turkey's Judicial Coup D'etat," Newsweek*, April 14, 2008.

17. Ihsan Dagi, "AK Party Survives Closure Case: What Is Next?" *SETA*, Policy Brief No. 19, August 2008.

18. Saban Kardas, "Turkey under the Justice and Development Party: Between Transformation of 'Islamism' and Democratic Consolidation?" *Critique: Critical Middle Eastern Studies* 17 (Summer 2008), pp. 175–87.

19. For background, see the collection of chapters in Umit Cizre, ed., *Secular and Islamic Politics in Turkey: The Making of the Justice and Development Party* (London: Routledge, 2007).

20. Michael M. Gunter, "The AKP Catalyst: Progressive Islamists and Ambitious Kurds," *Georgetown Journal of International Affairs* 9 (Summer/Fall 2008), pp. 59–68.

21. Cited in "The Sun Also Rises in the South East," *Briefing* (Ankara), August 15, 2005.

22. The Copenhagen Criteria required for EU membership mandate the stability of institutions guaranteeing democracy, the rule of law, human rights and protection of minority rights. To these political requirements are added economic ones regarding the functioning of a market economy. Copenhagen European Council, "Conclusions of the Presidency," June 21–22, 1993.

23. See the Turkish military's web site: http://www.tsk.mil.tr.

24. See Michael M. Gunter, "The Silent Coup: The Secularist-Islamist Struggle in Turkey," *Journal of South Asian and Middle Eastern Studies* 21 (Spring 1998), pp. 1–12.

25. See the detailed analysis in Walter Posch, "Crisis in Turkey: Just Another Bump on the Road to Europe?" Occasional Paper No. 67 (Paris: Institute for Security Studies, 2007), pp. 18ff. The prominent Turkish journal *Nokta* was forced to close down in April 2007 after publishing apparent details of the attempted coup.

26. See Frank Hyland, "Investigation of Turkey's 'Deep State' Ergenekon Plot Spreads to Military," Vol. 5, No. 26, *Terrorism Focus* (Jamestown Foundation), July 16, 2008; and Gareth Jenkins, "Murky Past of Turkey's Gendarmerie Intelligence Emerges in Ergenekon Investigation," Vol. 6, No. 17, *Terrorism Monitor* (Jamestown Foundation), September 4, 2008. For background, see Chapter 6 above and Michael M. Gunter, "Susurluk: The Connection between Turkey's Intelligence Community and

Organized Crime," *International Journal of Intelligence and CounterIntelligence* 11 (Summer 1998), pp. 119–41.

27. See, for example, Michael Rubin, "Erdogan, Ergenekon, and the Struggle for Turkey," *Mideast Monitor*, August 8, 2008, http://www.meforum.org/article/1968, accessed August 11, 2008.

28. Burhanettin Duran, "The Justice and Development Party's 'New Politics': Steering Toward Conservative Democracy—A Revised Islamic Agenda or Management of New Crises?" in Unit Cizre, ed., *Secular and Islamic Politics in Turkey: The Making of the Justice and Development Party* (London: Routledge, 2008), p. 91.

29. Cited in Sabrina Tavernise, "Turkey's Liberals Speaking Out as Reform Stalls," *New York Times*, November 24, 2008.

30. Cited in Emrullah Uslu, "Firat Resignation May Indicate a Hardening of AKP Kurdish Policy," Vol. 5, No. 216, *Eurasia Daily Monitor* (Jamestown Foundation), November 11, 2008.

31. This and the following citations were taken from Tavernise, "Turkey's Liberals Speaking Out as Reform Stalls."

32. Lale Sariibrahimoglu, "Kurdish Issue Is Deadlocked Again," *Today's Zaman,* November 14, 2008.

33. Commission of the European Communities, Commission Staff WorkingDocument, *Turkey 2008 Progress Report* {Com(2008)674}, Brussels, November 5, 2008. The following citations from this document are referred to in the text by page numbers in parentheses.

34. For a recent evaluation of the changing political role of the Turkish military, see Sule Toktas and Umit Kurt, "The Impact of EU Reform Process on Civil-Military Relations in Turkey," *SETA Policy Brief* No. 26, November 2008, which points out that "Turkey has traditionally regarded its military as [a] strength in international organizations such as NATO. Yet in the EU accession process, the Turkish military has come to be considered a weakness." Ibid., p. 2. The formal lessening of the role of

the National Security Council has been the most visible conces-
sion Turkey's military has made to the country's EU candidacy.

35. For background details concerning the Semdinli case, see
Chapter 6 above, pp. 122–26.

36. Cited in European Parliament, "Motion for a Resolution...on
Turkey's Progress Report 2008," (RE\748541EN.doc.
PE414.936v01–00), November 21, 2008, pp. 5/9.

37. "KHRP Publishes Response to European Commission Turkey
Progress Report," in email received from knklondon@gn.apc.
org. The most recent (2010) EU Progress Report on Turkey
broke little new ground, simply noting continuing problems
with freedom of expression and association, access to justice and
the independence of the judiciary, freedom of religion, children's
rights, gender rights, and harsh treatment of human rights
defenders, all of which affected the Kurds. See European
Commission, Commission Staff Working Document, *Turkey
2010 Progress Report* {COM(2010) 661}, Brussels, November 9,
2010. Also see the EU Turkey Civic Commission, "Final
Resolutions to the 7th International Conference on [the] EU,
Turkey and the Kurds," European Parliament, Brussels,
November 17–18, 2010, www.mesop@online.de, accessed
November 20, 2010.

38. This and the following citations were taken from Selcuk Gultasli,
"EU about to Lose Hope in Erdogan," *Today's Zaman*, November
11, 2008.

39. Cited in "Turkey: The Worrying Tayyip Erdogan," Economist.
com, http://www.economist.com/world/europe/PrinterFriendly.
cfm?story_id=12696853, accessed December 3, 2008.

40. Michael M. Gunter, "The U.S.-Turkish Alliance in Disarray,"
World Affairs 167 (Winter 2005), pp. 113–23.

41. U.S. Department of State, Bureau of Democracy, Human Rights,
and Labor, *Turkey: Country Reports on Human Rights Practices—2007*,

March 11, 2008. The following citations from this document are referred to in the text by page numbers in parentheses.

42. Mustafa Akyol, "Insulting Kurdishness (and Even More Than That)," *Turkish Daily News*, October 4, 2008.

43. "Leyla Zana Sentenced to 10 Years," *Yeniden Ozgur Politka*, December 6, 2008.

44. Turkish Economic and Social Studies Foundation (TESEV), *A Roadmap for a Solution to the Kurdish Question: Policy Proposals from the Region for the Government* (Istanbul: TESEV, 2008).

45. Turkish Chamber of Commerce and Commodity Exchange (TOBB), *Dogu Sorunu: Teshisler ve Tespitler [The Eastern Question: Diagnoses and Findings]* (Ankara: TOBB, 1995).

46. Cited in "Gul: Kurdish Problem is the Most Important Problem of Turkey," *Today's Zaman*, May 11, 2009.

47. These name changes may have been due in part to the felt need to answer criticisms that too much was being offered to only the Kurds, that the initiative was something positive for the entire state.

48. Cited in *Today's Zaman*, August 12, 2009.

49. *Hurriyet*, issues of November 18, 2009; December 2, 2009; December 9, 2009; and December 14, 2009; as cited in Menderes Cinar, "The Militarization of Secular Opposition in Turkey," *Insight Turkey* 12 (Spring 2010), p. 119. Also see E. Fuat Keyman, "The CHP and the 'Democratic Opening': Reactions to AK Party's Electoral Hegemony," *Insight Turkey* 12 (Spring 2010), pp. 91–108.

50. Odul Celep, "Turkey's Radical Right and the Kurdish Issue: The MHP's Reaction to the 'Democratic Opening,'" *Insight Turkey* 12 (Spring 2010), p. 136.

51. Rusen Cakir, "Kurdish Political Movement and the 'Democratic Opening,'" *Insight Turkey* 12 (Spring 2010), p. 185.

52. Actually, despite the government's Kurdish Initiative, arrests of Kurdish politicians and notables associated with the *Koma Civaken*

Kurdistan (KCK) or Kurdistan Communities Union, an umbrella PKK organization supposedly acting as the urban arm of the PKK, had been occurring since April 14, 2009 in apparent retaliation for the DTP local election victories at the end of March 2009. These DTP gains were largely at the expense of the AK Party.

53. For further background, see Marlies Casier, Andy Hilton, and Joost Jongerden, "'Road Maps' and Roadblocks in Turkey's Southeast," *Middle East Report Online*, http://www.merip.org/mero/mero103009, October 30, 2009. The reference to not even a mouse was made by now banned DTP leader Ahmet Turk. Ibid., p. 6.

54. "Resolution of the Tenth General Assembly Meeting of the Kurdistan National Congress KNK," Brussels, Belgium, May 24, 2010.

55. Cited in Jonathan Head, "Turkey's Kurdish War Reignites," BBC News, Istanbul, July 3, 2010.

56. Cited in Sebnem Arsu, "Step by Step, Gulf between Turkey and Kurds Narrows," *New York Times*, January 10, 2011.

57. The following suggestions were taken from Turkish Economic and Social Studies Foundation (TESEV [Delek Kurban and Yilmaz Ensaroglu]), *Towards a Solution to the Kurdish Question: Constitutional and Legal Recommendations* (Istanbul: TESEV, 2010).

58. These amendments barred gender discrimination, bolstered civil liberties, made it possible to prosecute the generals who had led the military coup in 1980, and provided for a major overhaul of the judiciary, among other items.

59. Cakir, "Kurdish Political Movement," p. 185.

60. "Peace in Kurdistan [Campaign] Welcomes Turkey's Talks with Abdullah Ocalan," Press Release, September 25, 2010; Middle East Online, "Turkey in Fresh Drive to End Kurdish Conflict," September 28, 2010, which states that Turkish authorities are "seeking contacts with the [PKK] rebels.... The authorities

appear to have included jailed PKK leader Abdullah Ocalan in the effort, with his lawyers acting as intermediaries and holding meetings with him in his cell on the prison island of Imrali." Http://www.middle-east-online.co.xn—ler-lla8h.net /english/?id=41597, accessed November 26, 2010; Lale Kemal, "Turkey's Paradigm Shift on Kurdish Question and KCK Trial," *Today's Zaman*, October 21, 2010, where the article refers to "state contacts with the imprisoned leader of the PKK, Abdullah Ocalan, on supposedly broader issues." Http:///www. todayszaman.com/columnist-224988-turkeys-paradigm-shift-on-kurdish-ques..., accessed November 26, 2010; and Lale Kemal, "It's Confidence-Building Time for Kurds," *Today's Zaman*, November 16, 2010, who refers "to increased media coverage of alleged dialogue between the PKK, its imprisoned leader Abdullah Ocalan and state officials." Http://www.todayszaman. com/columnist-227299-its-confidence-building-time-for-kurds..., accessed November 26, 2010.

61. See, for example, Abdullah Ocalan, *Declaration on the Democratic Solution of the Kurdish Question* (London: Mesopotamian Publishers, 1999).

62. Emre Uslu, "PKK's Strategy and the European Charter of Local Self-Government," *Today's Zaman*. June 28. 2010, Http://www. todayszaman.com/news-214416–109-pkks-strategy-and-the-european-charter-..., accessed November 26, 2010.

63. Cited in Emrullah Uslu, "PKK Muddies Turkey's Waters," Jamestown Foundation via *Asia Times*, July 14, 2010.

64. The following discussion is largely based on "BDP's Decentralization Proposal Debated in Turkey," *Hurriyet Daily News & Economic Review*, October 3, 2010. Http://www. hurriyetdailynews.com, accessed November 26, 2010.

65. Ayse Karabat, "Kurds Expect Gul's Diyarbakir Visit to Ease Recent Tension," *Today's Zaman*, December 29, 2010. Http://

www.todayszaman.com/news-230981..., accessed December 30, 2010.

66. Cited in "BDP's Decentralization Proposal Debated in Turkey."

67. This and the following statements were cited in "Turkish Deputies to Focus on New Charter in New Legislative Year," *Hurriyet Daily News & Economic Review*, October 1, 2010. Http:// www.hurriyetdailynews.com, accessed November 26, 2010.

68. Cited in "The Executive Council of the KCK/Statement in English, Arabic, Turkish," September 30, 2010. http://www. mesop.de/2010/10/01/.

69. Ihsan Dagi, "Ever Closer to a Kurdish Solution?" *Today's Zaman*, October 4, 2010.

70. Adam Liptak, "Court Affirms Ban on Aiding Groups Tied to Terror," *New York Times*, June 21, 2010.

SELECTED BIBLIOGRAPHY

This bibliography is a much revised and updated version of the one in the first edition of this book that was published in 2008. For the present bibliography, I have deleted the news media entries from the earlier edition, but added many new scholarly books, reports, and articles published since the release of the first edition. Please consult my current endnotes for the old and new news media sources I have used and cited, but not listed in this bibliography. Most of the works listed here (but not all) were published after the fall of Saddam Hussein in 2003. For a much more detailed bibliography on the Kurds, see the second edition of my *Historical Dictionary of the Kurds* (Lanham, MD: Scarecrow Press, 2011). For an even larger bibliography on the Kurds (but before 1997), see Lokman I. Meho, com., *The Kurds and Kurdistan: A Selective and Annotated Bibliography* (Westport, CT: Greenwood Press, 1997); and Lokman I. Meho and Kelly L. Maglaughlin, coms., *Kurdish Culture and Society: An Annotated Bibliography* (Westport, CT: Greenwood Press, 2001).

Acikyildiz, Birgul. *The Yezidis: The History of a Community, Culture and Religion.* London: I.B. Tauris, 2010.

Ahmed, Mohammed M. A. *America Unravels Iraq: Kurds, Shiites and Sunni Arabs Compete for Supremacy.* Costa Mesa, CA: Mazda Press, 2010.

Ahmed, Mohammed M. A., and Michael M. Gunter, eds. *The Kurdish Question and International Law*. Oakton, VA: Ahmed Foundation for Kurdish Studies, 2000.

———. *Kurdish Exodus: From Internal Displacement to Diaspora*. Sharon MA: Ahmed Foundation for Kurdish Studies, 2002.

———. *The Kurdish Question and the 2003 Iraqi War*. Costa Mesa, CA: Mazda Press, 2005.

———. *The Evolution of Kurdish Nationalism*. Costa Mesa, CA: Mazda Press, 2007.

Alkadiri, Raad. "Oil and the Question of Federalism in Iraq." *International Affairs* 86:6 (2010): 1315–28.

Anderson, Liam, and Gareth Stansfield. *The Future of Iraq: Dictatorship, Democracy, or Disivion?* New York: Palgrave Macmillan, 2004.

———. *Crisis in Kirkuk: The Ethnopolitics of Conflict and Compromise*. Philadelphia: University of Pennsylvania Press, 2009.

Arikan, Harun. *Turkey and the EU: An Awkward Candidate for EU Membership*, 2nd ed. Hampshire, England: Ashgate Publishing, 2006.

Baker, James A. III, and Lee H. Hamilton, Co-Chairs. *The Iraq Study Group Report: The Way Forward—A New Approach*. New York: Vintage Books, 2006.

Barkey, Henri J. "Turkey's New Engagement in Iraq." Washington, D.C.: United States Institute of Peace, May 2010.

Barkey, Henri J., and Graham E. Fuller. *Turkey's Kurdish Question*. New York: Rowman & Littlefield, 1998.

Barkey, Henri J., and Ellen Laipson. "Iraqi Kurds and Iraq's Future." *Middle East Policy* 12 (Winter 2005): 66–76.

Bellaigue, Christopher de. *Rebel Land: Among Turkey's Forgotten Peoples*. London: Bloomsbury, 2009.

Bodansky, Yossef. *The Secret History of the Iraq War*. New York: ReganBooks, 2004.

Brancati, Dawn. "Is Federalism a Panacea for Post-Saddam Iraq? *Washington Quarterly* 25 (Spring 2004): 7–21.

Branscheidt, Hans. "Turkish Accession to the European Union: Human Rights and the Kurds." mimeographed paper, August 25, 2005.

Bremer, Paul L. *My Year in Iraq: The Struggle to Build a Future of Hope*. New York: Simon & Shuster, 2004.

Bruinessen, Martin van. *Agha, Shaikh and State: The Social and Political Structures of Kurdistan*. London: Zed Books, 1992.

Casier, Marlies, Andy Hilton, and Joost Jongerden. "'Road Maps' and Roadblocks in Turkey's Southeast." *Middle East Report Online* http://www.merip.org/mero/mero103009, October 30, 2009.

Casier, Marlies, and Joost Jongerden, eds. *Nationalism and Politics in Turkey: Political Islam, Kemalism and the Kurdish Issue*. London and New York: Routledge, 2011.

Celep, Odul. "Turkey's Radical Right and the Kurdish Issue: The MHP's Reaction to the 'Democratic Opening.'" *Insight Turkey* 12 (Spring 2010): 125–42.

Chandrasekaran, Rajiv. *Imperial Life in the Emerald City: Inside Iraq's Green Zone*. New York: Vintage Books, 2007.

Charountaki, Marianna. *The Kurds and US Foreign Policy: International Relations in the Middle East since 1945*. London and New York: Routledge, 2010.

Chehab, Zaki. *Iraq Ablaze: Inside the Insurgency*. London & New York: I.B. Tauris, 2006.

Cinar, Menderes. "The Militarization of Secular Oppositioin in Turkey." *Insight Turkey* 12 (Spring 2010): 109–23.

Cizre, Umit, ed. *Secular and Islamic Politics in Turkey: The Making of the Justice and Development Party*. London: Routledge, 2007.

Cockburn, Patrick. *The Occupation: War and Resistance in Iraq*. London & New York: Verso, 2006.

Commission of the European Communities, Commission Staff Working Document. *Turkey 2008 Progress Report* {Com(2008)674}, Brussels, Belgium, November 5, 2008.

Cordesman, Anthony H. *Iraqi Security Forces: A Strategy for Success.* Westport, CT: Praeger Security International, 2006.

Dagi, Ihsan. "AK Party Survives Closure Case: What is Next?" *SETA,* Policy Brief No. 19, August 2008.

Diamond, Larry. *Squandered Victory: The American Occupation and the Bungled Effort to Bring Democracy to Iraq.* New York: Times Books, 2005.

Dodge, Toby. *Inventing Iraq: The Failure of Nation Building and a History Denied.* New York: Columbia University Press, 2003.

Eccarius-Kelly, Vera. *The Militant Kurds: A Dual Strategy for Freedom.* Westport, CT: Praeger Security International, 2010.

Entessar, Nader. *Kurdish Politics in the Middle East.* Lanham, MD: Lexington Books, 2010.

Etherington, Mark. *Revolt on the Tigris: The al-Sadr Uprising and the Governing of Iraq.* Ithaca, NY: Cornell University Press, 2005.

Fearon, James. "Iraq's Civil War." *Foreign Affairs* 80 (March/April 2007).

Galbraith, Peter W. *The End of Iraq: How American Incompetence Created a War without End.* New York: Simon & Schuster, 2006.

Gordon, Michael R., and General Bernard E. Trainor. *Cobra II: The Inside Story of the Invasion and Occupation of Iraq.* New York: Pantheon Books, 2006.

Guclu, Yucel. "Who Owns Kirkuk? The Turkoman Case." *Middle East Quarterly* 14 (Winter 2007).

Gunter, Michael M. *The Kurds of Iraq: Tragedy and Hope.* New York: St. Martin's Press, 1992.

———. *The Kurds and the Future of Turkey.* New York: St. Martin's Press, 1997.

———. "The Connection between Turkey's Intelligence Community and Organized Crime." *International Journal of Intelligence and CounterIntelligence* 11 (Summer 1998): 119–41.

———. "Abdullah Ocalan: We Are Fighting Turks Everywhere." *Middle East Quarterly* 5 (June 1998): 79–85.

———. *The Kurdish Predicament in Iraq: A Political Analysis.* New York: St. Martin's Press, 1999.

———. "Kurdish Future in a Post-Saddam Iraq." *Journal of Muslim Minority Affairs* 23 (April 2003): 9–23.

———. "Federalism and the Kurds: The Solution or the Problem?" *Orient* 46 (No. 1; 2005): 45–66.

———. "Kurdistan's Revival." *Worth (Robb Report),* May 2005.

Gunter, Michael M., and M. Hakan Yavuz. "The Continuing Crisis in Iraqi Kurdistan." *Middle East Policy* 12 (Spring 2005): 122–33.

———. "Turkish Paradox: Progressive Islamists versus Reactionary Secularists." *Critique: Critical Middle Eastern Studies* 16 (Fall 2007): 289–301.

Hassanpour, Amir. *Nationalism and Language in Kurdistan, 1918–1985.* San Francisco: Mellen Research University Press, 1992.

Heper, Metin. *The State and Kurds in Turkey: The Question of Assimilation.* New York: Palgrave Macmillan, 2007.

Herring, Eric, and Glen Rangwala. *Iraq in Fragments: The Occupation and Its Legacy.* Itacha, NY: Cornell University Press, 2006.

Horowitz, Donald L. *Ethnic Groups in Conflict.* Berkeley, CA: University of California Press, 1985.

Houston, Christopher. *Islam, Kurds and the Turkish Nation State.* Oxford and New York: Berg, 2001.

———. *Kurdistan: Crafting of National Selves.* Bloomington and Indianapolis: Indiana University Press, 2008.

Ibrahim, Ferhad, and Gulistan Gurbey, eds. *The Kurdish Conflict in Turkey: Obstacles and Chances for Peace and Democracy.* New York: St. Martin's Press, 2000.

International Crisis Group. "Iraq and the Kurds: Resolving the Kirkuk Crisis." Middle East Report No. 64. Kirkuk/Amman/Brussels: International Crisis Group, April 19, 2007.

———. "Oil for Soil: Toward a Grand Bargain on Iraq and the Kurds." Middle East Report No. 80. Kirkuk/Brussels: International Crisis Group, October 28, 2008.

International Crisis Group. "Turkey and Iraqi Kurds: Conflict or Cooperation?" Middle East Report No. 81. Istanbul/Brussels: International Crisis Group, November 13, 2008.

———. "Iraq and the Kurds: Trouble along the Trigger Line." Middle East Report No. 88. Baghdad/Erbil/Brussels: International Crisis Group, July 8, 2009.

———. "Iraq's New Battlefront: The Struggle over Ninewa." Middle East Report No. 90. Mosul/Brussels: International Crisis Group, September 28, 2009.

Jabar, Faleh A., and Hosham Dawod, eds. *The Kurds: Nationalism and Politics*. London: Saqi, 2006.

Jongerden, Joost. *The Settlement Issue in Turkey and the Kurds: An Analysis of Spatial Policies, Modernity and War*. Leiden and Boston: Brill, 2007.

Joseph, Joesph S., ed. *Turkey and the European Union: Internal Dynamics and External Challenges*. New York: Palgrave Macmillan, 2006.

Kardas, Saban. "Turkey under the Justice and Development Party: Between Transformation of 'Islamism' and Democratic Consolidation?" *Critique: Critical Middle Eastern Studies* 17 (Summer 2009): 175–87.

Keyman, E. Fuat. "The CHP and the 'Democratic Opening': Reactions to AK Party's Electoral Hegemony." *Insight Turkey* 12 (Spring 2010): 91–108.

Kirisci, Kemal, and Gareth M. Winrow. *The Kurdish Question and Turkey: An Example of a Trans-state Ethnic Conflict*. London: Frank Cass, 1997.

Kissinger, Henry. *Years of Renewal*. New York: Simon & Schuster, 1999.

Koker, Levent. "A Key to the 'Democratic Opening': Rethinking Citizenship, Ethnicity and Turkish Nation-State." *Insight Turkey* 12 (Spring 2010): 49–69.

Koohi-Kamali, Farideh. *The Political Development of the Kurds in Iran*. New York: Palgrave Macmillan, 2003.

Kurdistan Development Corporation. *Iraqi Kurdistan Business & Investment, 2004: Special Supplement*. London: Saffron Books, 2004.

Laciner, Sedat, Mehmet Ozcan, and Ihsan Bal. *European Union with Turkey: The Possible Impact of Turkey's Membership on the European Union.* Ankara: ISRO Publication, 2005.

Lake, Michael, ed. *The EU and Turkey: A Glittering Prize or a Millstone?* London: The Federal Trust for Education and Research, 2005.

Lawrence, Quil. *The Invisible Nation: How the Kurds' Quest for Statehood Is Shaping Iraq and the Middle East.* New York: Walker and Company, 2008.

Lijphart, Arend. *The Politics of Accommodation: Pluralism and Democracy in the Netherlands.* Berkeley, CA: University of California Press, 1968.

Lowe, Robert, and Gareth Stansfield, eds. *The Kurdish Policy Imperative.* London: Chatham House, 2010.

Lundgren, Asa. *The Unwelcome Neighbour: Turkey's Kurdish Policy.* London and New York: I.B. Tauris, 2007.

MacDonald, Charles G., and Carole A. O'Leary, eds. *Kurdish Identity: Human Rights and Political Status.* Gainesville: University Press of Florida, 2007.

Mango, Andrew. *Ataturk: The Biography of the Founder of Modern Turkey.* Woodstock & New York: Overlook Press, 2000.

Marr, Phebe. *The Modern History of Iraq,* 2nd ed. Boulder, CO: Westview Press, 2004.

McDowall, David. *A Modern History of the Kurds.* 3rd revised ed. London: I. B. Tauris, 2004.

McKiernan, Kevin. *The Kurds: A People in Search of Their Homeland.* New York: St. Martin's Press, 2006.

Muller, Mark, Claire Brigham, Kariane Westrheim, and Kerim Yildiz, eds. *International Conference on Turkey, the Kurds and the EU: European Parliament, Brussels, 22–23 November 2004—Conference Papers.* Great Britain: Kurdish Human Rights Project, 2005.

Mutlu, Servet. "Ethnic Kurds in Turkey: A Demographic Study." *International Journal of Middle East Studies* 28 (November 1996): 517–41.

Natali, Denise. *The Kurds and the State: Evolving National Identity in Iraq, Turkey, and Iran.* Syracuse: Syracuse University Press, 2005.

———. *The Kurdish Quasi-State: Development and Dependency in Post-Gulf War Iraq.* Syracuse: Syracuse University Press, 2010.

Ocalan, Abdullah. *Declaration on the Democratic Solution of the Kurdish Question.* London: Mesopotamian Publishers, 1999.

———. *Prison Writings: The Roots of Civilisation*, trans. by Klaus Happel. London: Pluto Press, 2007.

O'Leary, Brendan, John McGarry, and Khaled Salih, eds. *The Future of Kurdistan in Iraq.* Philadelphia: University of Pennsylvania Press, 2005.

O'Leary, Brendan. "Federalizing Natural Resources," in Ben Roswell, David Malone, and Markus Bouillon, eds. *Iraq: Preventing Another Generation of Conflict.* Boulder, CO: Lynne Rienner Press, 2007.

———. "Iraq's Future 101: The Failings of the Baker-Hamilton Report." *Strategic Insights* 6:2 (March 2007).

Olson, Robert. *The Emergence of Kurdish Nationalism and the Sheikh Said Rebellion, 1880–1925.* Austin: University Texas Press, 1989.

———. *Turkey's Relations with Iran, Syria, Israel, and Russia, 1991–2000.* Costa Mesa, CA: Mazda Press, 2001.

———. *Turkey-Iran Relations, 1979–2004: Revolution, Ideology, War, Coups and Geopolitics.* Costa Mesa, CA: Mazda Press, 2004.

———. *The Goat and the Butcher: Nationalism and State Formation in Kurdistan-Iraq since the Iraqi War.* Costa Mesa, CA: Mazda Press, 2005.

———. *Blood, Beliefs and Ballots: The Management of Kurdish Nationalism in Turkey, 2007–2009.* Costa Mesa, CA: Mazda Press, 2009.

Ozcan, Ali, Kemal. *Turkey's Kurds: A Theoretical Analysis of the PKK and Abdullah Ocalan.* London and New York: Routledge, 2006.

Ozoglu, Hakan. *Kurdish Notables and the Ottoman State: Evolving Identities, Competing Loyalties, and Shifting Boundaries.* Albany: State University of New York Press, 2004.

Packer, George. *The Assassins' Gate: America in Iraq.* New York: Farrar, Straus and Giroux, 2005.

Phillips, David. *Losing Iraq: Inside the Postwar Reconstruction Fiasco.* Boulder, CO: Westview Press, 2005.

Pollack, Kenneth M. *The Threatening Storm: The Case for Invading Iraq.* New York: Random House, 2002.

———. *A Path Out of the Desert: A Grand Strategy for America in the Middle East.* New York: Random House, 2008.

Posch, Walter. "Crisis in Turkey: Just Another Bump on the Road to Europe?" Occasional Paper No. 67. Paris: Institute for Security Studies, 2007.

Prunhuber, Carol. *The Passion and Death of Rahman the Kurd.* New York and Bloomington: iUniverse Inc., 2009.

Romano, David. *The Kurdish Nationalist Movement: Opportunity, Mobilization and Identity.* Cambridge: Cambridge University Press, 2006.

———. "An Outline of Kurdish Islamist Groups in Iraq." *Jamestown Occasional Papers Series.* Washington, D.C.: Jamestown Foundation, September 17, 2007.

Shadid, Anthony. *Night Draws Near: Iraq's People in the Shadows of America's War.* New York: Henry Holt, 2005.

Somer, Murat (with Evangelos G. Liaras). "Turkey's New Kurdish Opening: Religious versus Secular Values." *Middle East Policy* 17 (June 2010): 152–65.

Stansfield, Gareth. *Iraqi Kurdistan: Political Development and Emergent Democracy.* London: RoutledgeCurzon, 2003.

———. *Iraq: People, History, Politics.* Cambridge and Oxford: Polity, 2007.

Stansfield, Gareth, and Liam Anderson. "Kurds in Iraq: The Struggle between Baghdad and Erbil." *Middle East Policy* 16 (Spring 2009): 134–45.

Tahiri, Hussein. *The Structure of Kurdish Society and the Struggle for a Kurdish State*. Costa Mesa, CA: Mazda Press, 2007.

Talabany, Nouri. "Who Owns Kirkuk? The Kurdish Case." *Middle East Quarterly* 14 (Winter 2007).

Taspinar, Omer. "The Old Turks Revolt." *Foreign Affairs* 86 (November/January 2007): 114–30.

Tripp, Charles. *A History of Iraq*, 3rd ed. Cambridge: Cambridge University Press, 2007.

Turkish Economic and Social Studies Foundation (TESEV). *A Roadmap for a Solution to the Kurdish Question: Policy Proposals from the Region for the Government*. Istanbul: TESEV, 2008.

———. *Towards a Solution of the Kurdish Question: Constitutional and Legal Recommendations*. Istanbul: TESEV, 2010.

Ulusoy, Kivanc. "The 'Democratic Opening' in Turkey: A Historical/Comparative Perspective." *Insight Turkey* 12 (Spring 2010): 71–90.

U.S. Department of State, Bureau of Democracy, Human Rights, and Labor. *Turkey: Country Reports on Human Rights Practices—2007*. March 11, 2008.

Vali, Abbas, ed. *Essays on the Origins of Kurdish Nationalism*. Costa Mesa, CA: Mazda Press, 2003.

Wimmer, Andreas. "Democracy and Ethno-Religious Conflict in Iraq." *Survival* 45:4 (2003): 111–34.

Woodward, Bob. *Plan of Attack*. New York: Simon & Schuster, 2004.

———. *State of Denial: Bush at War, Part III*. New York: Simon & Schuster, 2006.

Yavuz, M. Hakan. "Five Stages of the Construction of Kurdish Nationalism in Turkey." *Nationalism & Ethnic Politics* 7 (Autumn 2001): 1–24.

———. "*Provincial* not *Ethnic* Federalism in Iraq." *Middle East Policy* 11 (Spring 2004): 126–31.

———. *Secularism and Muslim Democracy in Turkey*. New York: Cambridge University Press, 2009.

Yavuz, M. Hakan, and Michael M. Gunter. "The Kurdish Nation." *Current History* 100 (January 2001): 33–39.

Yavuz, M. Hakan, and Nihat Ali Ozcan. "Crisis in Turkey: The Conflict of Political Languages." *Middle East Policy* 14 (Fall 2007): 118–135.

Yildiz, Kerim. *The Kurds in Iraq: The Past, Present and Future.* London: Pluto Press, 2004.

———. *The Kurds in Turkey: EU Accession and Human Rights.* London: Pluto Press, 2005.

———. *The Kurds in Syria: The Forgotten People.* London: Pluto Press, 2005.

Yildiz, Kerim, and Susan Breau. *The Kurdish Conflict: International Humanitarian Law and Post-Conflict Mechanisms.* London and New York: Routledge, 2010.

Yildiz, Kerim, and Tanyel Taysi. *The Kurds in Iran: The Past, Present and Future.* London: Pluto Press, 2007.

Watts, Nicole F. *Activists in Office: Kurdish Politics and Protest in Turkey.* Seattle: University of Washington Press, 2010.

White, Paul. *Primitive Rebels or Revolutionary Modernizers? The Kurdish National Movement in Turkey.* London: Zed Books, 2000.

Zurcher, Eric. *Turkey: A Modern History,* 3rd revised ed. London: I. B. Tauris, 2004.

INDEX

9 780230 112872